SIMPLIFIED ACCOUNTING FOR NON-ACCOUNTANTS

Meet John Your, owner of Yourcompany, a small-business man who discovers one morning that all his company books have disappeared—and so has his bookkeeper!

As he uncovers a $200,000 theft and reconstructs how it happened, he learns everything about accounting that he needs to know in order to protect himself in the future. His experience will help you understand as never before the meaning, use and relevance of business theories and transactions.

If you want to develop a thorough understanding of accounting without getting into complex details; if you have a need for practical information in plain, accessible language—this book is for you.

Most Jove Books are available at special quantity discounts for bulk purchases for sales promotions, premiums, fund raising, or educational use. Special books or book excerpts can also be created to fit specific needs.

For details, write or telephone Special Markets, The Berkley Publishing Group, 200 Madison Avenue, New York, New York 10016; (212) 686-9820.

Simplified Accounting
for Non-accountants

Rick Stephan Hayes
and C. Richard Baker

ILLUSTRATIONS BY NANCY RAFFAELLI RICHARDS

JOVE BOOKS, NEW YORK

This publication is designed to provide accurate and authoritative information in regard to the subject matter covered. It is sold with the understanding that the publisher is not engaged in rendering legal, accounting, or other professional service. If legal advice or other expert assistance is required, the services of a competent professional person should be sought. *From a Declaration of Principles jointly adopted by a Committee of the American Bar Association and a Committee of Publishers.*

SIMPLIFIED ACCOUNTING FOR NON-ACCOUNTANTS

A Jove Book / published by arrangement with
John Wiley & Sons, Inc.

PRINTING HISTORY
John Wiley edition published 1980
Playboy Paperbacks edition / June 1982
Jove edition / November 1982

All rights reserved.
Copyright © 1980 by John Wiley & Sons, Inc.
Cover photo copyright © 1982 by PBJ Books, Inc.,
formerly PEI Books, Inc.
This book may not be reproduced in whole or in part,
by mimeograph or any other means, without permission.
For information address: John Wiley & Sons, Inc.
605 Third Avenue, New York, New York 10158.

ISBN: 0-515-09099-9

Jove Books are published by The Berkley Publishing Group,
200 Madison Avenue, New York, New York 10016.
The name "JOVE" and the "J" logo
are trademarks belonging to Jove Publications, Inc.

PRINTED IN THE UNITED STATES OF AMERICA

10   9   8   7   6   5

Preface

Accounting is of vital importance to all businesses. Everyone knows this. Yet, traditionally, accounting books have been so complex and frustrating that the businessperson is actually discouraged from learning. This is a shame—and a crime.

It was with the hope that we could create a simple, understandable, and practical book that C. Richard Baker and I started to write. Achieving these goals turned out to be a much more difficult task than we had first thought. We had to rewrite material many times before we were convinced that it was simple enough. By making extensive use of charts, illustrations, graphs, actual business forms, and copious examples we tried to communicate the day-to-day accounting needs of your business.

But dry facts, even simply stated, are not very exciting. And accounting, considered by itself, is not thrilling.

To make your reading not only practical, but also interesting, this book tells of a typical businessman. He comes to work one morning only to find that his company books are gone. So is the bookkeeper. This book is the story of how the businessman tracks down what has happened, how he discovers over $200,000 in accounting theft, and how he learns enough about accounting to control it—instead of vice versa.

The book covers such essential topics of accounting as original business accounting forms, journals, ledgers, trial balances, income statements, balance sheets, and sources and uses of funds. It defines and shows the tax implications of assets, liabilities, owner's capital, income, cost of sales, and operating expenses. It describes how to determine the value of assets, depreciation, tax credits, and bad debt expense. It explains which travel and entertainment expenses may be written off and what proper proof and documentation is required. But the book also goes beyond accounting and discusses loans, ratios, breakeven sales, and describes financial techniques that can be used to make your company more profitable. The book ends with a glossary of accounting terms. Many illustrations are provided.

In short, this book is written for the businessperson who wants a thorough understanding of accounting without getting into complex details, the person who hates reading matter that gets bogged down, and the person who has a great need for practical information.

RICK STEPHAN HAYES

Topanga, California
January 1980

Contents

1. Accounting and John Your — 1
2. Accounting and Accounts — 25
3. The First Transformation—The Books — 49
4. Assets, Cash, and Accounts Receivable — 98
5. Inventories, Fixed Assets, and Depreciation — 125
6. Liabilities — 146
7. Forms of Business Organizations — 168
8. Revenue and Expense — 187
9. The Second Transformation—The Work Papers and Closing the Books — 208
10. Business Financial Statements — 236
11. Business Finance and Ratios — 254

Index — 287

Chapter One
Accounting and John Your

John Your wished that what was happening to him was a nightmare. But it wasn't. If it was a nightmare, John could wake up, see the sun and know that what had been happening was only a product of his overworked mind and body. But he was awake, it was daylight, and his predicament was real. Very real.

During the past weekend someone had broken into the factory and stolen the books. Not any money. Not any of the products. Not even a gold ring that John had in his top drawer. They had stolen only the books.

What do you do when someone steals your company books? John had called the police right after he had discovered the loss. The police had come, searched around, and found no sign of entry, found nothing missing but the books.

All morning John had tried to get his bookkeeper, Martha Hunt, on the phone, but nobody answered at her house.

When John told the police that a CPA was coming today to do an audit, the policeman suggested that perhaps someone in the plant had something to hide that he or she didn't want discovered. After the police had made their report and left, John had sat at his desk wondering who could have done it.

John had told his secretary to hold all the calls and, except for the people at the plant, no one was aware of the theft. John sat at his desk, becoming nervous and worried. He got up out of his chair and began pacing the office floor. The thought of what all this could mean was buzzing through his brain like a hornet's nest.

His secretary, Mary, opened the office door a crack and said in a loud whisper: "Pete Popstein, the CPA, is here. What shall I do?"

In all the confusion John had forgotten to call the CPA and tell him the story. This was the first time John had ever had an audit. This was the first time the CPA, Popstein, had been at the plant. John almost felt relieved that Popstein had come. "Send him in, and don't let anyone disturb us," John told his secretary.

Pete Popstein was a round man with a very youthful face. He had curly brown hair and seemed to always carry twenty pens and pencils in his right-hand shirt pocket.

"Please sit down," John motioned for the chair. "We've got some problems. This morning when I came to work, I went into Martha's office to get the books so I would have them ready for you when you came in. They're gone. The police just left. I've been trying to call Martha—the bookkeeper—all morning and no one is at home. What should I do?"

"Whew . . . well," Pete Popstein answered, "What books were stolen: the journal, the ledger, the accounts receivable records, the checks—what?"

"Well," John felt embarrassed. "I don't know what what-you-said looks like. It is the big book that Martha makes entries in when she writes checks or when the business has income or borrows money or something. All I ever heard it called was 'the books.' Anyway, it's gone."

"Hmmm," Pete thought out loud, "Well, it could have been the ledger or the journal, but more likely it was both. . . . The checks and check stubs, sales slips, shipping orders, and payroll records—were they taken?"

"I don't know," John became even more embarrassed. "I think Martha keeps them in her office."

"Well," Pete got up out of his chair, "Let's take a look."

John Your and Pete Popstein went into the bookkeeper's office. John stood looking as Pete went through the file drawers, saying "Here's the checks . . . here's the sales slips . . . here's the bills from suppliers. . ." When Pete had looked into every drawer, he glanced at John. "Boy, you have a mess on your hands. I found your last year's income tax. Assuming that it is correct, then you have to go through a full 13 months of original material to find out where you are now, financially. The books that are gone seem to have been the ledger and journal combined. That means that you are going to have to take all the original documents and reconstruct your journal and ledger."

"Do you know why someone would have done this?" John asked.

"Yes. To hide something. Tell me about your bookkeeper." Pete replied.

"Martha? Why, she's been with me for almost two years. John Hart—our old CPA, before we called you—thought that she was a real good bookkeeper. He said all her entries were neat and accurate. And she came with a recommendation from Bill Gilbert who owns Brown Electric down the street. How could it be her?"

"Does anyone else make entries in the books?" Pete asked.

"No, but . . ."

"Who writes the checks?" Pete continued.

"Well, Martha does, but I sign them."

"Do you check the checks she gives you against invoices?" Pete asked.

"Well, no . . . not always."

"I'm not saying that your bookkeeper stole the books or that there is anything irregular," Pete continued. "But she seemed to have the most opportunities to pull something. Did Hart, your old accountant, ever look at your books or audit, or did he just take the trial balance from your bookkeeper?"

"I don't know," John looked down at the floor. "I don't know what you mean by a 'trial balance.' He didn't come to the plant and get the books or anything. Martha told me that it wasn't necessary to take the books to him. Anyway, he doesn't do audits; that's why I contacted your company."

Pete continued "You know how hard it has been for me to start the audit. We've postponed it three times. Each time you said that Martha didn't have the accounts receivable ready, or the company was in the middle of a mass production run, or something. When I finally said it was either today or never, I arrived here today to find that the books are gone."

"You don't think I . . ." John said.

"No. Why would you call for an audit if that was true." Pete Popstein answered. "Never mind that. You have some work to do. I've had this happen before. You could hire an attorney to pursue your bookkeeper in court, if she is the one who did it. You'll also have to go through all the original records and post them to a journal so you can reconstruct what happened.

"John, didn't you tell me that this was your slack season?"

"Yes—practically this whole month is slow. This is the month that they have the national convention. I generally spend my time this month getting ready for it."

Pete looked John in the face. "I suggest that you get someone else to prepare for the convention. This is serious business. What does your company have in gross sales?"

"About $1.2 million," John answered.

"What was your net profit last year?" Pete asked.

"About $100,000 I think."

"Well it's quite possible, John, that the company could have lost up to $150,000 this year from embezzlement. Maybe there was no embezzlement. Maybe someone stole your books as a prank. At any rate, you have to find out. And the faster, the better."

"Can you get started on it right away?" John asked Pete.

Pete answered. "This is my busiest season. I'm afraid that I don't have the time to take each document and enter it in a new journal. Besides which, to do what needs to be done would cost you over $10,000 in my time if I were to do it."

"Well, what do you suggest I do?" John asked Pete.

"There are three things you can do: (1) You can hire someone to go through all the records and make the entries and not bother with them yourself, or (2) you can do all the work yourself, or (3) you can start the work yourself and have someone else— your secretary or a part-time worker—do the repetitive entries. I suggest that you do the latter. This incident should make it clear to you that you don't know enough about accounting to have real control over all the monetary functions of this company.

Pete continued, "You are going to have to reconstruct your books to find out how much was lost, if any, and to pursue any legal aspects of this. I will help you. I will come here a couple of hours every day or so and see how you are doing. I'll give you instruction on what you have to do for the next couple of days, and when you finish that task I'll tell you what to do next. That way you will learn accounting and at the same time perhaps find out what happened to the books."

John thought for a while. He had always hated accounting. One of the first persons he had hired when he started his business was a bookkeeper. Yet he had always felt concerned that he didn't know what was happening. He was especially nervous when he had to talk to his bankers. They always asked him questions about his net worth, his receivables, inventory turnover, and other stuff that he didn't understand.

This was definitely a time of crisis for the company. This month his time might well be better spent on acounting than on the convention.

But who could handle the convention for him? How about his nephew? He had worked part time off and on. His nephew, Don Your, had always liked displays, organization, and so forth. Okay, he decided, Don could take over the convention work. John would still go to the convention, of course, but Don could do the ground work.

"Now, let me get this straight," John said after about five minutes of deliberation. "You tell me what to do; I get the process started to the point that it's just repetitive, then I get a part-timer to handle it. When I finish the first step, you look at it, tell me about it, then tell me what to do next. Right?"

"Right. Then I'll explain what you have to do next, and so on." Pete concluded.

"How much will it cost me?" John asked.

"I will charge you my regular fee of $60 per hour when I'm reviewing the work and giving you instruction. The part-timer will cost you $5 per hour."

"Okay," John extended his hand to Pete, "It's a deal. When do we start?"

"Since I was going to be here all morning for the audit, anyway, let's start now. Ready?"

"Okay."

John took a breath and began.

ORIGINAL TRANSACTION DOCUMENTS

The first step for an accountant of today is the same as it was for an accountant of 5000 years ago. The accountant must record and understand the original transaction documents. The original transaction documents are: sales slips, cash register receipts, checks, shipping documents, invoices, petty cash slips, deposit slips. They represent the first recording of a business transaction at the point of exchange.

The documents can be grouped as follows:

- Sales documents (cash register receipts, sales slips, daily cash summary, and invoices)
- Bank documents (checks, check register, deposit slips)
- Petty cash
- Purchasing documents
- Shipping and invoice documents
- Payroll records
- Travel and entertainment records

Sales Documents

Examples of sales documents include: a cash register receipt (tape), credit card receipts, and sales slips.

Most retail firms use a cash register for handling transactions where cash sales are involved. A cash register usually has two paper printouts of the transactions, one for the customer and one for the records of the business. These paper tapes are called "cash register receipts" or "detailed audit strips." Some businesses have terminals that are hooked up to a computer or some computer storage device. These cash registers will not only have the paper tape, but will relay this information directly to a computer.

Another recording method, the sales slip, is usually reserved for larger deals, such as the sales of Yourcompany owned by John Your. Here is a copy of a sales slip (see Figure 1.1).

The first line usually contains the department and/or salesperson number and an indication of whether it is a cash sale or a

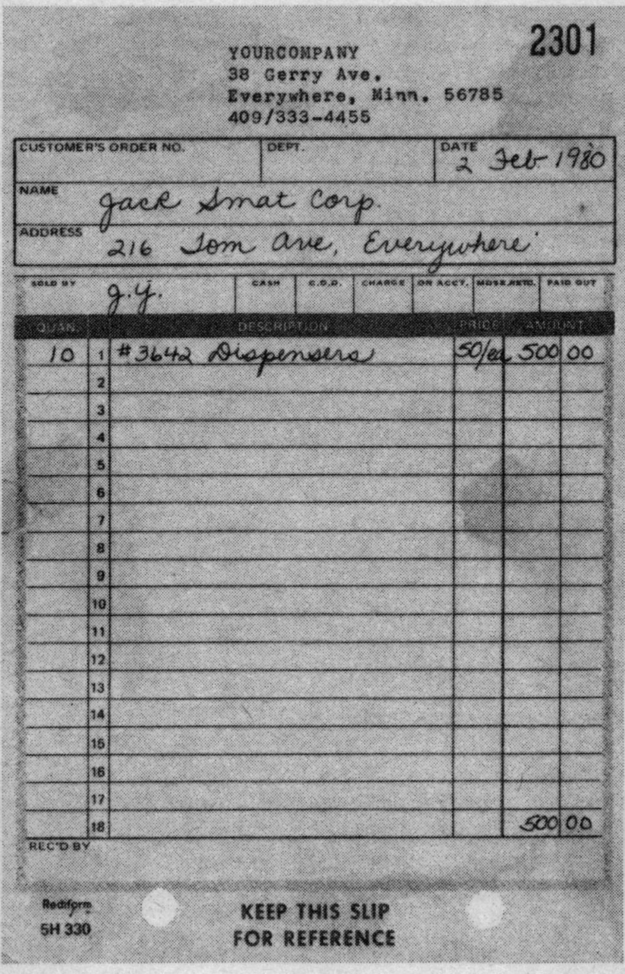
2301

YOURCOMPANY
38 Gerry Ave.
Everywhere, Minn. 56785
409/333-4455

CUSTOMER'S ORDER NO.	DEPT.	DATE 2 Feb 1980

NAME Jack Smat Corp.

ADDRESS 216 Tom Ave, Everywhere

SOLD BY	CASH	C.O.D.	CHARGE	ON ACCT.	MDSE.RETD.	PAID OUT
J.Y.						

QUAN.		DESCRIPTION	PRICE	AMOUNT	
10	1	#3642 Dispensers	50/ea	500	00
	2				
	3				
	4				
	5				
	6				
	7				
	8				
	9				
	10				
	11				
	12				
	13				
	14				
	15				
	16				
	17				
	18			500	00

REC'D BY

Rediform
5H 330

KEEP THIS SLIP
FOR REFERENCE

Figure 1.1. Sales slip.

credit sale. Credit sales are almost always recorded on a sales slip. The sales slip has a place for the name and address of the customer, followed by a space for any delivery instructions. Further spaces are allowed for a description of the item, including quantity, name, unit price, total price and sometimes inventory number.

The salesperson gives the customer a copy of the sales slip and retains a copy for the business (Yourcompany has four copies because shipping and special orders are sometimes required).

Today, many sales are not made for cash, but charged on a credit card in retail sales or charged to a receivable account for other types of industries. These sales are called *charge sales* or *credit sales*.

The documents for a charge account would include an application record, a charge-card slip, and a sales invoice or sales slip.

The first step in opening a credit line with a customer is to obtain application information from him. The application requires information such as address and name, past credit information, income (either company or personal), expected monthly orders, and so on.

The following is an example of a credit application for a business customer:

```
BUSINESS:  Zlapps Tulip Works
           34 Flower Street
           Weed, Calif. 90000
SALESMAN: Charles Smith
LAST YEAR SALES: $3,000,000
D&B RATING: 3A-2
TYPE: Tulip Fabricator
MERCHANDISE MOST
   FREQUENTLY ORDERED: f-719 Tulip Stems
PURCHASING MAN: Fred Zlapps
LAST YEAR PROFIT: $48,000
CREDIT LINE: $100,000
```

Credit cards are often used with retail customers. Credit cards have specific forms such as the one shown for Mastercharge

Original Transaction Documents

Figure 1.2. Masterchage form.

(Figure 1.2). Information required includes a description of the item purchased and the cost, the customer's signature, and sometimes a telephone number, driver's license number, or some other form of identification.

At the end of the business day, a retailer totals the cash in the cash register and compares it to the cash register tape (or detailed audit strip). This form (Figure 1.3) is a typical daily *cash summary form*.

The daily report may be in the form of an envelope which checks sales and payment on account against cash in the cash register. The day's total cash register receipts are usually put into the envelope.

Bank Documents

The most commonly used bank documents are the *check* and the *deposit slip*. Samples of a business check and a deposit slip are shown in Figures 1.4 and 1.5. The checks and deposit slips are usually coded at the bottom with the account number of the business so that it can be read by automated equipment. The name of the business and the address are usually printed in the top left-hand corner. The check has spaces for the date, the payee (person to whom the check is made out), a signature, and usually

DAILY REPORT

Date 15 Feb. 19 80

CASH RECEIPTS

Sales	$ 2,018.16	
MISC. - VENDING MACH	$ 20.00	
	$	
	$ 2,038.16	$ 2,038.16

RECEIVED ON ACCOUNT

Tabadda Trinkets	$ 346.18	
	$	
	$	
	$	
	$	
	$	
TOTAL RECEIPTS	$ 346.18	$ 2,384.34

CASH PAID OUT

Petty Cash	$ 100.00	
	$	
	$	
	$	
	$	
	$	
	$	$
	$ 100.00	$ 100.00
TOTAL PAID OUT	$	$ 100.00

NET RECEIPTS	$	$ 2,284.34
CASH IN REGISTER	$ 2,464.34	
Less Change Fund	$ 200.00	
NET CASH	$ 2,264.34	
CASH OVER OR (SHORT)	$ 20.00	
DEPOSITED IN BANK	$ 2,264.34	$ 2,264.34

Figure 1.3. Daily report.

Original Transaction Documents

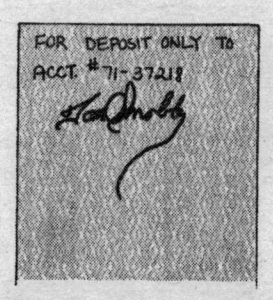

Figure 1.4. Check and endorsement.

has a comment space. The deposit slip lists all the currency, coin, and/or checks to be deposited.

Whenever a check is written by a company, it is recorded on a *check stub* or *check register*. In the check register (Figure 1.6), the amount of each check, date, check number, payee, and account number or explanation are recorded each time a check is written. The check register may also have a space for entering deposits. Deposits are recorded by date, who from, reason, and total.

Note. When depositing checks, there are two types of endorsements. One is just the signature of the payee (the person to whom the check is made to). The other is the "restrictive endorsement," which indicates that the check is for deposit only. The illustrated example of the endorsement of a check (Figure 1.4) is a restrictive endorsement.

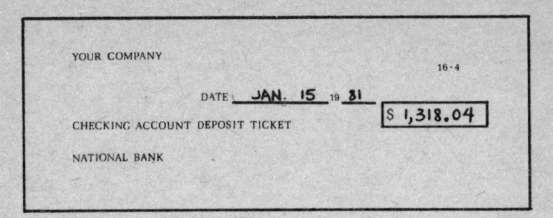

```
YOUR COMPANY
                                                16-4
              DATE  JAN. 15  19 81
CHECKING ACCOUNT DEPOSIT TICKET     $ 1,318.04

NATIONAL BANK
```

CHECKS	DOLLARS	CENTS
1 16-20	412	01
2 4-18	310	73
3 6-71	242	12
4		

35		
36		
Checks	964	86
Currency	321	00
Coin	32	18
TOTAL	1,318	04

Figure 1.5. Checking account deposit slip.

Other bank documents include a savings account *deposit slip* or a *withdrawal slip* (deposit slip is illustrated in Figure 1.7). A savings account slip requires the name of the depositor, account number, date, and total deposited or withdrawn.

A common accounting procedure of a small business is the reconciliation of a checking account. The next section is drawn from a booklet published by Bank of America,* which explains in simple language how this is accomplished.

---

* *Consumer Information Report 1*, "How to Balance Your Checkbook," Bank of America, 1975.

CHECK NO.	DATE	CHECK ISSUED TO	IN PAYMENT OF		AMOUNT OF CHECK	✓	DATE OF DEPOSIT	AMOUNT OF DEPOSIT	BALANCE	
	1981			BALANCE BROUGHT FORWARD →					1,016	72
1198	1/14	SNOBB SUPPLY	Invent.	(512)	518 03				498	69
1199	✓	ATOMIC EDISON	util.	(640)	112 18				386	51
1200	✓	WORLD TELEPHONE	util.	(640)	150 12				236	39
	1/15	DEPOSIT REGISTER					1/15	1,318 04	1,554	43

DESCRIPTION OF DEPOSITS

DATE OF DEP.	SOURCE OF ITEM		NATURE OF ITEM	AMOUNT OF ITEM	TOTAL AMOUNT OF DEPOSIT
1/15/81	ED SINALL	(ACCT #173)	PMT. ON ACCT.	42 01	
	JOHN BIG	(ACCT 195)	✓	310 73	
	S. W. FOX	(ACCT 100)	✓	242 12	
	CASH SALES			353 18	
					1,318 04

Figure 1.6. Check register.

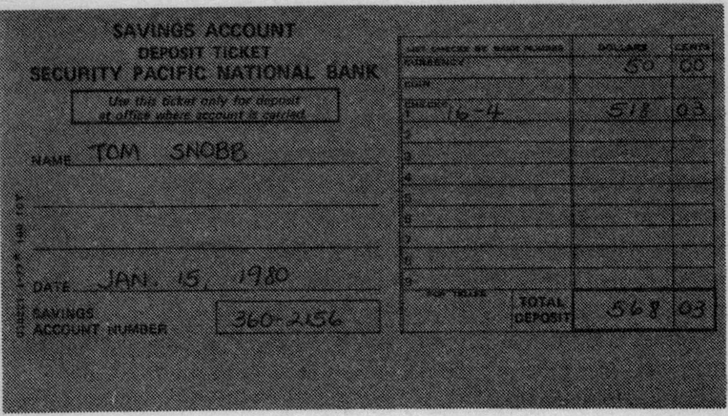

SAVINGS ACCOUNT
DEPOSIT TICKET
SECURITY PACIFIC NATIONAL BANK

Use this ticket only for deposit at office where account is carried

NAME TOM SNOBB

DATE JAN. 15, 1980

SAVINGS ACCOUNT NUMBER 360-2156

	DOLLARS	CENTS
CURRENCY	50	00
COIN		
CHECKS 1 16-4	518	03
2		
3		
4		
5		
6		
7		
8		
9		
TOTAL DEPOSIT	568	03

Figure 1.7. Savings account deposit slip.

Petty Cash

Most businesses set aside a small sum of cash for the payment of minor business expenses. This sum is called the "petty cash fund," and it is kept either in a cash box or an envelope. Items that are usually paid out of petty cash include postage, transportation, telegrams, incidental office supplies, and sometimes parking, duplicating, and entertainment expenses (for lunches, etc.).

Figure 1.8 is an illustration of a petty cash envelope or *office fund voucher,* as it is usually called. When money is paid out of petty cash, the receipt is placed in the envelope and a notation is made indicating the date, the receipt number (if any), to whom it was paid, the expense category it falls under, the account number, and the amount. At the bottom of the envelope in this particular illustration, there are columns for recording the "distribution" of the expenses to the different accounts. The first entry on the cash fund voucher envelope in the example is for postage expense—\$3.50 paid to the U.S. Post Office on 1/5/80. A notation is made that the postage account number is 510. At the bottom of the envelope the two entries recorded for postage are entered in a column under account 510.

The usual procedure is to issue a check for "petty cash" for

OFFICE FUND VOUCHER				No. 1		
From 1 JAN 19 80 to 19 Paid by Check No.						
AUDITED BY		APPROVED BY				
DATE	RECEIPT NO.	TO WHOM PAID	FOR WHAT	ACCOUNT	AMOUNT	
1/5/80		U.S. POST OFFICE	POSTAGE	510	3	50
1/7/80		COPY CROP	DUPLICATING	511	20	16
1/10/80		DOWNTOWN PARKING	PARKING	512	2	50
1/15/80		COPY CROP	DUPLICATING	511	7	40
1/20/80		U.S. POST OFFICE	POSTAGE	510	7	50
1/22/80		GREEN ONION	DINNER - C. ZAP	520	14	80
			TOTAL DISBURSED			
			CASH ON HAND			
			AMOUNT OF FUND			

Post.		Dupl.		Park.		Ent.		DISTRIBUTION									
510		511		512		520											
3	50	20	16	2	50	14	80										
7	50	7	40														

Figure 1.8. Envelope for petty cash receipts.

some dollar amount, usually $100, and keep it in the envelope, a cash box, or a cash register. The money is spent for the various cash expenses and recorded accordingly. When $100 (or whatever the fund amount is) is spent, another check is written for that amount and another envelope is started. The envelope that was just completed is entered in the general journal and the amount of each expense is posted to the proper account (e.g., postage, parking, entertainment) in the ledger.

Purchasing Documents

Sometimes a business can simply order inventory by telephone, but many suppliers require a firm to request merchandise by written order. The form for requesting goods is called a *purchase order*. The purchase order form is sent by the purchaser to the company which will supply the goods. Purchase orders are usually in triplicate, each sheet being a different color. One copy is sent to the vendor (supplier), the second copy is usually retained for the purchasing company files, and the third copy is furnished to the receiving department where the goods are to be delivered.

The purchase order usually contains the following information:

- Number of the purchase order
- Name and address of the vendor
- Name and address of where the goods are to be shipped
- Special shipping instructions
- Date
- Quantity, description and price of the items ordered

When the vendor ships the goods to the buyer, the vendor prepares an invoice, or bill, that he sends to the buyer (illustrated on Figure 1.9).

These invoices may be packed with the shipment and are then referred to as *packing slips,* or the vendors may simply mail the invoice directly to the buyer. This invoice transfers rights to property (providing the property is paid for) to the buyer.

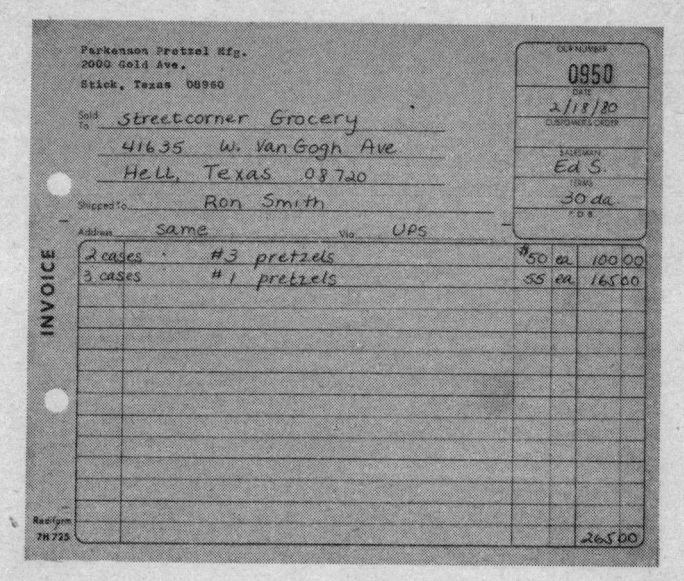

Figure 1.9. Sales invoice.

Travel and Entertainment Records

The Securities and Exchange Commission (SEC) requirement that businesses disclose "perks" (perquisites) given to employees that were previously considered company paid entertainment and travel expense, and pending Internal Revenue Service (IRS) regulations, have caused confusion about what constitutes legal travel and entertainment expense.

Figure 1.10 is an illustration of an expense report for travel and entertainment. It breaks down the cost for eleven separate items, one of which is not tax deductible as an expense:

1. *Transportation* includes airfare, trainfare, busfare, or transportation by automobile compensated at some rate per mile. Note that part of the way down the page this item is broken

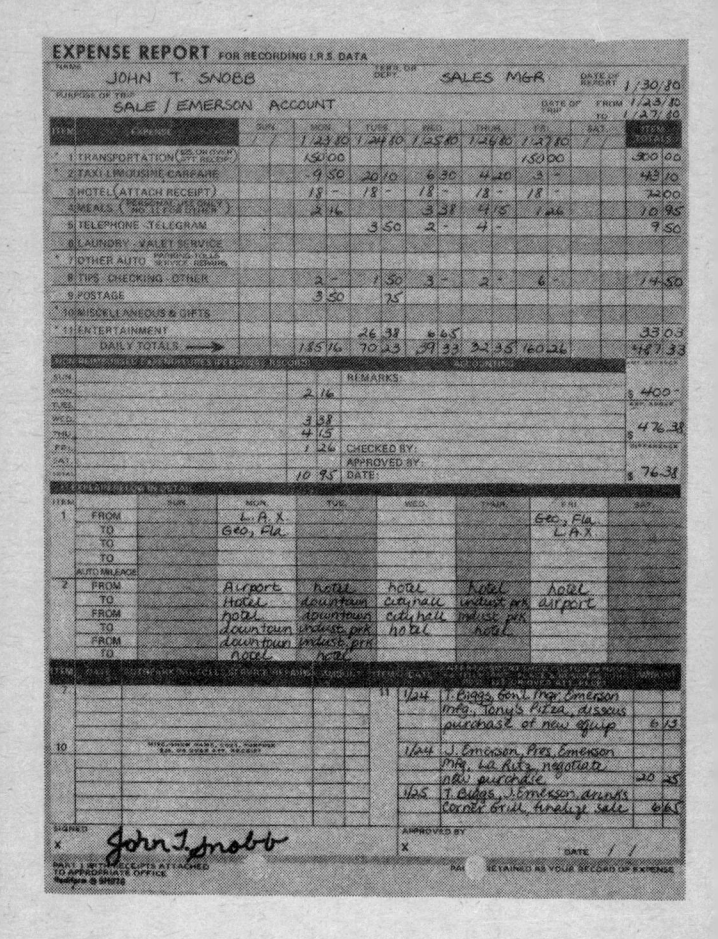

Figure 1.10. Expense report form.

into destination and departure points. If the amount of this transportation cost is over $25, receipts should be included, but it is wisest to include receipts no matter what the cost.

2. *Taxi-limousine fare* represents the cost of transportation by private or public transport at the destination or departure points. This is also broken down by departure and destination.
3. *Hotel* includes the cost of room at a hotel. Receipts are always required.
4. *Meals - personal.*
5. *Telephone-telegraph* includes business-related communication costs. Whenever possible receipts should be kept for this, too.
6. *Laundry-valet service* is for laundry costs required by business activities.
7. *Other auto* includes the cost of tools, parking, service, repairs, and so on. Receipts should be kept. These are itemized in a section at the bottom of the expense report.
8. *Tips* may be kept track of here.
9. *Postage* is for business correspondence.
10. *Miscellaneous and gifts* should be carefully itemized as to name of recipient, cost, and purpose. Gifts cannot be for more than $25 per person per year.
11. *Entertainment expense* requires careful attention to reporting details. In addition to the breakdown at the bottom of the report, we suggest that you attach receipts and give particulars as to customer's name and title, place of business, amount, and purpose of meeting. We would suggest that the reporter always prepare at least a one-paragraph summary of what was discussed at the meeting. If there are further tax restrictions on expenses, entertainment expense will be the area that is most likely to be affected. But as long as entertainment expense has been conducted for business purposes, and this is carefully documented, the business person has little to worry about.

Payroll Records

Because you have employees in your business, you have certain obligations to the federal government for payment of payroll taxes and withholding of income taxes. You have similar obligations for payroll and/or withholding taxes to state and to local jurisdictions.

Federal regulations do not prescribe the form in which your payroll records must be kept, but the records should include the following information and documents:

1. The amounts and dates of all wage payments subject to withholding taxes, and the amounts withheld.
2. The names, addresses, and occupations of employees receiving payments.
3. The periods of their employment.
4. The periods for which they are paid by you while they are absent because of sickness or personal injuries, and the amount and weekly rate of payments.
5. Their social security account numbers if they are subject to social security tax.
6. Their income-tax withholding exemption certificates.
7. Your employer-identification number.
8. Duplicate copies of returns filed.

Usually, an employee's earnings card is set up for each employee. Every wage payment to the employee is recorded on this card—all the information needed for meeting federal, state, and city requirements relating to payroll and withholding taxes, and all other amounts deducted from the employee's wages.

There are three types of federal payroll taxes: (1) income taxes withheld, (2) social security taxes, and (3) federal unemployment taxes. IRS *Publication 15*, "Employer's Tax Guide," should be consulted for additional information about employer-employee relationships, what constitutes taxable wages, the treatment of

EMPLOYER

EMP. NO. 318-92-8550	PAY FOR PERIOD ENDING 1/7/80
EMPLOYEE'S NAME JoAnne Topps	
DATE HIRED 1/1	DATE DISCHARGED
PLACE OF EMPLOYMENT	SCHEDULE HOURS THIS PERIOD

DAYS AND HOURS WORKED

HOURS	SUN.	MON.	TUES.	WED.	THURS.	FRI.	SAT.	TOTAL DAYS	TOTAL HOURS	RATE PER HR.	
		8	8	8	8	8		5	40	5.00	
OVER TIME											

SALARY (If paid on fixed Weekly or Monthly Basis)		
REMUNERATION OTHER THAN CASH (Room, Board, Tips, etc.)		
GROSS EARNINGS	200	00
DEDUCTIONS		
% WITHHOLDING TAX Table	21	40
1 % STATE DISABILITY INSURANCE	2	00
6.05 % FED. INS. CONTRIBUTION ACT	12	40
% STATE WITHHOLDING TAX	5	70
TOTAL DEDUCTIONS	41	50
NET EARNINGS	158	50
LESS: REMUNERATION OTHER THAN CASH		
☐ BY CASH ☒ BY CHECK NO. 138	NET PAY THIS PERIOD 158	50

I HEREBY CERTIFY THAT THE TIME SHOWN ABOVE IS CORRECT
EMPLOYEE SIGN HERE *JoAnne Topps*

4H417 Rediform ®

Figure 1.11. Employee deduction slip.

special types of employment and payments, and similar matters.

Income taxes are withheld on all wages paid an employee above a certain minimum. The minimum is governed by the number of exemptions claimed by an employee. The Tax Reduction and Simplification Act of 1977 changed the standard deduction to a flat rate of $2200 for single individuals and $3200 for married couples filing joint returns.

Social security taxes apply to the first $25,900 (in 1980) of wages paid an employee during a year. A percentage deduction (presently 6.13%) from the employee's wages is matched by an *equal amount* in taxes *paid by the employer*.

In addition to taxes withheld from employees' salaries and also paid by the employer, there is a tax that is paid by the employer *only*. This is the federal unemployment tax (FUTA), which is required only of employers who have: (1) paid wages of $1500 or more in any calendar quarter, or (2) employed one or more persons for some portion of at least one day during each of 20 different calendar weeks. The 20 weeks do not have to be consecutive. Individuals on vacation or sick leave are counted as employees in determining the businesses' status.

The FUTA tax is paid by you as the employer (no deduction is made from the employee's wages). The rate is 3.4% on the first $6,000 of wages paid to each employee.

Using the example of Jo-Ann Topps from Figure 1.11, a full accounting for the employees' taxes and the employer's taxes and payments would be made in a general journal entry, which we will discuss later.

Employer-paid items (social security, FUTA, and state unemployment) do not have to be paid in cash every week. Instead, the employer charges them to a payable account that is usually paid quarterly in cash. The employee items (except the net wage amount of $158.50) must be paid in cash on a quarterly basis.

If you are liable for social security taxes in excess of $200 quarterly, you must file a quarterly return, Form 941. This form combines the social security taxes and income tax withholding.

Due dates for Forms 941 and 941E and the full payment of tax are as follows:

Quarter	Due dates
January-February-March	April 30
April-May-June	July 31
July-August-September	October 31
October-November-December	January 31, next year

If you make timely deposits in full payment of the taxes due, you may file your quarterly return on or before the tenth day of the second month following the period for which it is made. In this case, the due dates are as follows:

Quarter	Due dates
January-February-March	May 10
April-May-June	August 10
July-August-September	November 10
October-November-December	February 10 next year

Deposits are made by sending a completed Form 501, "Federal Tax Deposit," together with a single remittance covering the taxes to be deposited to an authorized commercial bank or federal reserve bank. Names of authorized commercial bank depositories are available at your local bank.

John Your's Task

Pete Popstein looked at John Your. "Do you understand what you have to do now? You have to collect all these original documents and sort them into meaningful 'piles' with all the information in one spot."

John Your answered, "Let me see if I understand. I find all the original documents that show the original transactions in this business for the last year and I organize them in some fashion."

"Yes," Pete answered. "For now I just want you to put all the sales slips together, all the checks the company has written together, and so on. When you have finished this, I'll show you how to enter them into a journal, and later, how to enter them into a ledger. I'll also try to explain what each account means. Now, tell me, what original documents do you need?"

"I've made a list:

- *Sales documents*—that is, the purchase orders I receive
- *Bank documents* such as checks and deposit slips
- *Purchasing documents*—my orders from my suppliers and the bills they sent me
- *Records of our shipments*
- *Payroll records*—the records on each employee
- And *Travel and entertainment* records."

"Yes," Pete continued. "Be especially careful of the purchasing documents, records of shipment and checks. When there is a theft, these documents usually tell the story."

Pete Popstein shook hands with John Your and left the office. John picked up the phone and dialed his wife, "Honey, I'm gonna be late tonight."

Chapter Two
Accounting and Accounts

John Your was in the bookkeeper's—Martha Hunt's—office early in the morning on the day after the theft of the books. He came to work early and was busy finishing the task he had started the previous day—sorting out the original record-keeping documents.

At 8:00 sharp who should appear at the office door but Martha herself.

John was startled. Before he could say anything, Martha spoke.

"I'm sorry I couldn't come to work yesterday. I didn't call because it was all quite sudden. My mother had a heart attack and was taken into the hospital early Monday morning. Mother lives in Connecticut and I had to take an early flight out. But she's stable now. So I've come back to work."

John looked straight ahead, not knowing quite what to say.

"I'm sorry I missed the auditor, but the books were all ready, so I didn't think he'd need my help," Martha said.

John finally got control of himself. "Where were you this weekend?" he asked.

"I had a real nice weekend. I just sat at home and read and went to a couple of movies," she answered.

"Do you know anything about the books that were stolen over the weekend?" John asked with a slight quiver in his voice.

"What books?"

"The business books."

"They were stolen?"

"Yes, they were stolen, and there are no signs of entry. That means someone who works here at Yourcompany probably stole them," John concluded.

"You don't think that I . . ." Martha asked with tears coming to her eyes.

"I don't know who did it. That's why I'm tracing back through the books myself. With the CPA Popstein's help. I want to ask you some questions."

Martha's lip quivered as tears rolled down her face. "Okay."

"I don't know who these suppliers are. Who is Software Corporation? Who is Termafac?" John asked.

"Software makes micro assemblies. Thermafac makes heat-sensitive paper."

"I thought we got all our micro assemblies from Microism."

"We had to add another supplier—as a matter of fact several," Martha seemed more cool now. "Don't you remember when you said we were depending too much on one supplier? I think we have about forty suppliers now."

"How about Thermafac? I thought we bought paper from Simpson or Stonewell. I've never even heard of Thermafac," John asked.

"Thermafac is a new supplier. Hey, let me help you. You don't understand what all these papers mean. You don't understand anything about accounting. You always told me you hate accounting." Martha picked up some of the sales invoices from the stack.

"No," John grabbed the invoices, "Don't touch anything. Yes, I hate accounting, but I'm learning. I want you to go home. If I have any questions, I'll call you."

"Am I fired?"

"No. Until I find out a little more, I'm giving you a one-week leave. Go stay with your mother, but give me her number first."

"Please," Martha begged, "let me help you. If there is anything wrong, I can tell."

"Leave," John pointed to the door.

"Let me pick up some personal stuff."

"No," John repeated, "leave!"

After she had left, with tears again streaming down her face, John wondered if he had made the right decision. He had already begun to notice that there were many more suppliers than he had realized. But was it Martha who had made the decisions?

That day John finished collecting all the checks, purchase orders, and so on. He called Pete Popstein to come and see him the next day, which was a Wednesday.

Pete Popstein arrived at 9:00 Wednesday morning. John showed him the original documents he had collected. John still didn't know what he was supposed to do with the documents. He did, however, know that they were very important, and he took them home with him every night.

Pete looked at the folders of documents and began: "All accounts used by a business can be grouped into six major groups:

- Assets
- Liabilities
- Equity
- Income
- Cost of sales
- and Expenses . . . ."

THE SIX GROUPS OF ACCOUNTS

Assets

Assets are what a business owns. An asset is property that is used in your business. This property contributes toward earning the income of the business, whether directly or indirectly. Assets are productive items which contribute to income and are, generally speaking, tangible property or promises of future receipt of cash (such as accounts receivable), or investments made in the business that are not considered an expense.

The committee on terminology of the American Institute of Certified Public Accountants (AICPA), in Accounting Terminology Bulletin No. 1, defined assets as follows:

"The word *asset* is not synonymous with or limited to property but includes also that part of any cost or expense incurred which is properly carried forward upon a closing of books at a specific date. [An asset] represents whether a property right or value acquired, or an expenditure made, which has created a property right, is properly applicable to the future. Thus plant, accounts receivable, inventory, and a deferred charge are all assets."

Assets include the following items (accounts):

- Cash
- Accounts receivable
- Inventory
- Investments
- Prepaid expense (such as rent or utility deposits)
- Equipment
- Motor vehicles
- Furniture and fixtures
- Land and buildings
- Building improvements (or leasehold improvements if you are a renter
- Other tangible property
- Goodwill
- Patents and copyrights
- Organizational expense
- Research and development

All these items can be divided into three categories: current, fixed, and other assets.

Current assets are those items that can be readily converted into cash within a one-year period. With current assets, the flow of funds is one of continuous circulation or turnover in the short run. *Fixed assets* are items of property, plant, and equipment referred to as "fixed" because of their permanent nature and because they are not subject to rapid turnover. Fixed assets are used in connection with producing or earning revenue and are not for sale in the ordinary course of business. *Other assets* are all the assets that are not current and cannot fit into the fixed asset category (such as research and development or goodwill).

Liabilities

Liabilities are what a business owes to others. This includes debts of the company; amounts of money owed but not yet paid.

Liabilities include the following items (accounts):

- Accounts payable (money owed for inventory, outside labor, etc.)
- Notes payable (the notes—usually secured by some asset or personal guarantee—that require repayment, such as bank debt or mortgages)
- Accrued expenses (like income tax payable, salaries payable, rent payable—amounts that you now owe but haven't paid)
- Trade payables (generally called accounts payable)
- Provision for pensions
- Bonds
- Debentures

Liabilities are generally considered to be either current or long-term. *Current liabilities* are those debts existing as of the balance sheet date which are due for payment within one year or within the normal operating cycle of the business. *Long-term*, or *fixed*, *liabilities* are those debts that will be paid in a period longer than one year.

Equity

Owner's equity or capital is the owner's claim to funds invested in the business and the earnings kept in the business over the years. In a sole proprietorship (business owned by one person), owner's equity is shown as a single balance sheet figure covering both the capital an owner has put into the business and the net earnings left there. In a partnership, the owners' equity is usually shown on the balance sheet classified by individual partners. In a corporation, such as Yourcompany, the owner's equity is shown in a balance sheet in at least two parts: (1) capital stock (or paid-in capital), and (2) retained earnings. The capital stock is shown at "par" or "stated value." The difference between the par value and the amount paid initially for the stock by the stockholders, less costs, is shown as "paid-in surplus."

Owner's equity can be shown as:

- For sole proprietorships or partnerships—equity, one line
- For corporations—capital stock, paid-in surplus and retained earnings

Income

Income (or revenue) is the amount that a business receives for its goods and services. For the majority of companies—those that sell on credit, like Yourcompany—sales means the amount of goods shipped during a given accounting period. Sales may be extended to cover "fees" for services performed as well as other items of income such as commissions, rents, and royalties.

For sales involving the shipment of goods, there is normally a passing of legal title, which is evidence that a sale has in fact taken place. In other types of business transactions revenue recognition is not dependent on the passing of title. For example, service industries do not pass legal title when they perform a service for their customers.

Income usually includes the following items (accounts):

- Merchandise sales
- Rental income
- Commissions
- Royalties
- Fees for services

Operating Expenses

Operating expenses are the costs of operating a business that are not directly related to merchandise or inventory costs. Operating expenses include all overhead costs such as salaries and rent as well as the expenses of selling the product or service. Direct costs required to produce sales such as inventory costs or manufacturing costs are considered "cost of sales." Expenses are period costs and not inventory costs. Operating expenses are the costs to operate a business and are more or less independent of the sales level.

Clarence Nickerson, in *Accounting Handbook for Non-Accountants*, describes expense as "a term for a financial transaction or event resulting in a decrease in assets (such as cash) or an increase in liabilities (such as accounts payable) with a corresponding decrease in owner's equity."[1]

Expenses include the following items (accounts):

- Wages and salaries
- Rental expense (including equipment or premise leases)
- Repairs
- Replacements
- Depreciation
- Bad debt
- Travel and transportation
- Business entertainment
- Interest expense (on debt repayment)
- Insurance
- Taxes (payroll, social security, personal property, real property)
- Office supplies
- Accounting and legal expense
- Utilities (heat, gas, electric, telephone, etc.)
- Advertising
- Licenses and regulatory fees
- Charitable contributions
- Donations to business organizations and industry associations
- Management survey expenses
- Lobbying expenses

[1] Clarence B. Nickerson, *Accounting Handbook for Non-Accountants*, 2nd ed. Boston: CBI, 1979.

- Franchise, trademark, or trade name expenses
- Educational expenses for your employees or yourself
- Commitment fees or standby charges you incur in a mortgaging agreement
- Freight and postage

Cost of Sales

Cost of sales, sometimes considered to be an operating expense, is the cost of the merchandise sold. It does not cover the expenses of selling or shipping this merchandise nor, ordinarily, any storing, office, or general administrative expenses involved in company operations. These items are considered operating expense.

In professional and service businesses, there is usually no cost of sales because these companies receive income from fees, rents, and the like, and not from the sale of inventories.

In businesses that have inventories, such as retail, wholesale, and manufacturing businesses, there is a cost of sales.

Inventories are a major part of determining cost of sales. Inventory amounts include goods held for sale in the normal course of business as well as raw materials and supplies that will physically become a part of the merchandise intended for sale. In manufacturing companies like Yourcompany, the cost of labor, supplies, raw material, and certain other "factory overhead" items such as utilities make up finished inventories. Therefore, these items can be considered a cost of sales.

Cost of sales includes the following items (accounts):

- Merchandise inventory purchased and sold during the period
- Raw material
- Direct labor
- Supplies that become part of or are used up by the inventory manufacturing process
- Factory overhead including factory utility and supervisory costs
- Packaging and containers that are part of the product manufactured
- Freight-in, express-in, and cartage-in

Merchandise inventory purchased and sold during the year is usually determined by starting with the inventory at the beginning of the year, adding the purchases during the year, and subtracting out the ending inventory at the end of the year, as follows:

Beginning Inventory
plus Purchases during the period
minus Ending Inventory at the end of the period
equals Merchandise Inventory cost of sales

The following is a summary of the accounts, in groups and separately:

Assets:

Cash
Accounts receivable
Inventory
Investments
Pre-paid expense and deposits
Equipment
Motor vehicles
Furniture and fixtures
Land and buildings
Building improvements
Other tangible property
Goodwill
Patents and copyrights
Organizational expense
Research and development

Expenses:

Wages and salaries
Rental expense
Repairs
Replacements
Depreciation
Bad debt
Travel and transportation

Liabilities:

Accounts payable
Notes payable
Accrued expenses
Trade payables
Provision for pensions
Bonds
Debentures

Capital (equity):

Owners' equity
Capital stock
Paid-in surplus
Retained earnings

Income:

Merchandise sales
Rental income
Commissions
Royalties
Fees for services

Expenses (continued)

- Business entertainment
- Interest expense
- Insurance
- Taxes
- Office supplies
- Accounting and legal expense
- Utility expense
- Advertising
- Licenses and regulatory fees
- Charitable contributions
- Donations to business organizations and industry associations
- Management survey expense
- Lobbying expense
- Franchise, trademark, or trade name expense
- Educational expense
- Commitment fees
- Freight and postage

Cost of sales:

- Merchandise inventory
- Raw material
- Direct labor
- Supplies
- Factory overhead
- Packaging and containers
- Freight-in, express-in, and cartage-in

You now get the idea of what the accounts in accounting are. The early bookkeepers (going as far back as 3200 BC) were happy to stack or file all their original documents under these account headings.

As bookkeeping became more complicated, the practitioners decided to group these records under the proper account groups in a written record. This written record was a *journal*.

The more complex the system became, because of the number

of entries made, the greater the likelihood of mistakes. The question was: What can be done to minimize mistakes, to check each entry for accuracy, requires a minimum amount of time and is simple enough so that no great intellect is required to understand it?

The answer was the double-entry bookkeeping system.

BIRTH OF THE DOUBLE-ENTRY SYSTEM

The idea was simple and elegant. Take one transaction—for example a sale of merchandise—and write the number in a positive account. Then write the same number in a negative and opposite account.

Besides opposite balance, there was also another factor occurring at the same time: Movement in one account caused movement in another account. For instance, if a sale for cash was made, the asset cash increased by an amount equal to sales. It became apparent that all the different accounts affected each other directly or indirectly.

The first double-entry system we know of was the accounting of the Genoese communal stewards for the year 1340 AD (Figure 2.1). There is speculation as to whether the double-entry system could have been developed between 1278 and 1340 because a fire in 1339 destroyed all the books of state officials. The account book of the Commune for 1278 was based on the single-entry system. Because of the loss of all the volumes between 1278 and 1340 it is impossible to determine how early the double-entry system was introduced.

The original cartulary of 1340 which is now in the Genoese archives contains 478 pages. The accounts contained are of tax collectors and notaries.

Figure 2.1 is an account for soldiers. The entries are in medieval Latin. The debits are on the left half of the page and the credits on the right half. The formula for the debit side is "deve(n)t nobis pro" (or "in"). For the credit side "Recepimus" (we are recovered) is used even if there is no previous debit.

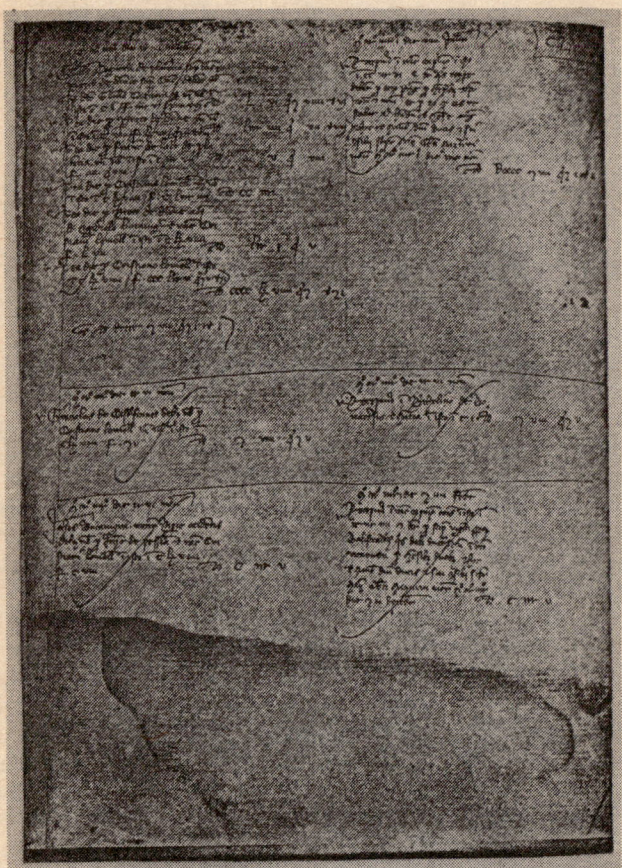

PHOTOSTAT OF A PAGE FROM THE ACCOUNTS OF THE GENOESE COMMUNAL STEWARDS FOR THE YEAR 1340, SHOWING THAT DOUBLE-ENTRY BOOKKEEPING WAS ALREADY IN USE IN THAT YEAR

Figure 2.1. First double-entry book.

[Early Italian text in historical typeface:]

> J reuerenti subditi de. V. D. S. Magnanimo. D. acio a pieno de tutto lordine mercantesco habino el bisogno: deliberai.(Olt'. le cose dinanze i qsta nra opa ditte) ancora particular tracrato grandemete necessario copillare. E in qsto solo lo iserto: p che a ogni loro occurreça el psente libro li possa seruire. Si vel mo / do a conti e scripture: como de ragion. E per esso intendo dar / li norma sufficiente e bastante in tenere ordinatamente tutti los conti e libri. Pero che. (como si fa) tre cose maxime sono opor tune: a chi vole con debita diligetia mercantare. De le qli la pori sima e la pecunia numerata e ogni altra faculta su stantiale. Ju xta illud phy vnu aliquid necessarioru e substantia. Sega el cui suffragio mal si po el maneggio traficante exercitare. Auega che molti gia nudi co bona fede comencando: de gra facede habio fatto. E mediante lo credito fedelmete seruato i magne richegge sieno peruenuti. Che asai p ytalia discurredo nabiamo cognoscuti. E piu gia nele gra republiche non si poteua dire: che la fede del bon mercatan te. E a quella si fermaua lor giuramento: dicedo. A la fe de real mercatante. E cio no deuel sere admiratione: cociosia che i la fede catolicamete ognuno si salui: e senza lei sia ipossibile piacere a dio. La secoda cosa che si recerca al debito trafico: sie che sia buon ragioneri: e prompto copurista. E p questo cosequire. (disopra como se ueduto) dal pricipio ala fine: ha uemo iducto regole e canoni a ciascuna opatione requisiti. Jn modo che da se: ogni dilige te lectore. tutto potra iprendere. E chi di questa pte non fosse bene armato: la sequete in ua no li serebbe. La 3a. e vltima cosa oportuna sic: che co bello ordine tutte sue facede debita

A PAGE FROM THE *Summa de Arithmetica* (1494)

Brother Lucas of the City of the Holy Sepulchre, as the author styles himself,
is said to be pictured in the capital letter.

Figure 2.2. First accounting book on the double-entry system.

The notations are in Roman numerals. Arabic numerals were known in Italy, but were not generally used in bookkeeping even during the fifteenth century, partly because of custom, but also because the Arabic figures offered a much greater possibility for fraudulent changes in postings than did the Roman numerals. As late as 1520, the municipality of Freiburg in Germany refused to accept as legal proof of debt entries in Arabic numerals.

The first book on accounting ever written was printed in Venice in 1494 bearing the title *Summa de Arithmetica, Geometria Proportioni e Proportionalita*, and written by a Franciscan friar called Frater Lucas de burgo Sancti Sepulchri (see Figure 2.2).

When the designer and early users of the double-entry system were deciding which entry would be a negative or a positive balance against another entry, they had to base the system on some logic. They had to consider how the accounts interacted with each other and then they had to consider the characteristics

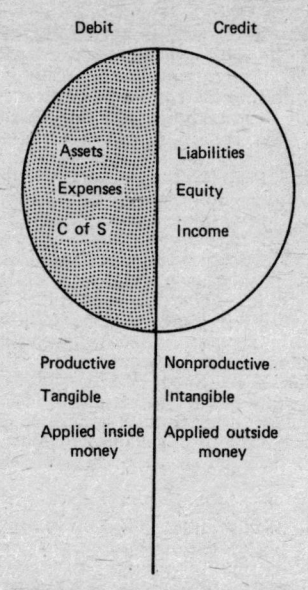

```
                    Debit        Credit

                    ┌─────────────────┐
                    │ Assets │ Liabilities │
                    │ Expenses │ Equity │
                    │ C of S │ Income │
                    └─────────────────┘

         Productive          Nonproductive
         Tangible            Intangible
         Applied inside      Applied outside
         money               money
```

Figure 2.3. The accounts circle.

of each account group: assets, liabilities, equity, income, expense, and cost of sales. They had to arbitrarily divide the accounts into "positive" and "negative" characteristics.

Looking at the six groups of accounts: assets, liabilities, equity, income, cost of sales, and expense, they were able to draw a few conclusions.

Assets, cost of sales, and expenses were account groups which had the characteristic of being money that the company had to spend to maintain business. Assets such as equipment, inventory, and so on, required that the company lay out money so that they could use these assets to produce income. Expenses such as rent and salaries also involved money that had to be spent in order to run the business. Cost of sales is the direct cost of either buying or purchasing inventory for sale. This was another use of money for business productivity. In short, what all these account

Birth of the Double-Entry System

groups (assets, expenses, cost of sales) had in common was that they represented *uses* of capital to produce income.

The characteristic that applies to the balance of the six accounts (liabilities, equity, and income) is that these accounts are sources of funds. The company gets money from income, of course, but the company also gets money from the owners in the form of owners' equity—the money that the business owners put in out of their pocket. Liabilities represent money that other people put into the business. If a bank loans the business some money, the money is from an outside source, the bank. When suppliers give you inventory on terms, they are supplying you with capital until they are paid. The common characteristic of liabilities, equity, and income is that they all represent *sources* of capital.

Figure 2.3 shows the accounts circle with assets, expense, and cost of sales on one side and liabilities, equity, and income on another side. In the illustration, we've put assets, expenses, and cost of sales on the left side and liabilities, equity, and income on the right side. We did that for a purpose.

Left and Right—The Debit and the Credit

In the double-entry bookkeeping system, each account has two possible entries, an entry on the left side (debit) and one on the right side (credit). Whether a left side (debit) entry increases the amount or decreases the amount in an account depends on what account the entry is made in, as we shall discuss shortly. But an entry in the *left* column is always a *debit* and an entry on the *right* side is always a *credit*.

Debit means left. Credit means right. Debit and credit have additional meanings when applied to the different accounts. Some accounts get a debit entry when they are increased, whereas other accounts are credited to increase them.

By now you might have guessed why assets, expense, and cost of sales are on the left (debit) side, and liabilities, equity, and income are on the right (credit) side. All of the *left* group generally have a debit (left) balance, and to increase the accounts you must *debit* them. For instance: to increase cash (an asset), you debit the account. Furthermore, since cash is generally more than zero it generally has a debit balance. To pay off (increase the amount spent on) an expense or cost of sales, you debit the account. Since rent, utilities, or salaries (expenses) are usually more than zero, there is usually a debit balance in these accounts. When you pay for containers in a manufacturing process, you increase the amount paid (from what it was before). Since cost of sales is rarely zero, you will generally have a debit balance.

Stated again: *Assets, expenses* and *cost of sales* generally have a *debit balance* and are *increased* by a *debit*.

You know that assets, expenses, and cost of sales are increased by debits, and liabilities, equity, and income are increased by credits. How are these accounts decreased? As you might guess; assets, expenses, and cost of sales (the left, debit group) are *decreased* by a *credit* to the account. Liabilities, equity, and income (the right, credit group) are *decreased* by a *debit*. In other words, if a debit increases an account, a credit decreases an account. If a credit increases an account, then it takes a debit to decrease the account. From the standpoint of balance this makes sense. Opposite account groups are increased in opposite ways and are decreased in opposite ways. A debit increases assets, expenses, and cost of sales and decreases liabilities, equity and income. A credit increases liabilities, equity, and income and decreases assets, expense, and cost of sales.

This can be summarized as follows:

Account group	Debit	Credit
Assets	Increases	Decreases
Expense	Increases	Decreases
Cost of Sales	Increases	Decreases
Liabilities	Decreases	Increases
Equity	Decreases	Increases
Income	Decreases	Increases

THE INTERRELATIONSHIPS OF THE ACCOUNTS

In accounting, if you debit one account you must credit another account. Conversely, if you credit one account you must debit

The Interrelationships of the Accounts

another account. In this way, transactions or movements in one account affect movements in another account.

Examples of Account Transactions

Let's take some examples: When an owner of a business puts his equity into a business, it increases (credit) his equity account and also increases (debit) the cash account. What happens is that the owner puts some cash into the business, but the accountant wants to keep tract of two facts: How much the owner put in and how much there is in the cash account because of this transaction. If the transaction were written in a journal, it would look like this:

Date	Explanation	Debit	Credit
1/20/80	Cash Owner's Equity To record the contribution of cash to the business of John Zipp	$5,000	$5,000

When a *sale* is made for *cash*, income is increased (credit) and cash is increased (debit). The journal entry would look like this:

Date	Explanation	Debit	Credit
1/21/80	Cash Income To record sales for cash	$ 500	$ 500

When an expense is paid, *cash* is decreased (credit) because the expense has to be paid out of cash, and *expense* is increased (debit). The journal transaction would look like this:

Date	Explanation	Debit	Credit
1/22/80	Expense Cash To record payment from cash of an expense	$ 400	$ 400

Assume that John Zipp, the owner of this business, is able to get inventory on credit; that is, he pays no money for a certain period of time, but he takes possession of the inventory. This would create an "account payable"; an account he owes money to. This transaction would increase (credit) *accounts payable* which is a liability and increase (debit) *inventory* which is an asset. The journal entries would look as follows:

Date	Explanation	Debit	Credit
1/23/80	Inventory	$1,000	
	Accounts payable		$1,000
	To record purchase of inventory on credit.		

Generalizations of Account Transactions

The following are some helpful generalizations:

First, every debit requires at least one credit and every credit requires at least one debit.

Second, there are three types of transactions between these account groups: increase-decrease, increase-increase, and decrease-decrease. Furthermore, any transaction between any of the account groups on one side of the accounts circle and any of the account groups on the *opposite* side of the circle will be either an increase-increase or decrease-decrease transaction [for example: debit (increase) cash and credit (increase) debt]. Any transaction between groups of accounts on the *same* side of the accounts circle will be an increase-decrease transaction [for example: debit (increase) expense and credit (decrease) cash].

Cash decreases (credit) whenever a check is written by the business.

- Most checks are written for expense items—debit (increase) expense and credit (decrease) cash.
- The second largest number of checks written is either to purchase inventory for cash (debit cost of sales, credit cash) or for the payment on accounts payable for merchandise already purchased on credit (debit accounts payable, credit cash).

- Almost every check written for debt repayment has an interest and a principal portion. The interest portion is an expense and the principal portion is considered a reduction in debt (debit interest expense, debit debt liability, and credit cash).
- Checks are occasionally written for owners' draw or dividends (debit dividends and credit cash).

With the exception of a reduction in accounts receivable (asset) caused by a payment on account by a customer, cash is almost always increased (debit) by increases in the account groups on the *right* side of the accounts circle (liabilities, equity, income). (For example: debit cash, credit liabilities, or debit cash, credit income; or debit cash, credit equity.) Only very rarely is cash increased from a cash rebate on expense or cost of sales or the proceeds from the sale of assets.

The Basic Accounting Equation and Permanent and Temporary Accounts

The basic accounting equation, the formula from which all accounting logic proceeds, is:

$$\text{ASSETS} = \text{LIABILITIES} + \text{EQUITY} \text{ (owner's capital)}$$

Using the rules of algebra, this can also be stated as:

Assets − Liabilities = Equity or
Assets − Equity = Liability or
Assets − Equity − Liabilities = 0 (zero)

In other words, the total dollar amount of assets equals the total dollar amount of equity plus liabilities. The dollar amount of assets minus the dollar amount of liabilities (or equity) equals the total dollar amount of equity (or liabilities). If you subtract the total dollar volume of liabilities and equity from assets, you get zero.

Both sides of the equation are in *balance;* the total of one side (assets) equals the total of the other side (liabilities plus equity). When these three accounts are put in document form, it is called a "balance sheet"—one of the basic documents of accounting.

The equation means that the value of the properties a business owns (assets) is equal to the value of the rights in those properties (liabilities and equity). Liabilities are the creditors' (banks, trade, etc.) rights in the business; equity is the owners' rights. So rights in properties equal the amount of properties.

We have discussed three of the six groups of accounts—assets, liabilities, and equity—let's now turn to the other three groups of accounts: income, cost of sales, and expense.

Income, cost of sales, and expense make up a second fundamental accounting document called an "income statement" or "profit and loss statement" (P&L for short). The income statement takes the sales (income) for a period and reduces it by cost of sales and expenses, resulting in a "net profit." This net profit, after such cash costs as loan principal reduction, taxes, and dividends or draw, is posted to the equity account as "retained earnings."

This process can be illustrated as follows:

```
        Income                        ⎫
minus   Cost of Sales                 ⎬  INCOME STATEMENT
minus   Expenses                      ⎪
equals  Net Profit (or Net Loss)      ⎭


                    Net Profit (or Net Loss)
APPLICATION OF  ⎰
FUNDS           ⎱   minus   Dividends
                    equals  RETAINED EARNINGS


        Retained Earnings             ⎫
plus    Previous Equity Balance       ⎬  EQUITY CALCULATION
equals  NEW EQUITY balance            ⎭
```

So, income, cost of sales, and expense are in effect part of the

The Interrelationships of the Accounts

equity account. The result of taking income and subtracting cost of sales, expenses, and dividends is either an increase (caused by net profit) or a decrease (caused by net loss) in the equity account.

Income, cost of sales, and expenses fit into the basic accounting equation of "assets = liabilities + equity" by being part of the equity account.

Let's expand the basic accounting equation to include income, cost of sales, and expense. The equation can be restated thusly: Assets = liabilities + previous equity + income − cost of sales − costs. ["Costs" include expense and cash costs (taxes, draw, etc.).]

The only way that a business can grow is by making money (profit after costs). If the business makes money, the worth (net worth or equity) of business is greater. If a company *loses* money, the worth of the company (equity) is less. The net cash that a company makes is the money that an owner has available from the business: it's the owner's equity.

The income, cost of sales, and expense accounts are a part of the equity account, but only a temporary part. Income less cost of sales less expense is only posted to equity *once* per period. If the accounting period for a business is one year, the income statement accounts (income, cost of sales, and expense) only become *incorporated into equity once per year*. This makes sense because it would be much too troublesome to incorporate these three large groups of accounts into the equity account constantly. This would cause the equity account to have a larger number of entries than the cash account. In short, it is accounting convention to incorporate income, cost of sales, and expense into equity no more than once per accounting period (month, quarter, year).

When income, cost of sales, and expense (the income statement accounts) are "posted" or put as part of equity, the separate accounts are zeroed out. All the entries in the income statement accounts are made zero and they start out with zero in the account to begin the next period.

The following is an example of an end of the period journal entry, closing various income and expense accounts to the income and expense summary, an equity account:

Date	Explanation	Debit	Credit
12/31/78	Income	$150,000	
	Income and Expense Summary		$150,000
	Income and Expense Summary	142,000	
	Merchandise purchases		120,000
	Salary expense		10,000
	Rental expense		4,000
	Utilities		2,000
	Supplies		1,000
	Taxes		500
	Accounting		1,200
	Entertainment		2,300
	Transportation and travel		1,000
	To record transfer of accounts to income and expense summary.		

The following shows how the salary expense *ledger* account is zeroed out by the above journal entries:

Date	Explanation	Debit	Credit	Date	Explanation	Debit	Credit
1/30/80	CDJ-2*	$1,000					
6/30/80	CDJ-10	1,000					
12/31/80	CDJ-21	1,000		12/31/80	GJ-† 12-3	$12,000	
	Total	10,000					

* CDJ stands for cash disbursements journal, the journal these entries came from. The number after the CDJ is the page number of the cash disbursements journal the entry was posted from.

† GJ means general journal. The number after GJ is the absolute number of the entry illustrated in the journal entry just above. General journal entries are usually numbered sequentially. The first number (12) stands for the month of the entry and the second number (3) is the number of the general journal entry that month, taken sequentially.

Income, cost of sales, and expense accounts are zeroed out and closed once per period. Therefore they are considered *temporary* accounts.

Assets, liabilities, and equity (to which the temporary accounts are closed once per period) and considered *permanent* accounts because they are never closed or zeroed out at the end of a period. These are the basic accounts of the business and the only time they will be zero is if they are physically reduced by some event such as selling off an asset, spending all the cash in the bank, paying off a debt, or taking all the money out of equity.

If all the assets are sold and all the asset accounts are reduced to zero, the business ceases to exist. If all the equity account equals zero, the business has as much debt as assets and the business is in trouble. If there were zero debt (no liabilities), the company would be considered unusual—this circumstance would generally exist only when a business is just starting. In short, it is a rare instance when any of the three account groups (assets, liabilities, and equity) are zero.

Assets, liabilities, and equity are permanent accounts that generally cease to exist only when the business ceases to exist.

SUMMARY

"Do you think you understand?" Pete Popstein asked John Your.

"Let me go over it with you and see," John answered. "There are six groups of accounts into which all accounts fall. These groups are:

- Assets
- Liabilities
- Equity
- Income
- Cost of sales
- Expense

"The groups of accounts fall into different categories. Assets, cost of sales, and expenses are money used inside the business—they are basically a *use* of money. All these accounts are increased by a debit and decreased by a credit.

"Liabilities, equity and income, on the other hand, are sources of money. They are increased by a credit and decreased by a debit.

"Assets, liabilities, and equity are the constituent accounts of the basic accounting equation:

$$\text{Assets} = \text{Liabilities} + \text{Equity}$$

"Assets, liabilities, and equity are *permanent* accounts—they are never closed out in accounting, but continue to be open as long as the business exists. Assets, liabilities, and equity are also the groups of accounts that make up the balance sheet.

"Income, cost of sales, and expenses are the group of accounts that make up the profit and loss statement. They are *temporary* accounts that are closed out at the end of each accounting period. They are all closed out to the equity account, which is a permanant account," John finished and took a long breath.

"Good," said Pete. "Now is there anything else you want to ask before we move on to the process of taking all the original documents and making them into accounts in the journal?"

"Yeah. Tell me again. How are the income, cost of sales, and expense accounts related to equity? I didn't quite understand that."

"Okay," Pete explained, "income, cost of sales, and the expense accounts make up the income statement. Income minus cost of sales minus operating expense equals net profit, or net loss. This net profit or loss is carried over to the equity account after taxes are paid. For instance, if Yourcompany makes a $10,000 net profit after taxes, then the equity is increased by $10,000."

"Okay," John sighed, "tell me about the journals."

Chapter Three
The First Transformation— the Books

Pete Popstein looked through the stacks of original documents that John had collected. He commented, "One thing that you need to do when you are journalizing [putting the amounts from the original documents into the journal] is to look very carefully at what was billed by your suppliers versus what was paid to them by check. Sometimes this is where the theft of money can be made. You should also call all of your suppliers, that is, everyone who has received a check from Yourcompany, and ask them what the present balance is that you owe them. It should be the same as the amount you will find after reconstructing the books, but the point is that some suppliers that Yourcompany has paid checks to may be nonexistent. Be especially careful that you have receipts for every check that you paid. These receipts may be in the form of credits to your account."

Pete Popstein continued, "When you are entering the accounts receivable ledger, check to see if you received all the money that the customer claims to have paid you."

"Okay, I think I can remember that. Not tell me how to use a journal."

"Okay," Pete began . . .

To make sense of all the thousands of transactions that the average business has during the year, these transactions are entered into a daily book called the *journal*. It allows the busi-

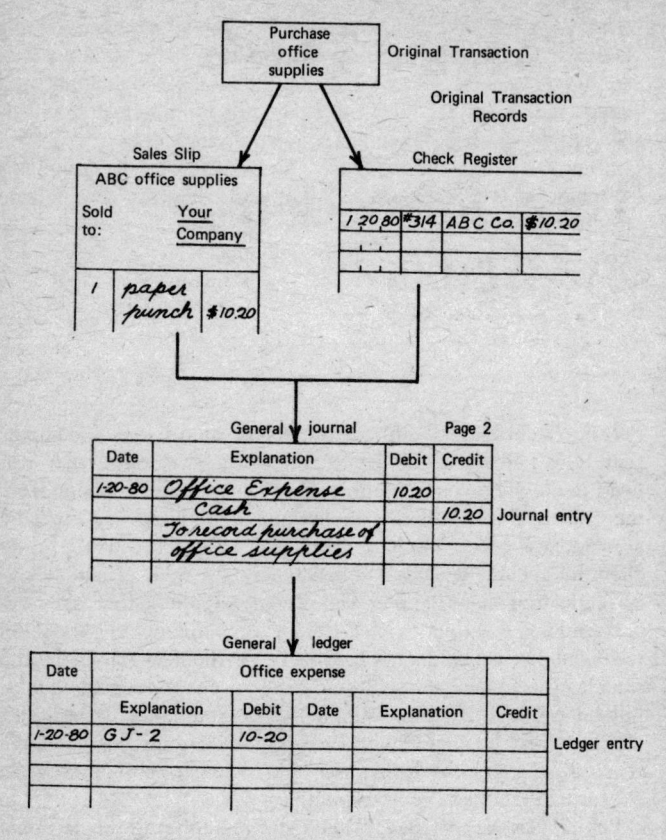

Figure 3.1. Flow of documentation in accounting.

Original Transaction: Purchase office supplies

Original Transaction Records:

Sales Slip — ABC office supplies
Sold to: Your Company
1 paper punch — $10.20

Check Register
1-20-80 | #314 | ABC Co. | $10.20

Journal entry — General journal, Page 2

Date	Explanation	Debit	Credit
1-20-80	Office Expense	10.20	
	Cash		10.20
	To record purchase of office supplies		

Ledger entry — General ledger

Date	Office expense				
	Explanation	Debit	Date	Explanation	Credit
1-20-80	G J - 2	10-20			

---

ness to keep track of every daily transaction in one place. Transactions are recorded sequentially, as they happen.

However, if a businessperson wants to find out, for instance, how much he or she paid for office supplies in the last two months, he or she would still have a problem. Even with the journal, he or she would have to look through every transaction in the last two months to pick out the supplies that were purchased in order to obtain a total. To solve this problem, another book that categorizes everything under specific topics, or accounts, is needed. He or she needs a book that has one page called "office supplies" that has every office supply expense listed. This summary book has come to be known as a *ledger*.

Figure 3.1 is an illustration of the transactions sequence, from purchase to original records of the transaction, to "journalizing" to entry in the ledger.

CHART OF ACCOUNTS

A common practice among most businessmen is to assign a number in addition to a name to various accounts. For instance, the cash account could have a number "101," so that when making entries the number would be used instead of writing out the name. Using numbers instead of—or in addition to—names of accounts is not only easier, but it also lends itself very readily to computerization.

When all the accounts are assigned numbers, the list of account names and numbers is called a *chart of accounts*.

The following is a list of assets, liabilities and expenses that are generally considered to be common account names:

Assets
Cash
Inventory
Accounts receivable (sales that have not been collected)
Notes receivable (short-term money owed to your company)
Prepaid expenses (money advanced for services or goods not yet received)
Short-term investments
Equipment (for business use)
Land and buildings (for business use)
Leasehold improvements
Goodwill paid when the business was acquired
Long-term investments
Certain development costs

Liabilities (money or goods not paid for but used for business purposes)

Accounts and notes payable
Provisions for pensions and taxes
Accrued items
Mortgages
Bonds and debentures
Long-term debt
Deferred taxes

Expenses (including cost of sales)

Rent or leases (for equipment or real property)
Outside services (accounting, consulting, janitorial, trash pickup, security, etc.)
Personnel salaries
Payroll taxes and benefit plans for employees
Travel required for business purposes
Material purchased
Supplies purchased
Inventory purchased
Freight
Utilities
Business license and local taxes
Equipment or tools with a life of one year or less
Repairs and maintenance
Certain clothing and laundry expense

Equity accounts represent money put into or retained by the business. Equity includes stock in the company (preferred, common, or treasury), paid-in, surplus, retained earnings, and interest in subsidiaries.

When you arrange all of these accounts under the basic groups: assets, liabilities, equity, income, expenses, and cost of sales, to simplify identification you have a chart of accounts.

Since there are likely to be many different accounts in business records, it is necessary to establish a plan for identifying each account and locating it quickly. If, besides listing all the accounts under the above groups, you are also assigning numbers to them, identification becomes that much easier. In developing an index or chart of accounts, blocks of numbers are assigned to each group of accounts.

For example, assets are assigned the block of numbers from 100 to 199 (or 1000 to 1999 for large companies with many accounts); liabilities have the numbers 200 to 299 (or 2000 to 2999); and so on.

Chart of Accounts

Account Number	Account Name
100–199	Assets
101	Cash
110	Accounts receivable
115	Notes receivable
120	Prepaid expense
120.1	Prepaid rent
150	Equipment
150.18	1970 Dodge pickup truck
. . .	Etc.
200–299	Liabilities
201	Accounts payable
201.29	Accounts payable— Associated Wagontongues
211	Notes payable
211.2	Notes payable Bank of Suez
221	Taxes payable
. . .	Etc.
300–399	Owners' equity
301	Capital stock
310	Preferred stock
330	Retained earnings
. . .	Etc.

400–499	Income
401	Income from operations
401.3	Income from Model B solid state mousetrap
401.5	Income from mousetrap accessories
410	Interest Income
450	Income from extraordinary items
. . .	Etc.
500–599	Operating expense
501	Salary expense
501.7	Officer's salary
505	Payroll taxes
505.2	Administrative employees' payroll tax
508	Rent expense
572	Small tool expense
. . .	Etc.
600–699	Cost of sales expense
601	Material purchases
601.62	Purchases of steel whatchets
610	Factory salaries
610.3	Factory salaries, Plant No. 3
. . .	Etc.

JOURNALS (THE DAILY BOOKS)

General Journal

The general journal is the original journal developed to cover all types of entries. The general journal (Figure 3.2) is a form that has a space for the date, a description of the entry, the account number (from the chart of accounts), a space to check off the entry when it is transferred to the ledger, and spaces for debit or credit entries.

Every accounting transaction can be recorded in the general journal, and for the very small one-person operation or service business, this general journal is all that is needed. For larger operations with lots of special transactions, such as credit sales and purchases and many cash transactions, it is advisable to have special journals such as the cash disbursements journal, the cash receipts journal, the sales journal, and the purchases journal. In Yourcompany special journals are used, and the general journal is only used to record transactions that do not fit into the special journals. For instance, such transactions as recording salaries and taxes or closing out the books at the end of the year would be recorded in the general journal because they have no place in the special journals (cash disbursements, receipts, sales, or purchases).

General Journal Examples

"Now," Pete Popstein reached into the documents that John Your had stacked on the desk, "now we are going to take some original documents and post them to the general ledger. At the beginning of this year you received a $25,000 loan from Bank Amerigold. Just to get you started we will make this entry and some others directly into the general journal. But as I just explained, it is better for a company of Yourcompany's size to use special journals.

Example One. You borrow $25,000 from Bank Amerigold at 11%.

The original transaction documents are the loan agreement and a deposit to Yourcompany by the bank.

The journal entry looks like Figure 3.3.

Cash is debited (increased) by $25,000 and the Bank Amerigold note is credited (increased). The transaction involves an increase in an asset (cash) and an increase in a liability (Bank Amerigold Note Payable).

Example Two. John Your, on January 3, purchased test equipment from Zarkoff Equipment for $10,000. He paid $5000 down

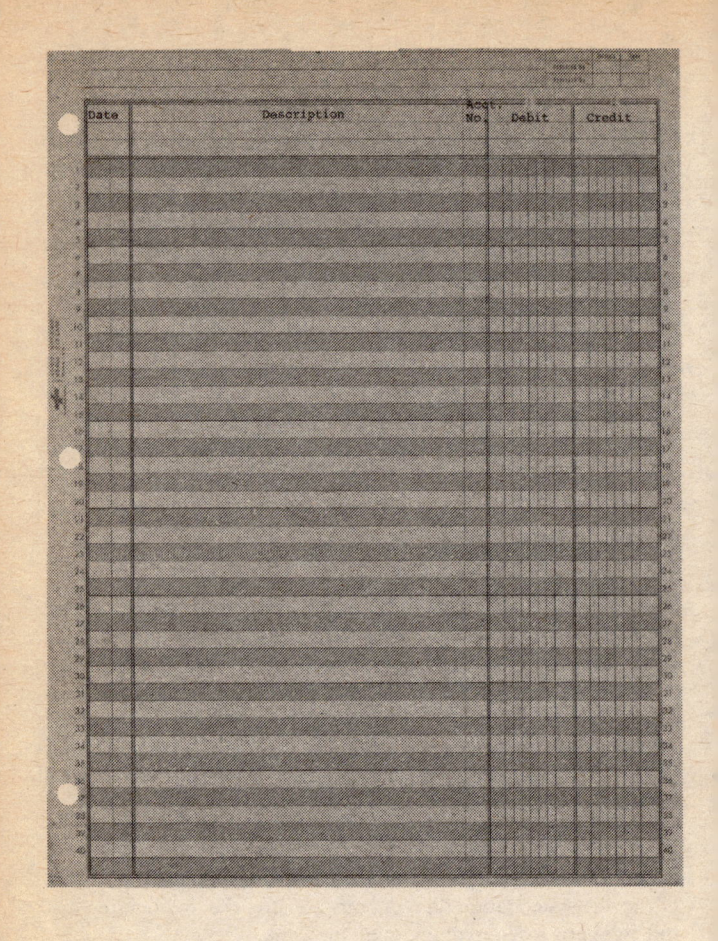

Figure 3.2. Trial balance sheet.

Journals (The Daily Books)

Date	Description	Acct.	Debit	Credit
1980	1-1			
1/2	CASH	101	25000	
	NOTE PAYABLE-BANK AMERIGOLD	211.1		25000
	TO RECORD LOAN NUMBER #378-14 FROM BANK AMERIGOLD			
	1-2			
1/3	TEST EQUIPMENT	150.1	10000	
	CASH	101		5000
	NOTE PAYABLE-ZARKOFF EQUIP.	211.2		5000
	TO RECORD PURCHASE OF TEST EQUIPMENT FROM ZARKOFF EQUIPMENT ON CREDIT AND FOR CASH.			
	1-3			
1/4	INVENTORY-PARTS	130	30000	
	ACCOUNTS PAYABLE-CCPSC	201.1		15000
	CASH	101		15000
	TO RECORD PURCHASE OF PARTS INVENTORY FROM CCPSC FOR CASH AND ON CREDIT			

Figure 3.3

and received a note to pay off the balance over a one-year period at 8%.

The original transaction documents are a sales slip from Zarkoff Equipment for $10,000, a note from Zarkoff for $5000, and a check from Yourcompany for $5000.

The journal entry is shown in Figure 3.3.

Test equipment is debited (increased) and both cash and notes payable to Zarkoff Equipment are credited (cash is decreased and notes payable are increased). The transaction involves both an increase (test equipment) and a decrease (cash) in an asset and an increase in a liability (notes payable—Zarkoff Equipment).

Example Three. On January 4, John Your bought $30,000 worth of parts inventory from Computer and Circuit Parts Supply Company (CCPSC). He paid cash for $15,000 worth of inventory and took $15,000 worth of inventory on thirty-day credit terms.

The original transaction documents are a check from Yourcompany for $15,000 and a sales slip from CCPSC for $30,000.

The journal entry is shown in Figure 3.3.

Parts inventory is debited (increased) and cash and accounts payable are credited (decrease cash, increase accounts payable). The transaction involves both an increase (inventory) and a decrease (cash) in an asset and an increase in a liability (accounts payable—CCPSC).

Example Four. On January 5, Yourcompany made a payment of $13,500 to Softfare.

The transaction documents include: a check and . . . Pete stopped.

"You don't seem to have a receipt for this payment. Do you have another bill from Software for a later date?"

John looked through the stack of bills. He found a billing for February for Softfare but it did not indicate on the billing that a payment had been made for January. The amount of the bill was different from the amount paid in January and there was no indication of a balance outstanding. John passed both the January and the February Softfare bills to Pete. Pete asked for all the Softfare bills for one year. None of them indicated previous payment, all were for different amounts, and none of them had a balance from a previous time.

"You better call these people," Pete told John. "Something is funny here." There was no phone number on the bill and information had no listing. "Well, we'll send them a letter asking for the present balance owed, copies of the past invoices, and a phone number so that we can contact them. I'll have my office handle that. Let's continue with our entries. . . ."

Here's how we would record the $13,500 payment to Softfare (Figure 3.4, 1–4).

Since, presumably, inventory from Softfare was ordered and received, you would debit (decrease) accounts payable—Soft-

Date	Description	Acct.	Debit	Credit
	1-4			
1/5	ACCOUNTS PAYABLE - SOFTFARE	201	13500	
	CASH	101		13500
	TO RECORD PAYMENT OF ACCOUNT BALANCE TO SOFTFARE [NOTE: MIGHT INVOLVE IRREGULARITIES]			
	1-5			
1/5	RENT EXPENSE	508	1200	
	CASH	101		1200
	TO RECORD PAYMENT OF PREMISES RENT TO SMITHREAL			

Figure 3.4

fare, and credit (decrease) cash for $13,500. This transaction involves a decrease in liabilities (accounts payable) and a decrease in an asset (cash).

Pete Popstein made an additional notation in brackets when recording the transaction because of possible irregularities.

Example Five. On January 5 Yourcompany wrote a check for its monthly rent of $1200.

The original transaction documents include a check from Yourcompany and a receipt from SmithReal, the landlord.

The journal entry is Figure 3.4.

Rent is debited (increased) by $1200 and cash is credited (decreased) by the same amount. The transaction involves both a decrease in an asset (cash) and an increase in an expense (rent).

Special Note on General Journals. As illustrated, in the standard format of the general journal a heading is placed over each entry with the month (January is 1) and the number of the entry

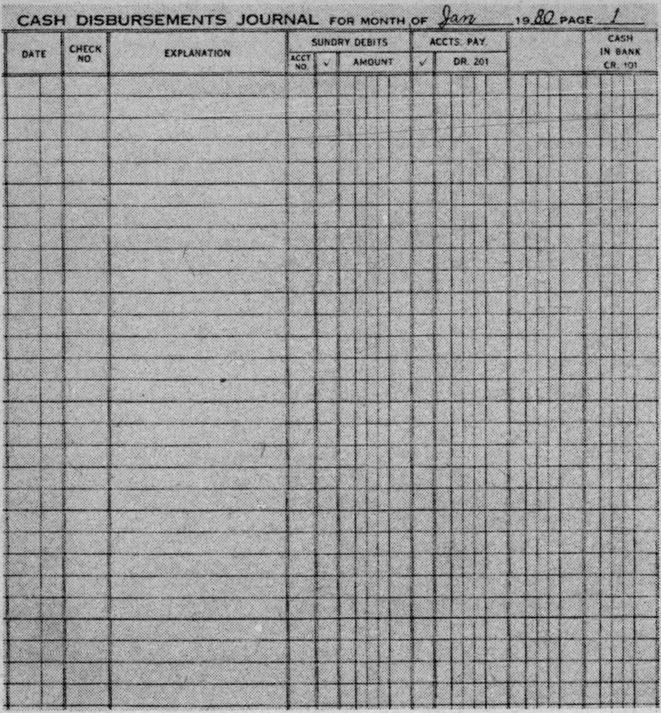

CASH DISBURSEMENTS JOURNAL FOR MONTH OF Jan 19 80 PAGE 1

DATE		CHECK NO.	EXPLANATION	SUNDRY DEBITS			ACCTS. PAY.			CASH IN BANK CR. 101
				ACCT NO.	✓	AMOUNT	✓	DR. 201		

Figure 3.5. Cash disbursements form.

CASH DISBURSEMENTS JOURNAL

Date	Check No.	Explanation	Acct. No.	Sundry Debits Amount	Accts. Pay. DR. 201	Sub-Contract CR 600-616	Cash In Bank CR. 101
1980							
Jan 6	104	Titan Telephone - Installation	510	300			
		Titan Telephone - Deposit	122	150			450
Jan 6	105	CCPSe	601		500		500
Jan 6	106	Assemblies, Inc.	601			1400	1400
Jan 7	107	Office Supplies	560	150 00			150
Jan 7	108	Business License	591	40			40

Figure 3.6. Cash disbursements journal form.

that month (1 through 5 in the example), and accounts are both named and numbered. There is a written summary of the transaction after the separate accounts are shown with the dollar amount of each entry. Also notice that the traditional method is to show the debits first, and the credits last. The debits are flush to the left and the credits are indented.

Cash Disbursements Journal

The cash disbursements journal is a specialized journal designed to record all cash disbursements—usually checks written. The cash disbursements journal is comparable to the check register because it records all the checks written and what accounts they represent. It differs from the check register in that it has special columns for accounts for which many checks are written. For instance, payments of accounts payable and purchases of inventory for cash might require a large number of checks to be written monthly, so the cash disbursements journal has special columns for these items.

The cash disbursements journal allows you to show on one line both the debit (to the account the check is made out to) and the credit (cash) in each transaction. The illustration following (Figure 3.5) is an example of a cash disbursement journal page.

The cash disbursement journal also has a check column to show when the accounts were posted to a ledger.

Cash Disbursements Journal Examples

Since Yourcompany, like most small businesses, pays out a lot of money and uses checks on the company account for this purpose, it is a good idea to have a cash disbursements journal. Using this special journal makes bookkeeping easier because summaries and general journal entries do not have to be made each time a check is written. You should have special columns for accounts payable and subcontract work. Here is how you would make entries into the special cash disbursements journal:

Journals (The Daily Books)

Example One. John wrote a check to Titan Telephone for new telephone installation and deposits. It is check number 104, dated January 6, for $430 as a deposit.

The original transaction documents include a receipt from Titan Telephone, Inc. and a check from Yourcompany.

The cash disbursements journal entry is shown in Figure 3.6.

Telephone expense and telephone deposits are debited (increased) and cash is credited (decreased). The transaction involves both an increase (deposits) and a decrease (cash) in assets and an increase in expense.

Example Two. Yourcompany pays off some of the money that it owes Computer and Circuit Parts Supply Company (CCPSC). Yourcompany wrote check 105 for $5000 to CCPSC on January 6.

The original transaction document is a check from Yourcompany.

The cash disbursements journal entry is shown in Figure 3.6.

CCPSC accounts payable (account number 201) is debited (decreased) and cash in the bank (account 101) is credited (decreased). The transaction involves a decrease in both a liability (accounts payable) and an asset (cash).

Example Three. Yourcompany paid Assemblies, Inc. for subcontract work they performed on the Yourcompany computer system. Yourcompany writes check 106 for $1200.

The transaction documents include a check from Yourcompany and a paid receipt from Assemblies, Inc.

The cash disbursements journal entry is shown in Figure 3.6.

Subcontract expense (610) is debited (increased) and cash is credited (decreased). The transaction involves an increase in a cost of sales (subcontract) and a decrease in an asset (cash).

Example Four. Yourcompany wrote check 107 on January 7 to ABC Office Supply for $150.

The transaction documents include a check from Yourcompany and a sales receipt from ABC Office Supply.

The cash disbursements journal entry is shown in Figure 3.6.

Sundry debits—office supplies (560) is debited (increased) and cash is credited (decreased). The transaction involves an increase in expense (office supplies) and a decrease in an asset (cash).

Example Five. Yourcompany paid $40 for a business license, check number 108.

The transaction documents are a check from Yourcompany and a receipt from the government for the license and a license.

The cash disbursements journal entry is shown in Figure 3.6.

Sundry debits—business license (591) is debited (increased) and cash is credited. The transaction involves an increase in an expense and a decrease in an asset—cash.

Note. The cash disbursements journal has columnar entries for accounts that will have many transactions (such as cash and accounts payable). Cash is credited in every entry because every time a check is written (a cash disbursement is made), cash is reduced.

The Cash Receipts Journal

For sales recording, it is better to use a cash receipts journal than the general journal. The cash receipts journal records your cash sales and can record sales from different categories in separate columns. For management reasons, you may want to keep track of which sales are for computer systems and which are for component sales, so we'll set separate columns in this cash receipts journal for these two groups of sales. An example of Pete's cash disbursements journal is shown in Figure 3.7.

For miscellaneous income there is a sundry credits column. Since Yourcompany does rent some of its systems, it is necessary to record this source of income under a miscellaneous (sundry) credits column.

The following are examples of cash receipts journal transactions.

Example One. On January 8, Yourcompany had cash sales of $378, all of which are sales of components.

Cash receipts journal for month of _____ 19____   Page ____

Date	Explanation	Sundry credits		Accounts receivable CR. 111	Systems sales CR. 410	Components sales CR. 420	Cash in bank DR. 101
		Acct. no.	Amount				

Figure 3.7. Cash receipts journal form.

CASH RECEIPTS JOURNAL

Date	Explanation	Loc No.	Sundry Credits Amount	Accounts Receivable CR. 111	Systems Sales CR. 410	Components Sales CR. 420	Cash in Bank DR. 101
1980							
Jan 8	Daily Sales					578	578
Jan 9	Daily Sales				510	630	1140
Jan 10	Daily Sales				540	816	
	Rental Income – K.K. Co.	430	150				1506
Jan 11	Daily Sales					530	
	John Kitt			75			605
Jan 12	Daily Sales				620	630	
	Rental Income – R.G.	430	150				1400

Figure 3.8

The transaction documents are sales receipts (a stack of sales slips) and a deposit slip for the amount of sales to Yourcompany's bank checking account.

The cash receipts journal entry is shown in Figure 3.8.

Cash in the bank (101) is debited (increased) and component sales (account 420) is credited (increased). The transaction involves an increase in both assets (cash) and income (component sales).

Example Two. The next day, January 9, Yourcompany had cash sales of both components ($630) and systems ($510).

Journals (The Daily Books)

The original transaction documents are the sales receipts and a deposit slip to Yourcompany's checking account.

The cash receipts journal entry is shown in Figure 3.8.

Cash in the bank is debited (increased) by $1140, and the total amount of both sales—component sales and systems sales—are credited (increased). This transaction involves an increase in cash (debit), and assets, and two income accounts—component sales and systems sales.

Example Three. On January 10, Yourcompany received not only cash sales from systems and components, but also rental income from a unit that was on lease to K. K. Company ($350), for total sales that day of $1506.

The original transaction documents are the sales receipts and the rental payment receipt from K. K. Company as well as the deposit slip to Yourcompany's bank for the total sales.

The entry is shown in Figure 3.8.

Cash in the bank is debited (increased) by $1506, the total amount of systems, components and rental income. Component and systems sales are both credited (increased) as in the previous example. Rental income, which is account number 430, is also credited (increased), but it is entered under the "Sundry Credits" column. The transaction involves an increase in the asset "cash" (debit), and an increase in the "systems sales," "component sales," and "rental income" accounts (credit).

Example Four. On January 11, Yourcompany received $530 in component sales and $75 in payment on a receivable from John Kitt, for a total of $605.

The original transaction documents included the sales receipts for component sales, a receipt to John Kitt for payment of a receivable, and the bank deposit slip for the total.

The entry is shown in Figure 3.8.

Cash in the bank is debited (increased) by the total from component sales and payment of receivables. Accounts receivable are decreased (credited) and component sales are increased (credited). The transaction involves an increase in the asset cash (debit) and in sales (credit) as well as a decrease in the asset accounts receivable (credit).

Example Five. On January 12, Yourcompany received money for component and systems sales as well as rental income.

The original transaction documents are the same as in Example Three above: deposit slip to the bank and receipts for sales and rentals.

The entry is shown in Figure 3.8.

Cash in the bank is debited (increased) and sales and rental accounts are credited (increased). The transaction involves an increase both in the asset cash (debit) and in component sales, system sales, and rental income (credit).

Note. The most active columns are the sales columns in the cash receipts journal. Remember that these are only cash sales and do not include sales made on credit (reserved for the "Sales Journal," discussed next). Cash receipts from whatever source (cash sales, rental income, or receipts of cash payments on accounts receivable owed) are entered in the Cash Receipts Journal. Every entry made requires debiting cash.

Pete looked closely at the stack of bank deposits.

"How many bank accounts does Yourcompany have?" Pete Popstein asked John Your.

"We have one checking account and one savings account at Bank Amerigold. The Everywhere, Minn., branch downtown," John answered.

"You don't have any accounts at the Chevy, Minn., branch in the suburbs?" Pete asked.

"No. I sometimes deposit there on the way home. Interbranch, you know."

"But you don't have an account there. And your deposit slips are not coded with their address?" Pete continued.

"No. What are all these questions about?" John asked.

"Let me see your bank deposit slips that you have with your checkbook," Pete asked John without answering. Pete looked at the blank deposit slips and at the deposit slips in the stack that

Sales journal for month of ______________ 19____ Page ______

Date	Sales slip no.	Customer's name	Accounts receivable DR. 111	Systems sales CR. 410	Components sales CR. 420

Figure 3.9

	Sales slip		Accounts Receivable	Systems Sales	Components Sales
Date	No.	Customer's Name	DR. 111	CR. 410	CR. 420
1976					
1/13	100	John Kitt	350	350	
1/14	101	Thompson Co.	160		160
	102	Rick Hayes	50		50
1/15	103	C. Richard Baker	50		50
1/16	104	Zipp and Co.	1250	1250	
	105	Thompson Co.	75		75
1/17	106	Richards Components	120		120

Figure 3.10

they were posting. Finally he said, "Someone has created an account at the Chevy, Minn., branch of your bank, Bank Amerigold. See this deposit slip? It has the branch address printed in the corner. The branch is in Chevy. The account number is 5-0987. Now look at your bank deposit slip and these other deposit slips. They are for the Everywhere branch of Bank Amerigold. See the address? And the account number is 1-3402. Let's call up the Chevy branch and ask them about this account number."

Pete called the Chevy branch of the bank and found that there was indeed an account for Yourcompany with the company's correct address—38 Gerry Avenue, Everywhere, Minn. The balance in the account was zero dollars. The last $500 had been withdrawn from the bank on the previous Friday. Pete told the branch manager that he was Yourcompany's CPA and that he and John Your would like to come to the bank and discuss the account with him.

"What does all this mean?" John was confused and worried.

"What this means," Pete explained, "is that someone created an account in the name of your company at a different branch of the same bank and probably used his or her own signature to draw from the account. They deposited checks from your customers, made out to "Yourcompany," and used their own signature on the account. This money from John Kitt—$75—is deposited in the Chevy branch. But it's getting late, so let's continue . . ."

Sales Journal

Since most of the customers of Yourcompany buy on credit, it is a good idea to have a special journal that will record this. Each time a credit sale is made—and only when a credit sale is made—this journal is used.

A sample sales journal is shown in Figure 3.9.

The purpose of the sales journal is to record all accounts receivable as they are created by the customer and record these sales on credit as part of the gross sales of the company.

The sales journal does not record *all* sales, only *those on credit*.

The particular format that Yourcompany uses has two separate columns for systems sales and component sales as well as a column for debits to accounts receivable.

Example One. Yourcompany on January 13 sold a system to John Kitt on credit.

The transaction document is a credit sales invoice (number 100).

The entry is shown in Figure 3.10.

Accounts receivable is debited (increased) and systems sales is credited (increased). The transaction involves an increase in the accounts receivable asset (debit) and in component sales (credit).

Example Two. In January both Thompson Company and Rick Jones are sold some components on credit.

The transaction documents are credit sales invoices (numbers 101 and 102).

The entry is shown in Figure 3.10.

Accounts receivable are debited (increased) for both the Thompson and Jones sales. Component sales are credited (increased) by the sales to both Thompson and Jones. The transaction increases the asset accounts receivable (debit) and component sales (credit).

Example Three. On January 15 Yourcompany sold components to George Baker on credit. The original transaction document is a credit sales slip and the entry is illustrated in Figure 3.10.

The asset accounts receivable is debited (increased) and the income account component sales is credited (increased).

Example Four. On January 16 Yourcompany sold a system worth $1250 to Zipp and Company and $75 more in components to Thompson Company. This is illustrated in Figure 3.10. The transaction document is again the credit sales slip.

The transaction involves debiting (increasing) accounts receivable and crediting (increasing) both the systems sales and component sales accounts.

Example Five. On January 17, Yourcompany sold Richards Components $120 worth of components on credit. The original transaction document is the sales slip (number 106). The example is illustrated in Figure 3.10.

The transaction is an increase in both accounts receivable (debit) and component sales (credit).

Note. The journal has a place for the sales slip number, which could save a lot of time if it has to be traced down at a later date. Accounts receivable is always debited when any entry is made.

Figure 3.11. Purchases journal form.

PURCHASES JOURNAL

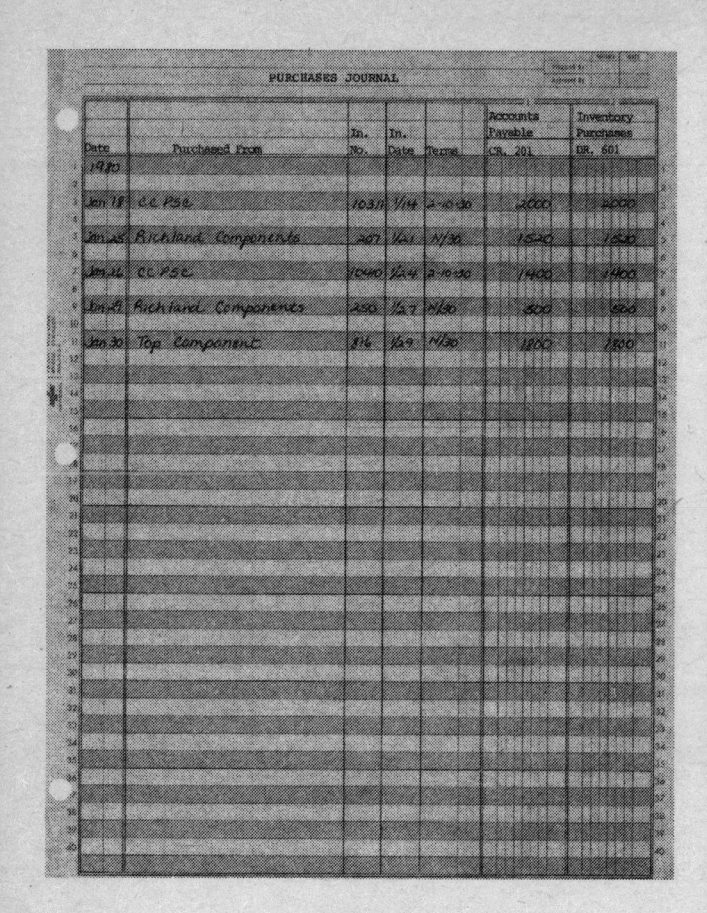

Date	Purchased From	In. No.	In. Date	Terms	Accounts Payable CR. 201	Inventory Purchases DR. 601
1970						
Jan 18	C.C. PSC	1031	1/14	2-10-30	2000	2000
Jan 25	Richland Components	207	1/21	N/30	1520	1520
Jan 26	C.C. PSC	1040	1/24	2-10-30	1400	1400
Jan 29	Richland Components	250	1/27	N/30	500	500
Jan 30	Top Component	816	1/29	N/30	1800	1800

Figure 3.12

Purchases Journal

The last commonly used special journal is the purchases journal. The purchases journal is for recording purchases made on *credit only*.

An example of the purchases journal form is shown in Figure 3.11.

Yourcompany needs a purchases journal to keep track of the goods bought from suppliers on credit. This is sometimes called trade credit. The purchases journal is for recording Yourcompany's accounts payable as they are incurred. The purchases journal only has entries for goods purchased on credit, and never records the payments to the suppliers on account. When money owed to the suppliers is paid off, the entry appears in the cash disbursements journal.

The purchases journal has a column for the date, the name of the supplier, the number of the supplier's invoice, the date of that invoice, the terms, and a column for credits to accounts payable and debits to inventory purchases.

Example One. On January 18, Yourcompany bought some merchandise from Computer and Circuits Parts Supply Company (CCPSC) for $2000 on credit.

The original transaction document is an invoice number 10311, dated 1/14/80, from CCPSC. The terms are 2/10 net 30. This means that if Yourcompany pays for the merchandise in 10 days, it will receive a 2% discount from the invoice amount. If Yourcompany does not take advantage of this discount, it has 30 days to pay for the merchandise.

This is illustrated in Figure 3.12.

The transaction involves an increase (debit) in the expense inventory purchases and an increase (credit) in the liability accounts payable.

Example Two. On January 25 Yourcompany bought merchandise on credit from Richland Components.

The original transaction document is Richland invoice number 207 dated 1/21/80 with net 30 day terms. Richland Components does not offer a discount and their normal terms are payment due in 30 days.

The example is shown in Figure 3.12.

The transaction, as in the case with all other examples in the purchases journal, increases inventory purchases (debit) and increases accounts payable (credit).

Example Three. On January 26, Yourcompany bought some more merchandise on credit from CCPSC. The original transaction document is the invoice number 10410 from CCPSC. This is illustrated in Figure 3.12.

The transaction is an increase in both inventory purchase (debit) and accounts payable (credit).

Example Four. On January 29, Yourcompany bought $500 worth of components on credit from Richland Components. The original transaction document is invoice 250 issued by Richland. It appears in Figure 3.12.

The transaction involves increases in the expense inventory purchases (debit) and the liability accounts payable (credit).

Example Five. On January 30, Yourcompany purchased $1800 worth of merchandise from Top Component, invoice number 816 with net 30 day terms. See Figure 3.12.

The transaction involves an increase (debit) in inventory purchases and an increase in accounts payable (credit).

Note. Every transaction involves a debit to inventory purchases and a credit to accounts payable. Listing the invoice number, date, and terms will help avoid unnecessary hassles in the future.

Ledgers (The Summary Books)

Now you have a good handle on all your accounting transactions because you have recorded them chronologically under the special journals. If you want to review the checks you have written in a given period, you check the cash disbursement journal. You can track Yourcompany's purchases, cash receipts, credit sales, and other transactions in total, and in chronological order without viewing the original checks.

But what if Yourcompany wants to find out what its total expenditure for the last month was for merchandise from Richland Components? What if you want to find out what John Kitt bought from you during the last year? How much did Yourcompany spend on utilities (telephone plus gas plus water)?

One way to find these totals is to go back through the journals during the whole period and take the separate items and total them. Another way would be to write or call the supplier, customer, or utility company and ask them for the total. The best way, however, is to keep a summary book during the period, transferring each entry to a particular category. In other words, if you had a book that listed each account separately (a page for utilities, a page for Richland Components, etc.) you could tell at a glance how much you owe, who owes you, or how much you've already paid.

A book that lists each account under a separate category is called a *ledger*.

Weekly, monthly, or quarterly, all the journals are totaled and "posted" into ledgers. Ledgers are summaries of activities under each account in the chart of accounts. Ledgers are divided into two groups: the general ledger and subsidiary ledgers.

Historically, there was only the *general ledger*. In this ledger, all the accounts were posted after a given period from their respective journal or journals. Entries in the journal indicate to the accountant what is to be debited and what is to be credited. With the journals as a guide, the information is entered into the respective individual accounts. The accountant uses printed forms for his account records as shown in Figure 3.13. Each account is kept on a separate form called a ledger sheet. All the accounts taken together constitute a ledger or "book of final entry." Some accountants make up a balance sheet and profit and loss statement and post from these statements into the ledger, but generally the ledger is posted from the journals. Eventually a "trial balance" is made and this is put into the form of a balance sheet and income statement (profit and loss statement). The ledger is the master reference book of the accounting system and provides

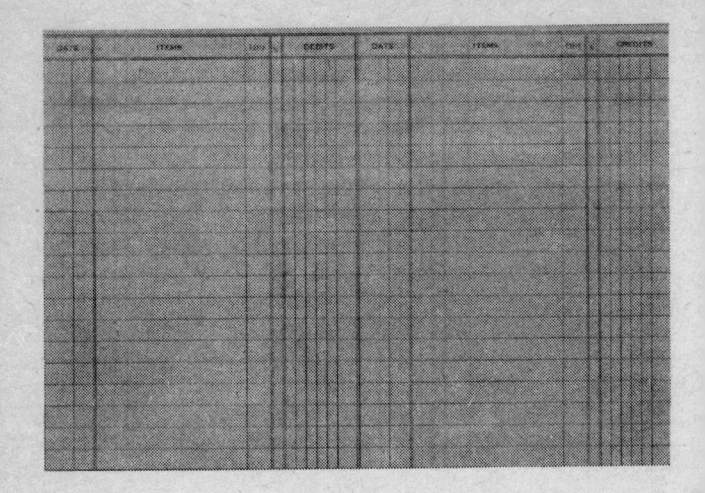

Figure 3.13. General ledger form.

a permanent and classified record of every element involved in the business operation.

The general ledger is divided into separate accounts (e.g., "cash 101") with a debit and credit column for each account. A look at the ledger account record will reveal a complete history of the increases and decreases of the items involved. Ledgers may be kept in book or card form in a ledger tray. Or, of course, these records may be kept on computer records.

Ledger Format

The following, Figure 3.13, is a general ledger format. Note that the format has a column for the date. The date used here may be either the date the entry was made in a journal or the date that the entry was transferred from the journal to the ledger. The former is preferable, but either is acceptable as long as the bookkeeper is consistent.

There are two columns for explanation and two for posting

Journals (The Daily Books)

reference. This allows an explanation and a posting reference for a debit and credit entry separately. The explanation is usually something like "total 1/15/78," or the name the check was made payable to, such as "Titan Telephone" for the telephone deposit entry.

The posting reference refers to the journal that is the source of the entry. Generally in the posting reference, the type of journal and the page number is given. However, in the case of the General Journal, the journal entry number is used. For instance, if a total for cash disbursed (credit to cash) is taken from the Cash Disbursement Journal at the end of the month, the post reference would be "CDJ-1," which means the entry comes from the Cash Disbursement Journal, page 1. General journal summaries would have a post reference like "GJ-1-5" meaning general journal, entry 1-5, which is the fifth entry (5) for the month of January (1).

Post Reference

CDJ	1
GJ	1-5
Abbreviation for the type of journal from which the entry comes	Page number of the journal from which the entry originates or in the case of the general journal the number of the entry

The abbreviations that are commonly used for the post reference are shown as follows:

Table of journal abbreviations

Name of Journal	Abbreviations Used
General journal	GJ
Cash disbursements journal	CDJ
Cash receipts journal	CRJ
Sales journal	SJ
Purchases journal	PJ

CASH   ACCOUNT NO. 101
SHEET NO. 1

DATE	ITEMS	folio	√	DEBITS	DATE	ITEMS	folio	√	CREDITS
1980					1980				
1/2	BANK LOAN	GJ1-1		25000 —	1/3	TEST EQUIP	GJ1-2		5000 —
1/12	TOTAL 1/1 – 1/12	CRJ-1		54429 —	1/4	INVENTORY PARTS	GJ1-3		15000 —
					1/6	RENT EXPENSE	GJ1-5		1200 —
					1/5	ACCTS. PAYABLE	GJ1-4		13500 —
					1/7	TOTAL 1/1 – 1/7	CDJ-1		6820 —

ACCOUNTS RECEIVABLE CONTROL   ACCOUNT NO. 111
SHEET NO. 1

DATE	ITEMS	folio	√	DEBITS	DATE	ITEMS	folio	√	CREDITS
1/17	TOTAL CR. SALES	SJ-1		2055	1/12	PAYMENTS	CRJ-1		75

DEPOSITS   ACCOUNT NO. 120
SHEET NO. 1

DATE	ITEMS	folio	√	DEBITS	DATE	ITEMS	folio	√	CREDITS
1/6	TITIAN TELE.	CDJ-1		1130					

Figure 3.14

The ledger format is divided into a debit and a credit side. If the entry is a credit, it is entered on the credit side; if a debit, it is entered on the debit side.

Note that in Figure 3.14 the format has a line at the top and a space for the number of the account. The line should be filled in with the name of the account and the number space should be filled in with the number of the account from the chart of accounts. The accounts are usually in the general journal in order of their chart-of-account numbers. The first account entered is

Journals (The Daily Books)

SYSTEM SALES — ACCOUNT NO. 410 — SHEET NO. 1

DATE	ITEMS	folio	✓	DEBITS	DATE	ITEMS	folio	✓	CREDITS
					1/12	TOTAL 1/1 – 1/12	CRJ-1		1680 –
					1/17	TOTAL 1/1 – 1/17	SJ-1		1600 –

COMPONENT SALES — ACCOUNT NO. 420 — SHEET NO. 1

DATE	ITEMS	folio	✓	DEBITS	DATE	ITEMS	folio	✓	CREDITS
					1/12	TOTAL 1/1 – 1/12	CRJ-1		2974
					1/17	TOTAL 1/1 – 1/17	SJ-1		455

RENTAL INCOME — ACCOUNT NO. 430 — SHEET NO. 1

DATE	ITEMS	folio	✓	DEBITS	DATE	ITEMS	folio	✓	CREDITS
					1/12	TOTAL 1/1 – 1/12	CRJ-1		700

RENTAL EXPENSE — ACCOUNT NO. 508 — SHEET NO. 1

DATE	ITEMS	folio	✓	DEBITS	DATE	ITEMS	folio	✓	CREDITS
1/5	FIRST MONTH	GJ-5		1200					

Figure 3.14 (*Continued*)

usually "Cash" or "Cash in Bank" or "Cash in Bank (Amerigold)" plus the account number such as "101."

Yourcompany Ledger Examples

The journal entries we used for Yourcompany (Figures 3.3 through 3.12) will now be posted to the proper general ledger and special ledger accounts. First, the completed general ledger is shown in Figure 3.14. A discussion of each account follows.

PARTS INVENTORY
ACCOUNT NO. 130
SHEET NO. 1

DATE	ITEMS	folio	√	DEBITS	DATE	ITEMS	folio	√	CREDITS
1/4	CCPSC	GJ1-4		30000					

TEST EQUIPMENT
ACCOUNT NO. 150.1
SHEET NO. 1

DATE	ITEMS	folio	√	DEBITS	DATE	ITEMS	folio	√	CREDITS
1/3	ZARKOFF	GJ1-3		10000					

ACCOUNTS PAYABLE
ACCOUNT NO. 201
SHEET NO. 1

DATE	ITEMS	folio	√	DEBITS	DATE	ITEMS	folio	√	CREDITS
1/5	SOFTFARE	GJ1-4		13500	1/4	CCPSC	GJ1-4		15000
1/7	TOTAL 1/1 - 1/7	CDJ-1		5000	1/30	TOTAL 1/1 - 1/30	PJ-1		7220

NOTES PAYABLE - BANK OF AMERIGOLD
ACCOUNT NO. 211.1
SHEET NO. 1

DATE	ITEMS	folio	√	DEBITS	DATE	ITEMS	folio	√	CREDITS
					1/4	FIRST LOAN	GJ1-2		25000

NOTE PAYABLE - ZARKOFF EQUIPMENT
ACCOUNT NO. 211.2
SHEET NO. 1

DATE	ITEMS	folio	√	DEBITS	DATE	ITEMS	folio	√	CREDITS
					1/3	INITIAL EQUIP.	GJ1-3		5000

Figure 3.14 (*Continued*)

TELEPHONE EXPENSE
ACCOUNT NO. 510
SHEET NO. 1

DATE	ITEMS	Folio	√	DEBITS	DATE	ITEMS	Folio	√	CREDITS
1/6	TITIAN TELE.	CDJ-1		300					

OFFICE SUPPLIES
ACCOUNT NO. 560
SHEET NO. 1

DATE	ITEMS	Folio	√	DEBITS	DATE	ITEMS	Folio	√	CREDITS
1/7		CDJ-1		150					

BUSINESS LICENSE
ACCOUNT NO. 591
SHEET NO. 1

DATE	ITEMS	Folio	√	DEBITS	DATE	ITEMS	Folio	√	CREDITS
1/7		CDJ-1		40					

INVENTORY PURCHASES
ACCOUNT NO. 601
SHEET NO. 1

DATE	ITEMS	Folio	√	DEBITS	DATE	ITEMS	Folio	√	CREDITS
1/30	TOTAL 1/1 - 1/30	PJ-1		7220					

SUB-CONTRACT
ACCOUNT NO. 610
SHEET NO. 1

DATE	ITEMS	Folio	√	DEBITS	DATE	ITEMS	Folio	√	CREDITS
1/7		CDJ-1		1200					

Figure 3.14 (*Continued*)

Journal	Account columns totaled and posted
General journal	None
Cash disbursements journal	(1) Cash in bank (2) Accounts payable (3) All other columns except sundry debits
Cash receipts journal	(1) Cash in bank (2) Accounts receivable (3) Income accounts except sundry credits
Sales journal	(1) Accounts receivable (2) All income accounts
Purchases journal	(1) Accounts payable (2) Inventory purchases

Figure 3.15. Account columns totaled.

General comments—All entries from the general journal are posted to the ledger. With the special journals such as the cash disbursements, cash receipts, sales, and purchases journals, it is different. In the special journals, the columns that have the most activity, especially those that require entries each time the journal is used, are *added up* at the end of a period and their *totals* are posted to the ledger. Figure 3.15 illustrates each journal and the columns from each journal that are totaled at the end of the period.

In the special journals, the columns that are *not* totaled are the "sundry" columns, either "sundry debits" or "sundry credits." In the general journal, no totals are obtained and each entry is posted to the ledger separately.

The traditional technique of totaling a column in a special journal is called footing. Footing is simply the process of drawing a line at the bottom of the column in pencil and writing the total under the line in pencil.

The cash account (account number 101) in the general ledger example has the most entries from the journals (7). This is a typical situation. The first entry on the debit side and the first three entries on the credit side came from the general ledger (GJ

Journals (The Daily Books)

in the post reference column). All entries from the general journal are posted to the ledger. The last (second) entry on the debit side is the cash debit total from January 1 through January 12, 1980 from the cash receipts journal (CRJ). The last (fourth) entry on the credit side is the cash credit total from the cash disbursements journal (CDJ). The total represents entries in the cash disbursements journal from January 1 through January 7.

The accounts receivable account (account number 111) has only two entries. One is a debit entry of $2055 which is the column total from the sales journal (SJ), page 1. The credit entry is $75 with the accounts receivable credit (payments) from the cash receipts journal (CRJ). Each separate customer account transaction is usually posted in a special ledger known as the accounts receivable ledger. Only the total of the accounts receivable *customer credit extended* and the payments made on these accounts are entered in the accounts receivable ledger account in the general journal. This account is sometimes called the "accounts receivable control account."

The deposits account (account number 122) has one entry for a telephone deposit from the cash disbursements journal, page 1 (CDJ-1). Since deposits are an asset that generally represents money that will not become an expense until some time in the future, most entries are debit (increasing) entries. This is also the case with prepaid expense (like prepaid rent).

The parts inventory account (account number 130) has one entry which represents the initial inventory purchase, or beginning inventory, which is an asset. The entry comes from the general journal, entry 1-4 (GJ 1-4).

The test equipment account (account number 150.1) represents the purchase of equipment from Zarkoff, entered in the general journal (GJ 1-3). The full amount of the value (purchase price) of the equipment is entered here, not just the amount paid out in cash as a down payment.

Note (on all 100 Accounts). All accounts from 100 to 199 are asset accounts. This means that generally they will have a debit balance, and the majority of the entries will be debit entries. Cash and accounts receivable are the only accounts that will receive frequent credit entries.

The accounts payable account (account number 201) has four entries. The two debit are the payment to Softfare from the general journal, entry 1-4 (GJ-1-4) and the total of all accounts payable paid in cash for that period from the cash disbursements journal, page one (CDJ-1). The first entry (January 4) on the credit side of the accounts payable ledger is from the general journal (GJ 1-4). The second entry is the total of all the merchandise credit Yourcompany received in the period from the purchases journal, page 1 (PJ-1).

The notes payable—Bank of Amerigold account (account number 211.1) has one credit entry. This entry records the total amount of the loan from the general journal (GJ 1-2). Each time the company secures a loan there will be a credit entry for the total amount. This account will have debit entries each time the principal portion of the loan is paid. Each month or quarter that a payment on the loan is made, the interest portion of that payment will be interest expense, and the principal portion of the payment will be a debit to this account.

Note payable—Zarkoff Equipment (account number 211.2) has one entry, the initial amount owed on the equipment purchased and recorded as an asset in account 150.1, test equipment. This is a credit entry from the general journal (GJ 1-3). As with the Note payable—Bank of Amerigold account above, each time the note is paid on, the principal portion of that payment will be entered as a debit to this account.

Note (on 200 accounts). All accounts from 200 to 299 are liability accounts. They generally have *credit* balances. Accounts payable and the notes payable accounts will, however, have frequent debit entries. The majority of the loan payable account entries will be debit entries for principal portion payment of debt.

Three hundred (300-399) accounts are equity accounts. There is generally activity in equity accounts only when money is contributed directly to the company by the owners or at the end of an accounting period.

Systems sales account (account number 410) has two entries: one from the cash receipts journal (CRJ-1) representing *cash* sales, and one from the sales journal (SJ-1) representing *credit* sales. Both entries are totals added up at the end of the period.

Component sales account (account number 420), like the systems sales account, above, has a cash sales and a credit sales entry. Both entries are credits; the cash sales entry comes from the cash receipts journal (CRJ-1) and the credit sales entry comes from the sales journal (SJ-1). Both entries are totals from the end of the period.

Rental income account (account number 430) has one entry. This entry is from the cash receipts journal, page 1 (CRJ-1) which is the total of rental income from January 1 through January 12, 1980.

Note (on 400 accounts). All accounts from 400 to 499 are income accounts. Income accounts always have a credit balance and very, very rarely receive a debit entry. The only debit entry posted in these accounts would be for sales returns or allowances.

Rent expense account (account number 508) has a single debit entry, from the general journal (GJ 1-5).

Telephone expense (account number 510) has a debit entry from the cash disbursements journal (CDJ-1) for a monthly telephone expense.

Office supplies (account number 560) has a debit entry from the cash disbursements journal dated January 7.

Business license expense (account number 591) has a debit entry for $40 from the cash disbursements journal.

Note (on 500 accounts). All accounts from 500 to 599 are expense accounts. They will always have a debit balance and will, except in rare circumstances, have only debit entries.

Inventory purchases (account number 601) has a debit entry for the purchases of merchandise from January 1 through January 30 from the purchases journal.

Subcontract (account number 610) has a debit entry from the cash disbursements journal from January 7.

Note (on 600 accounts). All accounts from 600 to 699 will have debit balances. Almost all of the entries in these accounts will be debit entries. The 600 accounts are the cost of sales accounts and the only credit entries will be for returns of merchandise or discounts.

Special Ledgers (Accounts Receivable and Accounts Payable Ledgers)

It is important for a company to keep careful track of who owes them what for product sales. You also want to know how much your customer owes you and for how long; when he bought and how much he bought. The total in the sales journal will tell you the total sales on credit you have, and if you trace through it and separate out the customers, you can find the individual statistics. Most people, however, find that it is much smarter to keep an account for each customer apart from the sales journal. The ledger that keeps track of what each customer purchases and later pays for under the customer's name is called the *accounts receivable ledger*.

The ledger that keeps track of what *you owe* to your suppliers under the suppliers' names is called the *accounts payable ledger*. The reasons for keeping the accounts payable ledger are the same as the reasons for keeping the accounts receivable ledger, although perhaps not as compelling. Since you are continually ordering and paying for merchandise it becomes difficult to keep track of the exact balance you owe each supplier and how much you typically buy from them. This is especially true of a company that has several suppliers. Although your suppliers will be glad to tell you how much you owe at any given time, it is a mistake to depend on their honesty and accuracy. There is not a company in the world who has not been billed for the wrong amount at one time or another.

Figures 3.16 and 3.17 are samples of the special ledger format. The same format is used for both the accounts receivable ledger and the accounts payable ledger.

The format has a place for the name of the account. This would be the customer's name in the case of an accounts receivable ledger and the supplier's name for the accounts payable ledger. It also includes a space for the terms such as net 30 days, 2/10 net 30, and so on.

General ledger sheet

Account:						No.	
Date	Description	PR	Items posted		Balance	
			Debit	Credit	Debit	Credit

Figure 3.16. General ledger sheet.

It also has a column for the description, which is generally pertinent information such as the invoice number. The post reference column could be used for the name and page number of the special journals or the entry number for the general journal. This is the same column used before in the general ledger. An example would be "PJ-1" which means that the entry is from the purchases journal, page 1.

The debit column in the accounts receivable ledger would list all credit sales to customers recorded in the sales journal. The credit column in the accounts receivable ledger would be used to record payments from the cash receipts journal. In the accounts payable ledger the debit column is for payments made to suppliers from the cash disbursements journal and the credit column is to record any trade credit that you receive from the suppliers recorded in the purchases journal.

The balance column is the amount now owed the supplier (in the case of the accounts payable ledger) or the amount the cus-

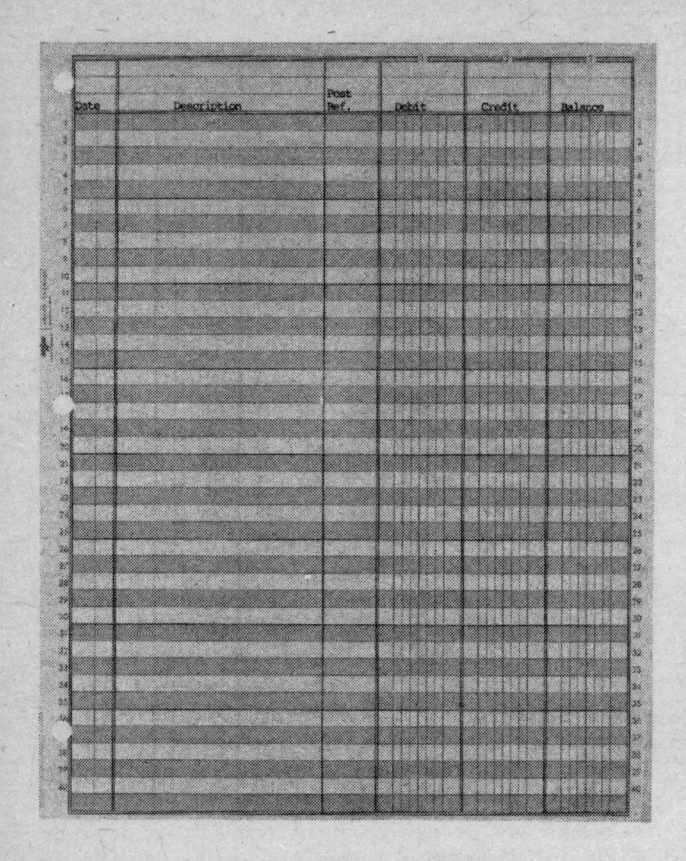

Figure 3.17. General ledger form.

Account	GEORGE BAKER				N 30
Date	Description	Post Ref.	Debit	Credit	Balance
1/15		SJ-1	50		50

Account	RICK JONES				N 30
Date	Description	Post Ref.	Debit	Credit	Balance
1/14		SJ-1	50		50

Account	JOHN KITT				N 30
Date	Description	Post Ref.	Debit	Credit	Balance
12/12/79	sales slip only	—	75		75
1/11/80		CRJ-1		75	-0-
1/13		SJ-1	350		350

Figure 3.18

Account RICHARDS COMPONENTS				N 30
Date	Description	Post Ref.	Debit	Credit	Balance
1/17		SJ-1	120		120

Account THOMPSON COMPANY				N 30
Date	Description	Post Ref.	Debit	Credit	Balance
1/14		SJ-1	160		160
1/16		SJ-1	75		235

Account ZIPP AND CO.				N 30
Date	Description	Post Ref.	Debit	Credit	Balance
1/16		SJ-1	1250		1250

Figure 3.18 (*Continued*)

tomer owes you (in the case of the accounts receivable ledger).

The accounts receivable ledger generally has a *debit* balance. The accounts payable ledger generally has a *credit* balance.

Examples of Special Ledgers

The following examples are from Yourcompany (see Figures 3.3 through 3.12). The special ledgers are posted directly from the journals. The *accounts receivable ledger* (Figure 3.18) shows six

Journals (The Daily Books)

customers: George Baker, Rick Jones, John Kitt, Richards Components, Thompson Company, and Zipp and Company. Yourcompany extends 30 day terms.

George Baker ordered $50 worth of merchandise on January 15. It was recorded in the sales journal, page 1 (SJ-1).

Rick Jones ordered and was delivered $50 worth of merchandise which was recorded in the sales journal, page 1 (SJ-1).

John Kitt was delivered $75 worth of merchandise on December 12, 1979. This transaction was recorded last year. Kitt paid off the credit on January 11 and it was recorded in the cash receipts journal (CRJ-1), bringing the balance to zero ($0). On January 13, Kitt was delivered $350 worth of merchandise, bringing the debit balance to $350.

Richards Components purchased merchandise on January 17, recorded the same day in the sales journal (SJ-1).

Thompson Company made two purchases from Yourcompany, on January 14 and 16, and has made no payments. Both purchases are from the sales journal, and the debit balance outstanding (how much they owe Yourcompany) is $235 as of January 16.

Zipp and Company made one purchase of $1250 on January 16, recorded in the sales journal (SJ-1).

The *accounts payable ledger* (Figure 3.19) has four accounts for suppliers who have sold to Yourcompany on credit: CCPSC with 2/10 net 30 terms; and Richland Components, Softfare, and Top Components with net 30 terms.

CCPSC is Yourcompany's most active supplier. On January 4, Yourcompany bought $15,000 worth of merchandise from CCPSC, recorded in the general journal (GJ-1-3). Yourcompany paid $5000 on that amount on January 6 with check number 105, recorded in the cash disbursements journal (CDJ-1), bringing the balance owed (credit balance) down to $10,000. Yourcompany ordered more merchandise on January 18 and January 26, both recorded in the purchases journal (PJ-1). The January 18 purchase was CCPSC invoice number 10311, dated 1/4/80, and brought the credit balance up to $12,000 owed. The next purchase was invoice number 10410, dated 1/24/80, and brought the credit balance owed up to $13,400.

Richland Components shipped two orders of merchandise to

C.C. PSC — 2/10 N 30

Date	Description	Post Ref.	Debit	Credit	Balance
1980					
Jan 4	INVENTORY	GJ1-3		15000 −	15000 −
6	CHECK #105	CD1-1	5000 −		10000 −
18	INVOICE #10311 1/14/80	PJ-1		2000 −	12000 −
26	INVOICE #10440 1/24/80	PJ-1		1400 −	13400 −

RICHLAND COMPONENTS — N 30

Date	Description	Post Ref.	Debit	Credit	Balance
1980					
Jan 25	INVOICE #207 1/21/80	PJ-1		1520 −	1520 −
29	INVOICE #250 1/27/80	PJ-1		500 −	2020 −

SOFTFARE — N 30

Date	Description	Post Ref.	Debit	Credit	Balance
1980					
Jan 6	CASH PAYMENT	GJ1-4	13500 −		−−−

TOP COMPONENTS — N 30

Date	Description	Post Ref.	Debit	Credit	Balance
1980					
Jan 30	INVOICE #816 1/28/80	PJ-1		1800 −	1800 −

Figure 3.19

Yourcompany, both recorded in the purchases journal (PJ-1). The first order was received January 25, invoice number 197, dated 1/21/80. The second order, invoice number 250, was for $500, bringing the credit balance owed up to $2,020.

Softfare was paid $13,500 by Yourcompany on account, bringing the balance owed to zero. John Your had looked at this invoice and found that there was no previous balance left unpaid. This is the company that Pete had tried to call, but whose number was unlisted.

Top Component sold $1,800 worth of merchandise to Yourcompany, invoice number 816, which was recorded in the purchases journal (PJ-1).

Special Note on Accounts Receivable and Accounts Payable Ledgers

The *accounts receivable ledger* generally has a *debit* balance because it is an asset account. All debit entries will come either from the sales journal or the general journal. Credit entries are made when the receivables are paid by your customer. Credit entries will always originate from the cash receipts journal or the general journal.

The *accounts payable ledger* will generally have *credit* balances because it is a liability account. All credit entries will come from the purchases journal or the general journal. Debit entries are made when the trade credit is paid off by Yourcompany and they are recorded either in the cash disbursements journal or the general journal.

Pete Popstein leaned back and lit up his pipe. He was smoking some kind of cherry tobacco. "Well, that's it with the journals and ledgers. I covered a lot of area. If there is something you don't understand, you should ask me. And, of course, you can call me any time you're working on this."

"This seems like a lot of detail work," John commented. "I don't know if I have the time to go through everything."

"What I suggest," Pete added, "is that you set up the different accounts yourself and do it for at least a couple of months, and maybe do some more every two or so months. The rest, the stuff in between, you can hire someone to do. Just explain to them what you want. I have a woman at the office who does this sort of work and she can train whoever you want to do it. The important thing is that you understand it yourself. You don't want to get your you-know-what in a ringer again."

"What is the biggest problem with getting someone else to enter the journals?" John asked.

"The biggest difficulty with journals and ledgers has always been inaccurate entries through human error. Therefore, one of the most important rules when making the entries is always to double check. One of the ways that has been traditionally used is the 'trial balance,' which I'll talk to you about when you get all the journals and ledgers completed for the year," Pete answered. "If you don't have any specific questions, let me summarize. Record keeping starts with the original documents. The original documents are recorded in a 'book of original entry'—the journal on a daily basis. Once every week, you take the totals of journal entries and enter them in a ledger under the specific title of the account. It's as simple as that."

"What about this theft problem?" John asked, "What should I look out for?"

"Good question," Pete answered. "From what I've seen so far, there is a distinct possibility that the person who was stealing from you had a 'Yourcompany' account at a different branch of your bank, and there are some irregularities in the people to whom payments were made—Softfare, for instance. You should be suspicious of any 'supplier' who is paid right away without waiting for the 30 or 10 days grace, especially if that supplier never indicates a previous balance. Also, you should have invoices or shipping slips that match the amount of the billing."

Pete continued, "If one of your customers shows that he has paid an amount and you don't show it as paid, this tells you something is wrong. For instance, your billing to a customer might show that he has paid a previous balance even though your cash receipts journal or your bank statements don't show any receipt of cash. If you find letters from customers saying that they have already paid an amount owed, this is another indicator. In these cases, the embezzler might be taking checks and depositing them to the other bank account—the one that you did *not* set up.

"Also keep your eyes open for other things that don't seem to make sense," Pete concluded.

"Pete, besides doing these books, I would like to find out a little more about the different accounts—assets, liabilities, capital, income, cost of sales, and expenses. Is there something I can read and study?"

"Yes," Pete said looking through his briefcase. "Here's a book called *Simplified Accounting* a couple of friends of mine just wrote. It's pretty good. In your spare time, what you have of it, you can read it."

"Thanks," John said looking at the manuscript. "I hope it *is* simplified."

Pete left for the day and John leaned back in his chair to see if he could find out about assets. He called his wife to tell her that he would be late for dinner.

Chapter Four
Assets, Cash and Accounts Receivable

"Well, I hope this accounting book isn't too technical," John Your said out loud as he opened to the first page of *Simplified Accounting*. Before he read the first word of the chapter on "Assets," John started thinking about the feelings that he had about accounting.

Things had been so busy the last couple of days that he didn't have much time to think about why he *didn't like* accounting. He had always figured accounting was a lot of mumbo-jumbo stuff that was just about as boring as any pursuit he could imagine. So here he was with an accounting book in his hand and he was actually going to read about it.

The most frightening thing about accounting was that it could either show a big profit or a big loss depending on who was interpreting the thing. He had a friend who ran a zapper manufacturing company. Well, actually the technical name for the thing was "lazer mask trimmer" and it was used in integrated circuit manufacture, but his friend always referred to it as the zapper. This zapper manufacturer had switched CPAs and the new CPA got him $10,000 in tax write-offs by switching from LIFO to FIFO inventory methods.

There was another friend who had a $100,000 *negative* net worth that an accountant made into a $20,000 *positive* net worth by changing the debt and the depreciation. And it was all legit.

"Well, I just hope that it's not too boring," John sighed as he started reading. . . .

ASSETS

Assets are what a company owns.

Assets are productive items which contribute to income. They are, generally speaking, tangible property or promises of future receipts of cash (like accounts receivable or investments).

Assets include the following items (accounts):

- Cash
- Accounts receivable
- Inventory
- Investments
- Prepaid expense (such as last month's rent or utility deposits)
- Equipment
- Motor vehicles
- Furniture and fixtures
- Land and buildings
- Building improvements (called leasehold improvements if you are a renter)
- Other tangible property
- Goodwill
- Patents and copyrights
- Organizational expense

All these items can be divided into three categories: (1) current, (2) fixed, and (3) other assets.

Current assets are those items that can be readily converted into cash within a one year period. With current assets the flow of funds is one of continuous circulation or turnover in the short run.

Fixed assets are items of property, plant, and equipment and are referred to as "fixed" because of their permanent nature and because they are not subject to rapid turnover. Fixed assets are used in connection with producing or earning revenue and not for sale in the ordinary course of business.

Other assets are all the assets that are not current and cannot fit into the fixed asset category (such as research and development, or goodwill).

Current assets include:

- Cash
- Accounts receivable
- Inventory
- Investments or notes receivable that can be converted to cash within one year
- Prepaid expense

Fixed assets include:

- Equipment
- Motor vehicles
- Furniture and fixtures
- Land and buildings
- Leasehold improvements (or building improvements)
- Any other property considered tangible or long-lasting

Other assets include:

- Goodwill
- Patents and copyrights
- Organizational expense
- *Sometimes* prototype costs

This chapter will cover the most important current assets—cash and accounts receivable.

CASH

The cash account is the most active of all business accounts. Receipts from sales (either in cash or payment of accounts receivable), receipts from the sale of assets, receipts from capital investment of the owners, and receipts of loan proceeds all go through the cash account. So will disbursement for payment of expenses, cost of goods sold, repayment of a liability, payment of dividends or owner's draw, and the purchase of assets.

The cash account is the *only* account that is used in transactions with all the other groups of accounts: assets, liabilities, capital, cost of goods sold, income, and expenses.

Cash transactions in the cash account can be roughly divided into (1) cash receipts and payments, and (2) cash documentation in original vouchers, journals, and ledgers. Cash receipts come from sales of products or assets, investment in the business, or proceeds from borrowing. Cash documentation involves all bookkeeping records, from the original transaction document (such as a sales receipt) to the journals to the ledgers.

Cash Receipts and Payments—The principal cash events and their related original transaction documents are in Figure 4.1.

These original transaction documents initiate the processing of cash information. A cash receipt document indicates the firm has received cash; a check indicates that a payment has been made.

The concept of cash receipt, relocation, and disbursement is shown in Figure 4.2 in terms of how it affects journal entries.

Typical origins of cash receipts and disbursements follow:

Receipts

1. From customers—that is, collections of accounts receivable or notes payable.
2. From cash sales.
3. From miscellaneous repetitive sources—for example, rent income, interest income, dividends, and royalties.
4. From miscellaneous repetitive sources—for example, sale of surplus assets or investments and new sources of finance (bank borrowings, loans, equity investment from outside).

Event	Original transaction document (see Chapter 1 for examples)
Cash is received	1. Receipt (sales receipt, check cash)
	2. Draft (bank deposit slip)
Cash is relocated or transferred	
	3. Record of deposit (relocation of cash to a bank account)
	4. Transfer (relocation of cash from one business or division to another, or from one bank account to another)
Cash is disbursed	5. Bank adjustment (reduction from bank account for bank service charges and adjustments)
	6. Petty cash fund
	7. Check or money order

Figure 4.1. Cash transactions.

Event/Voucher		Notation	Accounts	Debit $	Credit $
Cash is received:					
1. Receipt voucher	(a)	Cash provided as equity from owners	Cash	5000	
			Equity		5000
	(b)	Cash provided by long-term creditors	Cash	2500	
			Long-term liability		2500
	(c)	Customer pays cash on account	Cash	150	
			Accounts receivable		150
	(d)	Fixed assets sold for cash	Cash	1000	
			Fixed asset		1000
	(e)	A sale is made for cash	Cash	1500	
			Income		1500
Cash is relocated:					
3. Deposit	(f)	Cash is deposited in Bank	X Bank	9750	
			Cash		9750
	(g)	Cash is transferred from X Bank to Y Bank	Y Bank	5000	
			X Bank		5000

Figure 4.2. Cash actions and journal entries.

Cash

Cash is disbursed:

5. Adjustment	(h)	X Bank service charges are recorded	Bank Charges X Bank	5	5
6. Petty Cash	(i)	Postage stamps are purchased	Miscellaneous expense Cash	50	50
7. Checks	(j)	Merchandise is purchased with a check from X Bank	Inventory X Bank	900	900
	(k)	A payment is made to long-term creditors from X Bank	Long-term liability X Bank	500	500
	(l)	Owner takes draw from Y Bank	Owners draw (equity) Y Bank	1000	1000
	(m)	Payment is made to Vendor from Y Bank	Accounts payable Y Bank	250	250
	(n)	A fixed asset is purchased with a check/Y Bank	Fixed asset Y Bank	2500	2500
	(o)	Wages, rent, & exp./Y Bank	Expenses Y Bank TOTAL	400 30505	 400 30505

Figure 4.2 (*Continued*)

Payments

1. To suppliers of raw materials or other supplies—that is, reduction of accounts payable or notes payable.
2. To employees for salaries and labor related expenses—for example, taxes, insurance, pension, etc.
3. For utilities and other services where payment is made on a regular basis (telephone, accounting, maintenance, etc.).
4. For other operating expenses (supplies, small tools, fees, etc.).
5. To settle tax liabilities (federal, state, and local).

	Feeder tanks

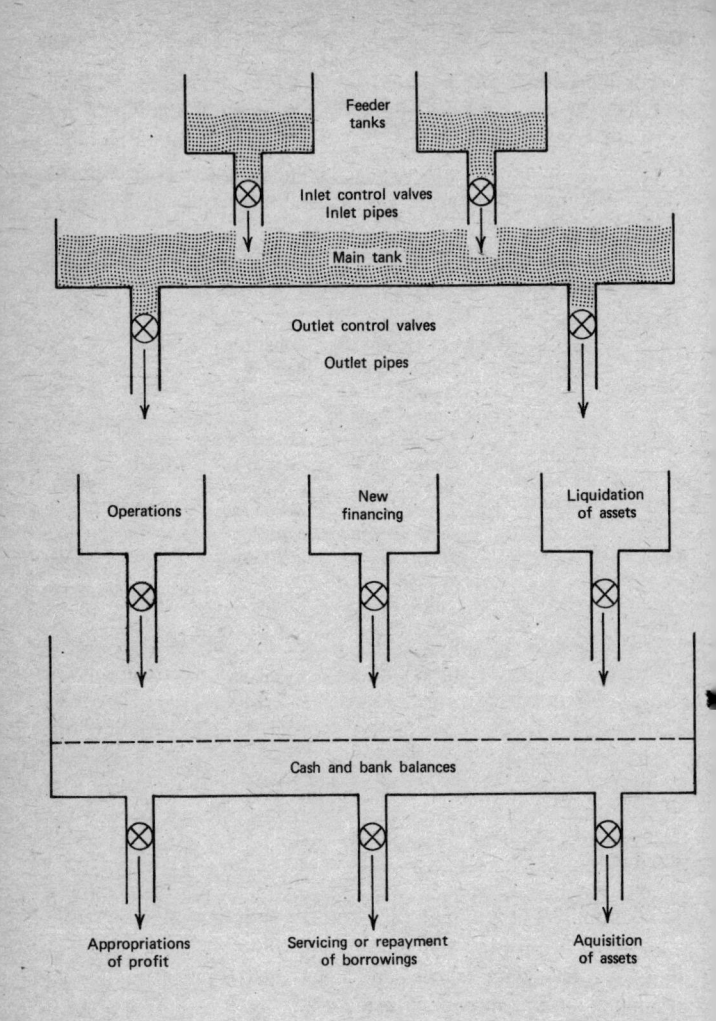

Inlet control valves
Inlet pipes

Main tank

Outlet control valves

Outlet pipes

Operations	New financing	Liquidation of assets

Cash and bank balances

Appropriations of profit	Servicing or repayment of borrowings	Aquisition of assets

6. For capital expenditures—for example, the acquisition of land, buildings, plant, and equipment—representing significant but irregular payments.
7. To meet financial obligations of a regular nature (e.g., interest and dividend payments), or of an irregular nature (e.g., repayment of loans).
8. For any other purpose of a significant, irregular or extraordinary nature—for example, settlement of litigation.

The Cash Tank Method of Cash Management

W.C.F. Hartley, in his book *Cash: Planning, Forecasting, and Control*,* describes an easy-to-visualize method of cash management called the "cash tank."

The level of liquid (cash) in the tank can be controlled only by one of two courses of action: (1) reducing or eliminating outflows by adjusting the valves on one or more of the outlet pipes, or (2) increasing inflows by adjusting the valves on one or more of the inlet pipes.

A schematic diagram of such a liquid flow system appears in Figure 4.3, showing the main tank, feeder tanks, inlet pipes, and outlet pipes, with the control valves pictured as a spoked wheel. The control valve regulates both the rate and timing of the flow.

Against the background of this physical model of liquid flow it is easy to visualize a cash flow system that adopts the same concepts. The main elements of such a system are incorporated into the second schematic diagram also shown in Figure 4.3. Only three feeder tanks have been used, representing the three major sources: income from operations, new financing (from debt or capital injection), and liquidation of assets.

Similarly, each group of inflows has its counterpart group of outflows: appropriations of profit (payment of all expenses out of income, plus payment of taxes, owners' draw, dividends, etc.); servicing or repayment of borrowings; and acquisition of assets.

---

* W.C.F. Hartley, *Cash: Planning, Forecasting, and Control* (London: Business Books Limited, 1976).

If management is to control the level of cash in the tank, these are the three primary groups of inflow and outflow to be addressed.

Forecasting Cash Movements

Because cash flow is critical to a firm, it is essential that management attempt to forecast the likely pattern of future cash flows, if only as a precaution against business failure. This forecast will not always prove to be precisely accurate, but it will still create reliable signals to indicate whether, when, and what type of action needs to be taken. A "good" forecast is not the one that turns out to be "right," but the one which provides the basis for guiding timely management action.

There are two types of forecasts, short-term and long-term.

The Short-Term Cash Forecast

The short-term (or short-range) cash budget covers the length of a cycle from investment of cash to its recovery in such terms as inventory and receivables. The period covered is generally one year.

The prime objective of a short-term cash forecast is to ensure that a firm can pay its debts in the immediate future. It is oriented towards the guidance of appropriate management control action in the short term. For this reason, it needs to be up to date and reasonably detailed. It should be prepared at frequent intervals over the next 6 to 12 months.

Long-Term Cash Forecast

A long-term (or long-range) cash forecast covers the length of a cycle from investment of cash to its recovery from such items as plant and equipment, market development, and research. The period most commonly used for this purpose is from 3 to 5 years, because this is viewed as being the maximum length of time in which sales trends, technology, and the products of market development and research can be projected. In cases where long-term cash flow is certain, as with ground rents, mortage loans or long-term leases, cash flow may be projected accurately for longer periods.

The object of preparing a cash forecast over the longer term is to indicate the future financial consequences of present courses of action. The long-term forecast is usually prepared annually. Its orientation is toward the financial consequences of and interrelationships of strategic management decisions.

Management Cash Control

There are generally considered to be two types of control in the cash system: (1) stewardship controls, and (2) management controls.

Stewardship Controls. Stewardship controls are designed to accomplish two things: the proper receipt of all cash to the organization, and the proper disbursement of all cash by the organization.

Cash is more susceptible to theft than any other asset.

John Your reread the passage he had just read. "Cash is more susceptible to theft than any other asset. . . . Amen. Stewardship controls must be what I need to learn about." Now there was something that John could use. He continued to read. . . .

For this reason, strict stewardship controls are needed to prevent misappropriation of cash. Two forms of embezzlement should be noted:

- *Lapping:* The theft of cash received from one customer, but credited to that customer's account at a later date by using cash received from another customer.

- *Kiting:* Cashing an unrecorded check in one bank, and covering it with a check drawn on another bank. Or, opening a bank account with a fraudulent check (usually originating in a different city or state to lengthen clearing time), and then drawing most of the amount out before the bank discovers the error.

Embezzlement using the methods just mentioned, as well as other techniques, may be guarded against by maintaining a system of internal controls over the handling of cash. The following are general principles for controlling cash receipts and cash disbursements.

General principles for controlling *cash receipts:*

1. The immediate separation of cash from its documentation. For instance, people who record cash transactions should not write checks or make deposits. Documentation is channeled to the accounting department and cash to the cashier. Their records can be compared.
2. The function of cash handling must be distinct from maintaining the accounting records. Neither party should have access to or supervise the record keeping of the other.
3. If possible, there should be a daily deposit of all cash receipts into the bank.
4. The person responsible for cash receipts should not be responsible for cash disbursements.

General principles for controlling *cash disbursements:*

1. All disbursements should be made by check. Issuing a check should require approval of more than one person. A cancelled check is proof that payment was made, and payment by check provides a permanent record of disbursements.
2. Checks should be prenumbered. Spoiled checks should be marked "void."
3. If possible, checks should be signed by one person and countersigned by another.
4. Supporting invoices and other documentation should be perforated or marked "paid," in order to prevent double payment for the same item.
5. A system for approving payments should underlie the issuance of checks. The person who approved payment should not be the person who issues the check.

Note that stewardship controls place a repeated emphasis on the principle of *separation of duties*. Underlying this principle is the fact that the probability of embezzlement is decreased significantly where an act of dishonesty requires the collusion of two or more persons.

Management Controls. Management control has as its principal purpose of *optimizing* the company's cash position. This is true if the company has a cash surplus or a cash deficit.

Excess cash may denote poor management because these cash resources can usually produce a higher return if they are converted to some other form of asset (such as investments). Contrary to popular thinking, a large cash balance is not a reliable indicator of an organization's good state of health; it may be just the opposite. Too little cash is also hazardous and may require unscheduled borrowing of funds or the untimely sale of the firm's assets.

Cash forecasts and budgets are the principal techniques for management control of cash. They serve as management controls for the following reasons:

1. They emphasize the timing of future cash events.
2. They indicate periods when cash surpluses or shortages are likely to occur, thus enabling management to convert temporary surplus cash into investments or arrange in advance for financing for periods where shortages are indicated.
3. They facilitate the scheduling of loan repayments.
4. By distinguishing postponable from nonpostponable expenditures, they provide management with a basis for deciding priorities and for relegating postponable needs to periods where better financing is available.
5. They provide guidelines for controlling disbursements, in that expenditures for a particular account cannot exceed budget without special approval.

Money Float

Money float is also a very effective management cash control technique. "Float" is cash in transit. For example, the period between the time a check is written and the time it clears is called float. Many large companies pay their employees on the West Coast with checks drawn on East Coast banks so that the time between when the check is written, cashed at a West Coast bank, shipped to an East Coast bank, and subtracted from the company's account is lengthy. The company can use the cash during this time interval. The following are some more examples of float:

1. *Disneyland coupons:* Visitors to Disneyland exchange money for coupons at the gate. If they do not use all of the coupons in one day, they keep the rest for a return visit days, weeks, or months later (or never). Disneyland, of course, has been paid for the unused coupons so that it gets float on the money.
2. *Traveler's checks:* Bank of America, Citibank, Cook's, and American Express Company trade their traveler's checks for cash (the money you pay for the checks, if any, goes to the bank as a handling fee). The person who exchanges cash for traveler's checks takes a vacation, during which he or she periodically cashes the checks. Meanwhile, the issuing company (e.g., American Express) has invested the cash it received. With a continuing stream of clients, the issuing company always has a substantial amount of "float" invested, earnings from which constitutes the company's source of income.
3. *Trade dollars:* A group of merchants wish to encourage business among themselves as a group. The promoters issue trade association dollars in exchange for real money. For as long as the "trade dollars" remain in circulation within the group, the promoters can benefit from the investment of the float.
4. *Gift certificates:* Rather than purchase an item from a retail store, many people buy gift certificates for relatives and friends. Until the relatives and friends spend these certificates, however, the company that issues them (the retailer) can use the money as float.

The above are examples of how float can be created. While most businesses do not create float, they can utilize it. For example, analysis of check-clearing processes can permit a pairing of cash reserves.

Float works two ways in a checking account: When deposits are made, a float of from 2 to 3 days is usually required before the checks clear the payer's account. This is "negative float," for until the deposits are cleared the firm may not issue checks or make withdrawals. On the other hand, checks issued by the firm are "float" until they have cleared the firm's bank account. This is "positive float." To refine our measurement of float you can analyze checks outstanding at the end of each month and "age" them according to various time periods shown:

Checks outstanding	0–30 days	31–60 days	61–90 days	Over 90 days
No. 1012				$ 500
1015			$1,000	
1023			500	
1032		$1,500		
1035		500		
1041	$ 500			
1046	2,000			
1048	2,500			
Total	$5,000	$2,000	$1,500	$ 500

With sufficient aging data and experience, you have a basis for calculating probable float. You can calculate the percentage of total checks cashed in less than 30 days, less than 60 days, and so on. You could then figure that a certain amount of your checks are going to be outstanding, so that you could actually write checks for that percentage more than your cash balance in the bank. You could also get an idea of how long a certain company takes to cash checks. In this way float analysis can be a useful management cash control tool.

RECEIVABLES

The term "receivables" indicates claims for money and goods due from other businesses. There are various types or categories of receivables, including:

- Accounts receivable (due from customers)
- Notes receivable (due from those who owe money and who have signed a negotiable instrument or note)
- Deposits receivable or returnable
- Claims against various parties (governments, lawsuits)
- Advances to employees, officers, stockholders

Current Versus Noncurrent

Receivables may be listed as current assets or as long-term assets. To be classified as a current asset, a receivable should be convertible into cash within one year's time, otherwise it should be classified as a noncurrent asset.

Receivables should be stated at their net realizable cash value. Initially, receivables may be stated at the invoice price of the sale if, for example, a credit sale for $100 is recorded. However, not all receivables are collectable; therefore, to state receivables at their net realizable cash value requires an estimate of the amounts of receivables that will not be collected. In other words, an *allowance for bad debts* or allowance for *uncollectable accounts* should be deducted from receivables.

Discounting

It is commonly understood that a dollar today is worth more than a dollar tomorrow. This is because a dollar today can be invested or loaned, and thus interest can be earned.

For example, if you have $100 and you can lend this money at 6%, at the end of a year you will have $106.

On the other hand, if a customer buys some goods from you worth $100, but says that he will pay in one year's time, you haven't sold for $100. You only sold for $94 (100 × .94), assuming you could have loaned the money at 6% interest.

A ruling by the Accounting Principles Boad, APB Opinion No. 21,[1] requires that interest be imputed on receivables. This means

[1] The APB was the official rule-making body of the accounting profession between 1959 and 1973. It has been replaced by the Financial Standards Board. Opinion No. 21 was issued in 1971.

that if you sell to a customer and allow liberal or lengthy terms for payment (1) without interest on the amounts owed, or (2) with interest at an unrealistically low amount, then the amount of the sale and the amount of the receivable should both be reduced. They are reduced by a realistic level of interest on the amounts receivable. This interest is taken into account over the term of the receivable.

Example: Yourcompany sells a machine to a customer for $1000 with the following terms: $100 down, balance payable in three annual installments of $300 each, plus accrued interest. The unpaid balance will accrue at 4%. However, similar loans to Yourcompany's class of customers would normally require interest at 6%.

Amount of sale:	$ 968	composed of:
	$ 100	down payment
	900	receivable
	72	interest at 4%[2]
	$1,072	
	(104)	less interest at 6%[3]
	$ 968	
Amount of receivable composed of:	$ 868	
Amount of sale	$ 968	
Less: Cash down	100	
	$ 868	

[2] $(900 \times .04) + (600 \times .04) + (300 \times .04)$
[3] $(900 \times .06) + (600 \times .06) + (300 \times .06)$

At the end of the first year you would record cash received of $336. And interest income of $52.

It should be noted that reducing sales and receivables for imputed interest is required for companies which issue financial statements that conform to generally accepted accounting principles. This is not a procedure that is acceptable for tax purposes, except in certain limited circumstances.

Bad Debts Expense

When you sell on credit, you must expect some customers not to pay, unless you have an extraordinarily effective collection procedure.

There are three principal methods of calculating estimates of bad debt expense:

- Percentage of sales
- Percentage of outstanding receivables
- Aging receivables

All of these methods are currently in use. The percentage of credit sales and percentage of outstanding receivables are most commonly used. The aging method probably gives the most accurate figure for bad debts expense and—with increased use of computers—should become widely used.

Percentage of Credit Sales. When a percentage of sales approach is employed, a company's past experience with uncollectable accounts is analyzed. If there is a stable relationship between previous year's charge sales and bad debts, that relationship can be turned into a percentage and used to determine the current year's bad debt expense (see Figure 4.4).

Year	Credit Sales	Actual Bad Debts
19X3	$1,000,000	$15,000
19X2	900,000	12,000
19X1	800,000	12,000
TOTAL	$2,700,000	$39,000

Percentage = $\dfrac{\$39,000}{2,700,000} = 1.44\%$

19X4 Credit sales: $1,200,000
19X4 Estimated bad debt expense: 1.44% × $1,200,000 = $17,280

Figure 4.4. Percentage of credit sales method of estimating bad debt expense.

Percentage of Outstanding Receivables. Using past experience, a company can estimate the percentage of its outstanding accounts receivables that will become uncollectable. This procedure provides a reasonably accurate picture of the value of the receivables at any time, but does not fit the concept of matching costs and revenues as well as the percentage of sales approach. This is because in the percentage of outstanding receivables method you must rely on the past to predict the future (see Figure 4.5).

Year	Accounts receivable (End of year)	Accounts receivable that become bad debts
19X3	$150,000	$15,000
19X2	140,000	12,000
19X1	135,000	12,000
TOTAL	$425,000	$39,000

Percentage: $\dfrac{\$39,000}{\$425,000} = 9.2\%$

19X4 *Ending accounts receivable:* $160,000
19X4 *Estimated bad debt expense:* 9.2% × $160,000 = $14,720

Figure 4.5. **Percentage of accounts receivable method of estimating bad debt expense.**

Aging of Accounts Receivable. A more sophisticated approach than the percentage of outstanding receivables method is to set up an aging schedule. Such a schedule indicates which accounts require special attention by providing the age of the receivable (see Figure 4.6).

Looking at the figure you can see that the amount $189 indicates the bad debt expense to be reported for the year. But only if this is the first year the company has been in operation. In subsequent years, the allowance for doubtful accounts is adjusted to the amount determined by the aging schedule. An aging schedule is not only prepared to determine bad debts expense, but it may also serve as a control device, to determine the composition of receivables and to identify delinquent accounts. The estimated loss percentage developed for each age category is based on pre-

Assets, Cash and Accounts Receivable

Name of customer	Balance 12/31	Under 60 days	61–90 days	91–120 days	Over 120 days
Customer A	$1,000	$ 800	$200	$	$
Customer B	3,000	3,000			
Customer C	600				600
Customer D	750	600		150	
	$5,350	$4,400	$200	$150	$600

Summary

Age	Amount	Percentage	
Under 60 days	$4,400	1%	$444.00
61–90 days	200	5%	10.00
91–120 days	150	10%	15.00
Over 120 days	600	20%	120.00
		Bad debts expense or allowance for doubtful accounts:	$189.00

Figure 4.6. Aging schedule.

vious loss experience and the advice of persons in your business who are responsible for granting credit. The aging approach is sensitive to the actual status of receivables, but as with all estimates, it may overstate or understate the actual loss from uncollectable accounts.

Designing a Credit Policy

Receivables result from selling on credit, and the essence of credit sales lies in the trade-off between increased sales and increased collection costs. Credit sales can be increased indefinitely in most businesses simply by liberalizing credit agreements. However, the increased sales become unprofitable when the costs of collection exceed the profit margin. Therefore, a balance between increased sales and collection costs must be sought.

Credit rating services, such as Dun and Bradstreet and TRW Credit Data, are helpful for making credit decisions, but rating services cannot themselves make credit granting decisions. They only provide the historical background on a prospective customer.

Receivables

Receivables Information System

A credit policy should be based on the typical credit terms in your industry. You should expect to meet the terms offered by the competition in the industry. Customers that are poor credit risks require stricter terms. One way to formulate a sound credit policy is to develop a credit information system, sometimes called a credit scoring system. This is based on the five C's of credit: character, capacity, capital, collateral and conditions.

- *Character*—Defined as the probability that a customer will try to honor his obligations, and measured by past payment history. Interviews and references can supply relevant information.
- *Capital*—Measured by the financial position of the firm as indicated by total assets, net worth, or debt to equity ratio.
- *Collateral*—Represented by assets the customer may offer as security.
- *Capacity*—Measured by the consistency of profitable operations.
- *Conditions*—The state of the economy and the state of the industry in which the customer operates.

An illustration of a credit scoring sheet appears in Figure 4.7.

How to Develop Credit Scores

Based on data supplied in the customer's credit applications, assign points in each rating category, then decide a cutoff point. The sum of the points in each category provides the customer's credit score. (In the example in Figure 4.7, points range from 1–5, but you can set your own range to suit the facts of your industry.)

As previously indicated, aging accounts is a useful technique, because it directs attention to the most troublesome areas, and may indicate necessary changes in credit granting policy. If the data is available, another useful technique would be analysis of payment history by customer class or category. Results of this technique may disclose that certain categories of customers are

Character				
Subjective measure	Excellent	Good	Fair	Marginal
	5	3	1	0
Capacity				
Years of profit	15+	10–15	5–10	2–5
	5	4	3	2
Capital				
Debt/equity ratio	0–.10	.10–.25	.25–.80	.50–1.00
	5	3	3	1
Collateral				
Type	Mortgage	Securities	Pledge	None
	5	4	2	1
Conditions				
Sales growth in customer's industry	Growth in past 4 quarters	Growth in past 2 quarters	Stable	Decline
	5	4	2	0
				TOTAL SCORE

Figure 4.7. Credit scoring chart.

more trouble than they are worth, and that credit should either not be granted or granted only on restricted terms.

Payment Stimulation Techniques

Ways to speed up the payment of receivables include:

- Offering discounts for early payment
- Adding on interest for payment after a certain date
- Dunning letters that become increasingly threatening as time passes
- Personal telephone calls
- Outside collection services
- Legal action

Receivables

You would like to stimulate payment with the method that costs least in terms of expense and customer alienation. There is a trade-off between the severity of the stimulation technique and maintenance of customer satisfaction. You should relate the severity of the technique to the age of the receivable.

Bad Debts and the IRS. The tax law divides potential bad debts into three general categories: (1) business bad debts, (2) nonbusiness bad debts, and (3) personal bad debts.

Personal bad debts are generally not deductible at all unless they are fully supported by signed, legal agreements for repayment and evidence a business purpose. These agreements convert the bad debt from a personal one into a *nonbusiness bad debt* with an investment purpose. For example, a father makes a loan to his son, so that the son can start a business. If there are no signed agreements, with specific repayment terms, the debt would not be deductible in the event the son could not repay. However, if the agreement is specific as to times and terms of repayment, if the father did expect repayment, and if the son could not repay, then the debt would be deductible as a capital loss. This capital loss from personal bad debts could offset capital gains to be subtracted in arriving at adjusted gross income up to a limit of $1000 per year.

Business bad debts are deductible in full against ordinary income. There are two methods used to determine the amount of the bad debt deduction. One is the specific debt method. Under the specific debt method, the taxpayer deducts in each year the specific debts that become uncollectible in that year. This is used primarily by taxpayers who do not want to estimate a reserve for bad debts. It is not a generally accepted accounting principle for audited statements, and therefore should be used only by businesses not issuing audited statements.

The other accepted method of deducting bad debts for tax purpose is the reserve method, under which the taxpayer carries a reserve in the amount that he (and the IRS) considers sufficient to cover his bad debt losses. Under this method, the taxpayer makes an addition to the reserve each year so that the reserve remains at a figure sufficient to cover expected bad debts (see Figure 4.8).

Assume:

Volume of charge sales	$1,000,000
Notes and accounts receivable	
Beginning of year	$ 80,000
End of year	$ 90,000
Amount of debts which have become wholly or partially worthless and have been charged against reserve account	$ 2,500
Reserve for bad debts	
Beginning	$ 2,700
Estimated percentage of bad debts	3%
Calculation of reserve:	
Beginning	$ 2,700
Less: Charge-offs	(2,500)
	$ 200
Add: Addition to Reserve (3% × $1,000,000)	3,000
Ending balance	$ 3,200

Figure 4.8. Calculation of reserve for bad debts.

Deferring Tax on Installment Sales Receivable

Though it is not a generally accepted accounting principle to which auditors will attach a clean opinion, the *Internal Revenue Code* provides that the installment method of accounting can be used for tax purposes. This means that taxes on the uncollected portion of installment contracts receivable do not have to be paid until the cash is collected. This provision is available to all dealers in personal property who regularly sell on the installment basis, and to others who occasionally sell real property or personal property, if the amount received in the year of sale is 30% or less of the selling price.

An individual sells a house for $100,000. The buyer assumes a $20,000 mortgage, makes a down payment of $30,000 and agrees to pay the balance of $50,000 over 10 years. The house cost the seller $60,000. How much profit would the individual report in the year of sale?

Answer: $15,000

Explanation: The gross profit is $40,000 ($100,000 − $60,000). The installment method of reporting may be used because the cash received ($30,000) is not greater than 30% of the selling price ($100,000). The profit to be reported is the ratio of the gross profit ($40,000) to the contract price ($80,000).

Accounts Receivable Financing and Factoring

If you are in a business that is growing rapidly, you may find that there is a need for additional working capital, but that your balance sheet does not support unsecured borrowing from a bank. It is often possible, in similar circumstances, to borrow on a secured basis by pledging or assigning valid accounts receivable as collateral for the loan. This type of loan is available from your bank or from a subsidiary of a bank that specializes in commercial financing. For businesses with higher degrees of risk, commercial finance companies may be the appropriate source of funds.

The type of financing and the terms of the loan will vary according to the type of the industry you are in and the institution providing the financing. There are two types of financing: receivables financing and factoring.

Receivable Financing. In receivables financing, receivables act as collateral for a loan. Typically, the company that uses this type of financing is growing fast or is highly seasonal and needs cash in order to operate. Financial institutions will take considerable care in validating the value of receivables as collateral. The cost of receivables financing is high compared to the cost of term loans. Whereas the rate on term loans is typically about prime plus 1–2%, the rate on receivables loans may be prime plus 4–5%.

There are considerations that make receivables loan attractive. Interest is computed on an average daily balance basis with receivables loans, whereas with term loans, interest is computed based on the term. No compensating balances are required with receivables loans. Interest on the nonusable compensating balance at a rate of prime plus one may exceed the additional interest required on a receivables loan.

Factoring. Factoring is distinguished from receivables financing by the fact that in factoring the outstanding receivables are typically sold outright, and without recourse, to the factor. There are two types of factoring: maturity factoring and discount factoring.

In maturity factoring no funds are remitted by the factor until the receivables are collected. The factor, in essence, serves as the credit department of his customer. Typically the factor knows the customers of the client better than the client knows them, and is able to determine the credit worthiness of a customer and the collectibility of the receivable. The factor maintains credit files on customers in industries where factoring is common, and has staffs of auditors and loan officers to assist collection procedures. In discount factoring, the factor in essence buys the receivables for cash, at a discount.

For this service the client pays approximately 1% of outstanding receivables as a factoring fee, but is relieved of collection and credit burdens. Factoring is not widespread outside of the textile and garment industries.

Improvement of Financial Ratios by Factoring. Balance sheet financial ratios may be made to appear more favorable through factoring. Figure 4.9 presents an example of comparative balance sheets, with and without factoring. Without factoring, the company requires a $100,000 bank loan and incurs $200,000 of payables, while having $300,000 receivables outstanding.

The current ratio is 1.53:1 without factoring. With factoring, the receivables are sold, and $200,000 is applied to reduce the accounts payable to $100,000 and pay off the note. The current ratio is increased to 2.6:1.

John looked at the last page of the chapter on assets. So that's the story on cash and accounts receivable. John thought about all the management decisions that were based on receivables or the availability of cash. Budgeting, cash flow, the ability to collect money due the company—all these were important.

John glanced back through the chapter and tried to summarize in his mind.

Without factoring				With factoring			
Assets		Liabilities		Assets		Liabilities	
Cash	$ 10,000	Accounts payable	$200,000	Cash	$ 10,000	Accounts payable	$100,000
Accounts receivable	300,000	Note payable	100,000	Due from factor	100,000	Net worth	160,000
Inventory	150,000	Net worth	160,000	Inventory	150,000		
Total	$460,000	Total	$460,000	Total	$260,000	Total	$260,000

Figure 4.9. Comparative balance sheets with and without factoring.

Cash transactions involve cash receipts and payments and the accompanying documentation. Cash movements could be forecast on a short-term (1 year) or long-term basis (more than 1 year). Cash forecasting offered you the option of determining what the future situation would look like in your company before you got into trouble.

One of the things about cash that interested John most was the cash control suggestions. The first principle of managing cash receipts was to not allow people who keep the books to write out checks or make deposits. Also, the person who handles cash deposits should not handle cash receipts. John was learning that lesson right now with a vengeance. But how could he make sure this would happen? He would have to have his secretary and not the bookkeeper make the deposits. He would have to handle the verification of payments and make out the checks himself. Maybe he could have different people—maybe his wife—make out the checks. In any case he was not going to let the bookkeeper do it again.

It was possible to age the checks he wrote to see how fast they came back so he would know how much time he had before he needed to have the necessary cash at the bank. This would allow him "float" time.

It seemed that one of the most important things about accounts receivable was determining the bad debt allowance that should be used to get a better idea of exactly how much would be collected.

After reading this chapter John realized that he didn't have a credit policy. Basically he gave credit to just about anyone who gave him repeat orders. He had had problems before collecting the receivables and maybe that was one of the reasons. He was going to try to be more selective. He might use the credit scores that the chapter suggested. The last thing was accounts receivable financing. He didn't fully understand it, so he made a mental note to ask Pete about it the next day. He was also going to ask Pete about setting up some "stewardship" cash controls.

John went around the plant locking up and turning out the lights. It had been a tough day and his head was spinning.

Chapter Five
Inventories, Fixed Assets, and Depreciation

The alarm rang and John Your woke up with a headache. Today wasn't going to be an easy one. He had to set up the books and do the entries for the first couple of months. He also had to find someone to do the balance of the entries.

And John was getting sick of accounting. The subject was getting to be a really painful one for him. He didn't think finding documentation that showed how he had been ripped off would make him feel any better, either.

John sat at the kitchen table staring into his coffee. The rest of the house was dark. He realized that he hadn't played with his kids in . . . in . . . hell, since last summer. And now this accounting thing was hanging over his head. How much was gone from the company? Pete had guessed at $100,000. John felt sick when he thought of it. That $100,000 would have done a real nice job putting in the extra bedroom, or replacing that old milling machine at the plant. That machine must cost him $30,000 a year in down time and repairs.

John's mind shifted to cash controls. Maybe he would have his secretary write out the checks. The bookkeeper could give her a list. He would make the entries of all the receipts in the cash receipts journal himself. It would take time, but this would allow him to keep his hand in when and if customers were paying. He'd check with Pete.

John arrived early at the shop and went to the bookkeeper's office to start in with the books again. "What a drag," John thought as he opened the door.

All morning John made the entries in the journals. He discovered that payments had been made in February and March to Softfare. As with the first time he saw the books, these payments did not have any supporting shipping documents. And as before, there was no previous balance shown on the bills. He also noticed that there were two more deposits made to the "other" bank account in Chevy. John started getting upset and angry at Martha, the bookkeeper. He felt like smashing furniture. He called Pete Popstein instead.

"Pete, I'm really fed up. I'm at the end of my rope with this thing. I found two more checks made out to Softfare and two more deposits made to the wrong bank acount," John spat out in one breath over the phone.

"Hey, calm down, John. You're gonna get a stroke along with everything else. Look, it isn't gonna help to get mad. All you can do is document it. . . ." Pete quickly changed the subject, "How's your reading going?"

"Good. I want to ask you a question." John told him about his idea on having the secretary, bookkeeper, and himself divide up the work. Pete agreed that that was a good plan. John then asked Pete about accounts receivable financing.

"Well," Pete answered, "accounts receivable financing is simply a loan that the bank makes to you using your accounts receivable as the collateral. They take accounts receivable as collateral instead of, say, a house. In accounts receivable financing, when you get the money from your customer, you sign the back of the check and give it to the bank. They take out their advance and interest, and you get the rest. The advance is usually 80%; the interest is high. In factoring, the lender buys the accounts receivable at a discount. Just like you would sell inventory to someone at a big discount if you wanted to get rid of all of it at once. Factoring is even more expensive than accounts receivable financing. Since the factor owns your accounts receivable, he tells your customers that he now owns the receivable and the customer pays him directly. That's basically it."

"Yeah, that makes sense. I got to get back to these books. I'll call you later." John ended the conversation.

John continued making entries until about three o'clock. By then John was sick and tired of making entries. He took care of correspondence, payments, and phone calling until about five o'clock.

John took a walk around the plant and then went back to his office. He picked up *Simplified Accounting* and started to read. He would get in a couple of hours before he left for home . . .

In addition to cash and accounts receivable, there are other assets that are important to business.

The other important current asset is inventory. How inventory is calculated and valued (last-in-first-out, first-in-first-out, etc.), affects net profit directly. Unlike cash, accounts receivable, and other assets, inventories appear both on the balance sheet and on the income statement (profit and loss statement).

The most important consideration for fixed assets such as equipment, leasehold improvements, building, and so on, is the determination of their value and their depreciation. The method of depreciation one chooses directly affects net profit. The higher the depreciation, the faster the fixed assets are depreciated, and the less profit the company will show. Also, since depreciation is the only expense that does not require a cash outlay, it figures predominantly in cash planning. Similar expenses are investment tax credit, depletion, and amortization.

These topics will be discussed in depth in this chapter.

INVENTORIES

Inventories are defined as assets which are (1) held for sale in the ordinary course of business, or (2) goods that will be used or consumed in the production of goods to be sold. Assets that are to be resold are excluded from inventory because they are not normally sold in the ordinary course of business. Assets held for resale might include building and equipment items that are being retired or stocks and bonds held for investment.

Inventories are typically considered within the setting of a trading business. A trading business purchases its merchandise in a ready-to-sell form and considers unsold units on hand at the end of the period as merchandise inventory. Usually only one inventory account appears in the financial statements of a trading business.

Most larger businesses are not merchandising operations, but rather are manufacturing concerns whose purpose is to produce goods to be sold to merchandising firms (either wholesale or retail). A manufacturing firm normally has three inventory accounts—raw materials, work in process, and finished goods.

The cost of goods and materials on hand, but not yet placed into production, is considered *raw materials inventory*. Raw materials are items such as plastic to make toys or steel to make a car. These materials can be traced directly to the end product. At any given point in a continuous production process, some units are not completely processed. The cost of the raw material for a partially completed product, plus the cost of labor applied specifically to the material and a share of the overhead costs, constitute the *work in process inventory*. The costs of completed but unsold units on hand at the end of the period are reported as *finished goods inventory*.

An example of the four categories of inventories:

Finished goods	$200,000
Work in process	15,000
Raw materials	20,000
Other materials and supplies	30,000

Inventories are distinct from *supplies* because inventories typically become products to be sold, or at least part of a product to be sold, and supplies are consumed. Supplies would include lubrication oil for a machine, while inventory would include products manufactured by the machine.

The investment in inventories is usually the largest current asset in manufacturing and retail firms, and it may often be a significant portion of the firm's total assets.

If unsalable items accumulate in inventory, a potential loss exists. If products ordered or desired by the customers are not

Inventories

readily available in the style, quality, and quantity required, sales and customers may be lost. Inefficient purchasing, faulty manufacturing, or inadequate sales efforts result in excessive or unsalable inventories.

Inventories are more sensitive to general business fluctuations than other assets. When sales demand is great, merchandise can be disposed of quickly, and large quantities of inventories are appropriate. Yet, during a downward trend in the business cycle, lines of merchandise will move slowly, stocks will pile up, and obsolescence becomes a specter hovering over the manager's shoulder.

One essential of inventory planning and control is an accounting of information required by management to make manufacturing, merchandising, and financial decisions. Such an accounting system is often referred to as a perpetual inventory system.

In a perpetual inventory system, information is available at any time on the quantity of each item of material or type of merchandise on hand. There are basically two types of perpetual inventory systems: detailed inventory records that support the general ledger inventory account, and detailed records that constitute an information system outside the accounting double entry system.

In the first type of perpetual inventory system, purchases of raw materials or inventory are debited directly to an inventory account. As the inventory is sold or transferred to a work-in-process account, it is credited from the inventory account and debited to a work-in-process or cost of sales account. Thus, the balance in the inventory account at any time should equal the dollar value of inventory on hand. Figure 5.1 shows an example of this perpetual inventory system.

In the second type of perpetual inventory system, the records are similar to the first type. The basic difference is that dollar values are not maintained and debits or credits do not enter into the accounting system.

Computers have greatly facilitated the process of inventory control and planning. Because of the data processing capability of computers, additional information can be kept and maintained

Manufacturing concern

```
Raw materials          Work in process         Finished goods
     $                       $                       $
    ↗ ↘                     ↗ ↘                     ↗ ↘
Purchases  Transfers   Transfers   Transfers  Sales
           to work in               to
           process                  finished
                                    goods
```

Trading concern

```
        Merchandise
             $
            ↗ ↘
      Purchases  Sales
```

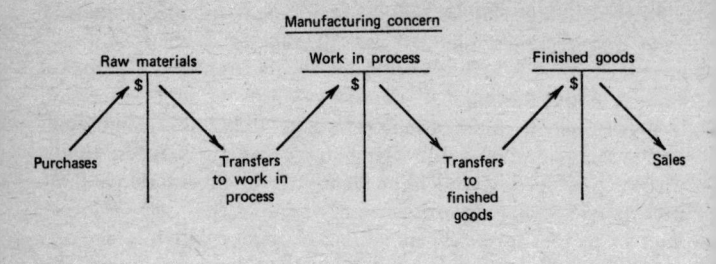

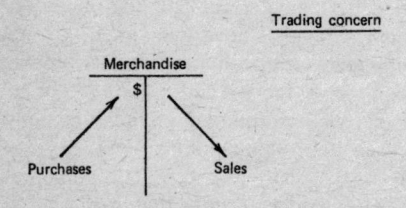

Figure 5.1. **Perpetual inventory system.**

in the perpetual inventory system. Some types of information that you might want to maintain are: a description of the inventory item, item number, location, minimum and maximum quantities to be maintained in inventory, vendor, amount and cost of items on hand.

Regardless of whether the perpetual inventory system is tied into the accounting system or is a separate information system, it is necessary to periodically take a physical inventory. A physical inventory must be taken at least once a year for all inventories. Merchandising firms take inventories more often in order to maintain control over inventories which can be stolen easily by customers or employees.

In recent years, some companies have developed inventory controls that are effective in determining inventory quantities. These methods are typically based on statistical sampling. The methods may be reliable enough so that an annual physical count of each inventory item is unnecessary.

Another inventory control possibility is to take the physical inventories throughout the year on a rotating basis. Thus, instead of taking one annual physical inventory, there is a continued physical inventory throughout the year so that all inventory items are counted and the detailed records corrected at least once during the year.

FIFO versus LIFO

There are three primary methods of valuing inventory and costs of goods sold for accounting and for tax purposes: (1) first-in, first-out (FIFO), (2) weighted average, and (3) last-in, first-out (LIFO).

Figure 5.2 presents an example of the calculation of the ending inventory values and the cost of goods sold under the three methods. As you can see, in a period of rising prices, LIFO produces a cost-of-goods-sold dollar figure that is higher than the cost-of-goods-sold figure produced by FIFO. This is the principal advantage of LIFO. In inflationary times, the effect of LIFO is to increase cost-of-goods-sold, thereby reducing your reported net income and your tax burden.

In certain situations, the LIFO cost flow will be representative of the physical flow of the goods into and out of the inventory. In most situations, however, LIFO will simply be an accounting and tax convention and will not be useful for control of inventory. An advantage of the LIFO method is that it reflects current disposable income. Essentially though, LIFO has become popular for a practical reason: the income tax benefits.

As long as the price level of inventories increases and the inventory quantities do not decrease, an indefinite deferral of income taxes occurs with LIFO. Even if the price level later decreases, your company will have been given a temporary deferral of its income taxes.

There are some criticisms of LIFO that should be mentioned. First, the inventory valuation on the balance sheet is outdated and irrelevant because the oldest costs remain in the inventory.

Assume:	Units	Unit cost	Total
Beginning inventory	2	$10	$20
Purchases:			
1	1	11	11
2	1	10	10
3	1	12	12
4	1	13	13
Cost of goods available for sale			$66
Total quantity available for sale	6		
Total sold during period	4		
Ending inventory units	2		

(1) Weighted average
Cost of goods available for sale $66
Total units available for sale 6
Average cost $11
Ending inventory value (2 × $11) $22
Cost of goods sold (4 × $11) $44

(2) First-in, first-out (FIFO)
Ending Inventory: 1 @ $13 = $13
                1 @ 12 = 12
                         $25

Cost of goods sold:
  Cost of goods available for sale $66
  Less: Value of ending inventory   25
                                 $41

(3) Last-in, first-out (LIFO)
Ending inventory: 2 @ $10 = $20
Cost of goods sold:
  Cost of goods available for sale $66
  Less: Value of ending inventory   20
                                 $46

Figure 5.2. Example of inventory valuation.

This causes several problems, especially regarding the measurement of working capital in the company. The difference between identical companies, one on FIFO and one on LIFO with respect to working capital will in general be that the working capital under LIFO will be smaller.

Second, LIFO does not measure "real income" in the economic sense. In order to measure "real income" as opposed to monetary

Inventories

income, the cost of goods sold should consist of the costs required to replace goods that have been sold. The FASB, through its statement No. 33, requires an estimate of this "real income" number for approximately the 1000 largest companies in the United States.

Third, with LIFO you face the involuntary liquidation problem. The involuntary liquidation problem occurs if the base layers, which have the old costs, are sold (liquidated). There can be bizarre results on income because old costs lead to an overstatement of reported income for the period and detrimental income tax consequences.

Fourth, in an attempt to avoid the negative consequences of the third criticism above, management may be induced into making poor judgments with respect to inventory purchases. At year end, unnecessary purchases may be made in order to restore liquidated LIFO inventory base layers.

Retail Inventory

Retail merchants often have difficulties when it comes to financial control, decision making, and the tax consequences of inventories. A special method of inventory measurement and valuation has been developed to aid the retail merchant. This method is called the conventional retail method. There is also a LIFO variation on the conventional retail method.

Under the conventional retail method, goods in inventory are valued at the *retail selling price*. This inventory value is then reduced to approximate cost through multiplication by a cost to retail ratio. A separate ratio must be determined for each department or class of goods. Figure 5.3 presents an example of a conventional retail method calculation of ending inventory.

Looking at Figure 5.3, notice that all costs—including costs in the beginning inventory, freight-in, and purchases—are added to the cost side (or numerator) of the ratio. The retail value of the beginning inventory, the retail value of the purchases, and additional mark-ups are added to form the retail side (denominator). The ratio is applied to the ending retail inventory to convert it to inventory at cost.

	Cost	Retail
Beginning inventory	$10,000	$20,000
Purchases	80,000	160,000
Freight-in	500	
Purchase returns	(2,000)	(4,000)
Mark-ups		1,000
	$88,500	$177,000

Cost/Retail Ratio: $\frac{88,500}{177,000} = .50$

	Cost	Retail
Sales		(100,000)
Mark-downs		(1,500)
Ending inventory	$37,750	$75,500

Figure 5.3. Conventional retail inventory method.

NONCURRENT ASSETS AND DEPRECIATION

The primary category of noncurrent assets for most businesses is *property, plant, and equipment,* which is also referred to as *fixed assets.* Fixed assets are machines, desks, typewriters, buildings, trucks, and land. Virtually all businesses have fixed assets of some sort.

The interesting thing about fixed assets is that all of them except land are subject to depreciation. That is, fixed assets at some point wear out from use. Even apartment or office buildings, which seem to appreciate—rather than depreciate—in value, wear out at some point. Therefore, the Internal Revenue Code allows a deduction on all fixed assets for depreciation.

DEPRECIATION

The remainder of this chapter will be concerned with the topic of depreciation. Depreciation, and the related topics of depletion and amortization are defined below:

Depreciation—In accounting terms, depreciation is defined as the process of allocating the cost expiration of tangible property against income. Depreciation also carries the connotation of decline in value due to use or wear and tear.

Depletion—Depletion is defined as the process of allocating against revenue the cost expiration of a natural resource, such as an oil well.

Amortization—Amortization is defined as the process of allocating the cost expiration of tangibles (such as patents or leaseholds) against revenue.

In order to determine the amount of depreciation, depletion, or amortization to be recorded for a period, or to be deducted for tax purposes, it is essential to know first: (1) the cost of the asset, (2) the estimated economic useful life of the asset, and (3) the estimated salvage or residual value of the asset at the end of its useful life.

Determining The Cost of an Asset

The acquisition cost of an asset is measured by the cash outlay made to acquire the asset. If something other than cash is exchanged for the asset, the fair market value of the noncash consideration at the time of the transaction is the measure of cost. If the fair market value of the noncash consideration cannot be determined, the asset is recorded at *its* fair market value.

An asset is generally not considered to be acquired for accounting or tax purposes until it has been placed in the position where it is ready to be used. Thus, all reasonable and legitimate costs incurred in placing an asset in service are considered to be part of the cost.

Cash Purchase. If an asset is purchased for cash, any other necessary outlay—including installation costs—should be capitalized. The capitalizable costs include the invoice price plus incidental costs (such as insurance during transit, freight, duties, title search, registration fees, and installation costs).

Credit Purchases. For assets acquired on a deferred payment basis, the cash equivalent price of the asset, excluding interest, should be capitalized. Actual or imputed interest on the note payable is written off as a current expense when it is paid. Even if the purchase contract does not specify interest on the liability, imputed interest should be deducted in determining the cost of the *asset*.

Example: To illustrate the purchase of an asset on credit, assume your company purchased a machine under a contract that required equal payments of $3,154.70 at the end of each 4 years when the prevailing interest rate was 10% per annum. To record the asset as $12,618.80 ($3,154.70 × 4) would include interest in the cost of the asset. The actual cost of the asset is the present value of the four payments discounted at 10%.

$$PV = Annual\ Payment \times Present\ Value\ of\ an\ Annuity^*$$
$$= \$3,154.70 \times 3.1699$$
$$= \$10,000$$

Therefore, the cost of the machine would be $10,000. Likewise, the difference between the $10,000 cost and the total of the installment payments ($12,618.80) represents interest expense which may be deducted as it is paid.

Assets Acquired in Exchange for Stocks or Bonds. If assets are acquired in exchange for stocks, the determination of cost may be difficult. This is because there may be no readily determinable fair market value for the stocks or the assets involved. The exchange is often a related party transaction, where the owners of the company are contributing assets to the company. As a consequence, the *Internal Revenue Code* indicates that, where assets are transferred to a corporation or a partnership in exchange for ownership interests, the cost basis of the asset will be the same for the corporation as it was for the transferrer/stockholder.

Assets Acquired in Exchange for Other Assets. If assets are acquired in exchange for other assets, further problems arise regarding the determination of the cost of the acquired assets. Items of property, plant, and equipment are frequently acquired by

---

* See Chapter 4 on Receivables.

trading in an old asset in full or as part payment for another asset. In some cases, an asset is acquired by exchanging another asset plus cash. Cash paid or received in an exchange transaction is often referred to as "boot."

For tax purposes, the cost basis of an asset acquired through an exchange is equal to the cost of the asset given up, plus any cash boot given.

Example: Your company acquired a truck 3 years ago for $9000 that had an estimated life of 6 years, with *no* salvage value, and you used straight-line depreciation. The current *book value*, or *basis*, of the truck would be $4500:

(1) $\dfrac{\$9000}{6} = \$1500$ depreciation per year

(2) 3 years × $1500 = $4500 depreciation for 3 years

(3) $9000 Cost − $4500 depreciation = $4500 basis

If you traded in the old truck for a new truck and paid $3000 cash in addition, you would then have a new truck with a book value, or basis, for accounting and tax depreciation purposes of $7500, despite the fact that the new truck might have a list price higher or lower than that amount:

$4500	Present basis of old truck traded
+ 3000	Additional money paid
$7500	Value of new truck purchased

Investment Tax Credit. It is important to determine the cost of an asset not only for depreciation purposes, but for an equally valuable reason, the Investment Tax Credit. The Investment Tax Credit was established by Congress in order to stimulate the purchase of machinery and equipment throughout the economy. It was first created in 1962 and has been modified subsequently several times. An investment credit is allowed against your tax liability when certain qualified business property is placed into service. The credit may also apply to progress payments made during the course of building or acquiring qualified property. The credit has no effect on regular depreciation.

Taxpayers can take a 10% credit for investments in qualified business property acquired after January 2, 1975. A corporate taxpayer may elect an 11% credit in an amount equal to 1% of the investment if it is contributed to an *employee stock ownership plan*. The maximum amount of credit that can be taken in any one taxable year is $25,000, plus 70% of your tax liability in excess of $25,000. The maximum credit allowable is $77,500 ($25,000 + 70% of $75,000). The credit can be carried over up to 7 years.

Example: Your company's tax liability before the investment tax credit is $100,000. If you buy qualified property costing $200,000, your credit would be $20,000 and your tax liability would be $80,000. The limit on investment credit will increase to 80% of the excess tax liability over $25,000 in 1981 and to 90% in years after 1981.

The amount of qualified investment depends on the useful life of the property to which the credit applies. Useful life is determined from the cost of the property. This is why the cost of an asset, discussed previously, is quite important.

For example, if you trade in a machine with a book value of $4000 and pay $1000 in additional cash for a new machine, the cost of the new machine would be $5000, and you would be allowed an investment credit of $500 (10% of $5000).

However, if the machine you acquire is used, rather than new, then only the excess cost above the book value qualifies for the investment credit. Therefore, in the example above, your investment credit would be reduced to $100 ($5000 − $4000 × 10%).

The rule about used property applies even if you sell an asset and then later reinvest the proceeds in a used asset of a similar type. For example, if you sell a truck, which has a book value of $3000, and then later you buy a truck for $5000, the amount of cost that qualifies for the investment credit is limited to $2000 ($5000 − $3000).

The investment tax credit applies to *depreciable tangible personal property*, which means it applies to property used in your trade or business which has a physical existence and which is not inventory, supplies, or real estate. Livestock of a farmer, except for horses, is considered to be qualified property.

Examples of qualified property include: office equipment, machinery in a factory, computers in a store, neon signs for advertising. Even the cost of producing a motion picture or television film has been considered to be qualified property though it is more intangible than tangible.

The investment credit does apply to real estate in certain circumstances. In order to qualifiy, the real property must be an integral part of either a manufacturing, production, mining, or utility operation, or constitute a research facility or a facility for bulk storage of commodities. Examples of real property qualifying for the investment credit include blast furnaces, oil derricks, oil and gas pipelines, broadcasting towers, and railroad tracks.

The credit is allowed for the year that the qualifying property is placed into service. This is the earlier of either (1) the first year that depreciation on the asset can be taken, or (2) the year the asset becomes ready for its intended purpose.

There is a limit on the amount of investment in used property and equipment that will qualify for the investment tax credit. The limit is $100,000 for corporations and for individuals. However, if you are married and file a separate tax return, the limit is $50,000. For a partnership, the limitation is $100,000 for the partnership as a whole.

No investment credit is allowed for property with a useful life of less than three years. Used property will not be qualified if, after you acquire it, it is used by the person from whom you acquired it. An example of this might be a sale and lease-back arrangement. Property which you have used before or property you repossessed will not qualify. Property that you acquire from your subsidiary, or from your parent company if you are a more than 50% owned subsidiary, would not qualify. If you sell or give personally owned property to a business which you control, the business cannot take a credit.

No credit is allowed for property that is used primarily for housing or to provide lodging, such as a hotel or motel. However, facilities related to housing or lodging may qualify, such as a restaurant in a hotel, or laundry machines in an apartment building.

Useful Life Limitations. In order to qualify for the full investment credit, the useful life of the asset must be at least 7 years.

If the useful life is 5 or 6 years, then only two-thirds of the cost of the asset qualifies for the credit. If the useful life is 3 or 4 years, then only one-third of the cost qualifies. If the useful life is less than 3 years, the asset does not qualify for the credit.

For example: Assume that you purchase a delivery truck, a small computer, and a lathe.

Asset	Useful life	Cost	Percentage	Qualified amount
Delivery truck	3	$ 9,000	33⅓%	$ 3,000
Computer	5	12,000	66⅔%	8,000
Lathe	7	15,000	100%	15,000
				$26,000

Investment credit ($26,000 × 10%) = $2,600

If the credit is not used in the period when it is earned, it may be carried back to offset taxes already paid up to 3 years previously, and may be carried forward up to 7 years.

The investment credit may have to be recaptured if the asset is not held at least 7 years. Even if the asset is destroyed, recapture of the credit will occur.

Example: If you bought a machine in 1978 which has a useful life of 10 years and cost $8000, in 1978 you could have taken an $800 credit. However, if the machine is destroyed by fire in 1980, the $800 will be added to your tax liability for 1980.

Depreciation and the IRS

Once you have acquired a depreciable asset and have determined its cost, then the question of depreciation arises.

The Internal Revenue Code recognizes that a depreciation allowance is necessary because property gradually approaches a point when its usefulness is exhausted. Therefore, depreciation is allowed only on property that has a definitely limited useful life. Depreciation may even be allowed on fruit trees if it can be shown that the trees have a limited life.

Intangible property can be depreciated, if its use in a business is of limited duration. Examples of depreciable intangibles in-

Depreciation

clude licenses, franchises, patents, and copyrights. Ordinarily, depreciation of intangibles is referred to as amortization.

Depreciation Methods. The Internal Revenue Code specifies three particular methods of computing depreciation. However, others may be used. The three methods are:

1. Straight line
2. Declining balance
3. Sum of the years digits

You do not need to use the same method for all your depreciable property, but once you choose a method for a particular property you must continue to use that method unless you obtain approval from the Internal Revenue Service to change methods. Obtaining approval to change is not a problem. You simply file Form 3115 during the first 180 days of the year of the change.

Useful Life. You may enter into an agreement with the IRS as to the useful life, depreciation method, and salvage value of any property. However, there are classes of property that have been established by Internal Revenue Regulations. These classes each have asset depreciation ranges. If you choose a useful life within the limits of the asset depreciation range for a given asset, you will not be challenged by the IRS.

Salvage value, established at the point when property is acquired, is the amount that can be realized when the property is no longer useful to the taxpayer. It may be no more than junk value, or it may be a large portion of the original cost, depending on the length of time before the end of the asset's useful economic life. The length of time for useful life is determined by when the taxpayer plans to dispose of the property. An estimated salvage value of *less than 10%* of the original cost may be *disregarded* in computing depreciation. However, no asset may be depreciated below a reasonable salvage value.

Salvage value must be subtracted from original cost in computing straight line and sum of the years digits depreciation. It is *not* subtracted in computing declining balance depreciation. *Ex-*

ample: A machine is purchased for $10,000 which has a salvage value of $2000 and a useful life of 5 years. The first year of depreciation under each of the three methods is as follows:

Straight line: $10,000 − $2000 ÷ 5 = $1600

Sum-of-the-years digits: $10,000 − $2000 × 5/15 = $2667

Double declining balance: $10,000 × 40% = $4000

Straight line: The formula for straight line depreciation is: Cost minus salvage value divided by useful life equals depreciation for each year.

Sum-of-the-years-digits: This method of depreciation allocates a declining portion of the total cost to depreciation expense in each year. In the example just shown where a machine was purchased for $10,000 and had a salvage value of $2000 and a useful life of 5 years, sum-of-the-years digits depreciation would be calculated as follows:

Year	Factor	×	Cost Minus Salvage	=	Depreciation Expense
1	5/15		$8000		$2667
2	4/15		8000		2133
3	3/15		8000		1600
4	2/15		8000		1067
5	1/15		8000		533
				Total	$8000

The formula for calculating the denominator of the sum-of-the-years digits fraction (which is '15' in the example) is:

$$\frac{n(n+1)}{2}$$

Where n = useful life

Example: Useful life = 5 years

$$\frac{5 \times 6}{2} = \frac{30}{2} = 15$$

Sum-of-the-years-digits cannot be used for real estate, except for new residential rental buildings such as apartment houses.

Depreciation

Declining Balance: This method applies a constant percentage to the declining book value of the asset. *Example:* Same asumptions as above. Cost of machine = $10,000, useful life = 5 years.

Double Declining Balance

Year	Percentage	Book value	Depreciation
1	40%	$10,000	$4,000
2	40%	6,000	2,400
3	40%	3,600	1,400
4	40%	2,160	864
5	40%	1,296	518.40

Note. The total depreciation exceeds the original cost minus salvage of $8000. This would *not* be allowed for tax purposes. Therefore, in the fourth year only $160 of depreciation could be taken (in order to bring the book value equal to the salvage value), and in the fifth year no depreciation would be taken.

The maximum rate on declining balance depreciation is specified by the following table. The factor is multiplied by the straight line rate in order to find the maximum declining balance rate.

Type of property	Factor
New equipment	2
Used equipment	1½
New real estate	1½
Used real estate	1
Used residential rental property	1¼

Example: You buy a new apartment building with a 50-year useful life. The maximum percentage you can use on declining balance depreciation is 3% (1½ times 1/50).

Depreciation for Periods Shorter Than One Year

Usually when you acquire an asset during a year, you prorate the depreciation that you owe on the asset.

Example: On April 1, you acquire a machine for $12,000 which has a useful life of 10 years. You decide to use straight line depreciation. The depreciation expense for the year of acquisition would be $900 ($12,000 / 10 × 9/12).

Gains and Losses on Sales

The rules regarding the computation of gains and losses upon sale or retirement of depreciable assets are somewhat complicated. In general, capital gains and losses are taxed at different rates than gains and losses on the sale of other assets. Depreciable property is not a capital asset; therefore, capital gains and losses are not allowable when depreciable property is sold. However, Congress decided in Section 1231 of the Internal Revenue Code to extend capital gain treatment to depreciable assets while preserving the benefits of ordinary loss treatment. Later, Congress changed its mind and added Section 1245 of the Code, which provides that for equipment that you sell, you have ordinary gain treatment to the extent of any depreciation taken on the equipment.

Example: You buy a machine in 1978 for $10,000 and decide to depreciate it on the straight-line method over 10 years. By the end of 1980 you have taken $2000 in depreciation. If you then sell the machine for $11,000, you must record $2000 of ordinary income gain and $1000 of capital gain.

Example: On January 1, 1971 you bought a machine for $6000. You claimed $600 depreciation on it for each year and sold it for $2000 on July 1, 1980. Your adjusted basis on the date of sale was $300 [$6000 less $5700, which represents $600 per year depreciation between 1971 and 1980 (9 years) plus $300 for the half year in 1980]. Therefore your gain was $1700 on the sale. Since the gain ($1700) was less than the total depreciation ($5700), the entire gain must be included as ordinary income.

On *real property*, gain or loss is calculated in the same way as personal property if either of the following applies: (1) you compute depreciation on the property using the straight-line methods (or any other method resulting in depreciation not in excess of that computed by the straight-line method), and you have held the property more than a year; or (2) you realize a loss on the sale of property. Otherwise, real property disposal by sale or exchange must be calculated by a special formula to determine what portion of the gain is to be treated as ordinary income.

Some thoughts on assets rattled through John's mind. LIFO

Depreciation

inventory shows a lower profit in time of inflation; FIFO shows a higher profit in times of inflation. If I want to show a higher profit I use FIFO; if I want to show a lower profit, I use LIFO. I know that my inventory is in three stages. First the raw material comes in the door—my people turn it into finished products and that becomes my "finished goods inventory." When inventory is counted, the goods that are only half finished are considered "work-in-process inventory." There are ways to keep track of your inventory on an ongoing basis—that's called "perpetual inventory system." This is done by an ongoing count and documentation.

All fixed assets and some intangible assets have a value that can be depreciated for tax and accounting purposes. The cost of an asset is the amount you pay for it plus tax plus shipping plus installation. If you buy an asset for something besides cash (like, in exchange for inventory), the value of the asset is equal to the value of the things you exchange (the inventory).

The cost of an asset acquired through an exchange is equal to the cost of the asset given up plus any additional cash paid, regardless of the value of the asset purchased. If I trade an old truck worth $4500 on the books plus $3000 in cash, for a *new* truck, the new truck is worth $7500. It doesn't matter what price the new truck lists for.

I can take an income tax credit of 10% on all new personal property I buy that has a life of at least 7 years.

Assets have different expected lives according to length of time you expect to wait before you dispose of the property, and assuming it is not less than IRS guidelines. Whatever value that you think the assets will have at the end of their life is the salvage value.

There are three methods of depreciation that are usually used: straight line, declining balance, and sum-of-the-years digits.

The formula for straight line depreciation—the simplest form—is: value of asset minus salvage value divided by the number of years in the asset's life. The formula for double declining balance depreciation is: depreciated value of the asset times the years of asset life times two divided by one hundred.

John Your looked at the stack of original documents and the uncompleted ledgers and decided he would have to come to work early again tomorrow morning.

Chapter Six
Liabilities

A second phony supplier, Thermafac, began to show up as the payee on Yourcompany checks. And their billing wasn't even professional. The letterhead was stamped with a rubber stamp.

It was bad enough that John Your's company had been paying out money since January to Softfare, but in June Thermafac appeared as a supplier. Each company had no telephone and an address that didn't exist.

John had driven past the address given for Softfare on his way home last night. The address was for a little one-bedroom shack that seemed to be vacant.

So far Yourcompany had paid Softfare, headquartered in a vacant one-bedroom house, $24,680. John felt sick.

John had done the books up to June, and so far he figured that there was about $38,000 missing. This included the money to Softfare, $3500 to Thermafac, and the balance—customers' checks deposited to the "other" bank account.

John should have been suspicious that something was going on when his profits seemed to be dropping so sharply; when, after four clean years, the checks started bouncing. John had dismissed it as higher cost of materials. He had been so stupid that he hated to admit it.

Now he was in a real fix, and he was going to have to get some more money quick. He was running behind on all his accounts payable and his account was about $20,000 overdrawn at the bank. Some of his materials had to be paid for in advance—this slowed down his production and upset his customers.

This damn theft was costing him more than money; it was costing the reputation of his company.

Liabilities

John was on pretty good terms with Fred Stoneface, his banker, but John didn't know how old Fred was going to take the news about this theft. At best Fred would simply think that John was a bad businessman. At worst, Stoneface might not bail him and Yourcompany out of this jam.

The more John thought about the bank, the more upset he got. For the last two days John had eaten nothing but boiled rice. This whole affair—the theft, the lost money, the unhappy suppliers, the upset customers, and the absolute need for a loan—had brought back his colitis. His stomach felt like someone was chewing on it. He was smoking two and a half packs of cigarettes a day.

John didn't feel like doing the books again. He got a cup of coffee and pulled out the *Simplified Accounting* book. He didn't feel like reading that, either, but he wanted to get his mind off his stomach and his anguish. And it was the only book in his office except for technical manuals.

John opened the book. He laughed. "Well, just what I needed, a chapter on liabilities and debt. . . ."

Liabilities are the amounts your company owes.

Liabilities are obligations that result from past transactions that require payment in the future. The amounts are either stated or implied in oral or written contracts.

Liabilities can be classified into current and noncurrent.

Current liabilities are those which are due and payable within one year. They include such things as: salaries and wages payable; other accrued expenses (utilities, taxes, supplies, etc.); accounts payable for inventories; and short-term notes payable to banks and others.

Salaries and wages payable and other accrued expenses are really another side of expenses and cash disbursements. We have already discussed cash disbursements arising from operating expenses. The main thing to remember with accrued expenses is to keep track of cash disbursements by using a check register and cash disbursements journal.

The other current liabilities typically represent debt due to banks and others, and are usually documented by a note. A note is a form of I.O.U., and is usually a legal document. This means that the holder of the note can take it to a court in order to have its provisions enforced.

Noncurrent liabilities are those which are due and payable in *more* than one year's time. Noncurrent liabilities are also referred to as *long-term debt*. Nearly all long-term debt is documented by a note. Notes pertain to both long-term and short-term debt.

DEBT

Every business in the United States—regardless of size—must from time to time borrow money. Usually a business will borrow from a bank, but it may also borrow from commercial finance companies; state, local, and federal governments; and the public bond market. The larger the business, the more likely that it can tap all of these debt sources. The smaller the business, the more likely it will only be able to use bank, government, and commercial loan sources.

Because this chapter of necessity is limited in scope, we shall not discuss publicly issued bonds. This is a specialty operation that requires accountants, lawyers and underwriters. We will limit the discussion in this chapter to the traditional sources of debt capital: banks, commercial financial lenders, and government (such as Small Business Administration's loans).

This chapter will offer a discussion of financial leverage, the types of loans that are available from different sources, the physical requirements of loan applications, and the accounting implications of debt financing.

Financial Leverage

Financial leverage is usually defined as the ratio of total debt to total assets. For example, a firm having assets of $1 million and total debt of $500,000 has a leverage factor of 50% ($500,000/$1,000,000).

The best way to understand the proper use of financial lever-

		Itscompany	
		Total debt	$-0-
		Net worth	$100
Total assets	$100	Total liability and worth	$100

		Hiscompany	
		Total debt	$ 50
		Net worth	$ 50
Total assets	$100	Total liability and worth	$100

		Theircompany	
		Total debt @ 8%	$ 75
		Net worth	$ 25
Total assets	$100	Total liability and worth	$100

Figure 6.1. Balance sheets comparing leverages.

age is to analyze its impact on profitability under varying conditions. Let's take the example of three firms in the electronic supply industry that are identical except for their debt percentage. Itscompany has used no debt and consequently has a leverage factor of zero. Hiscompany has financed their firm half by debt and half by equity so they have a leverage factor of 50%. Theircompany has a leverage factor of 75%. The companies' balance sheets are shown in Figure 6.1.

How a company's capitalization affects stockholder returns depends on the state of the economy. Let us assume that when the economy is depressed the firms can earn 4% on assets because sales and profit margins are low. When the economy is brighter, the firms can earn 8%. Under normal conditions they will earn 11%, 15% under good conditions, and 20% rate of return on assets if the economy is very good. The following table (Figure 6.2) illustrates how the use of financial leverage magnifies the impact on stockholders (or firm owners).

As shown in the illustrations, when economic conditions go from normal to good, return on assets for Itscompany (no leverage) goes up 36.4%, return on equity for Hiscompany (50% leverage) increases 57.1%, and return on equity for Theircompany (75% leverage) goes up a full 80%. Just the reverse happens when

	Very poor	Poor	Normal	Good	Very good
Rate of return on total assets before interest	4%	8%	11%	15%	20%
Dollar return on total assets before interest	$4	$8	$11	$15	$20
Itscompany: No Leverage					
Earnings in dollars	$4	8	11	15	20
Less: Interest expense	$0	0	0	0	0
Gross income	$4	8	11	15	20
taxes (50%)°	$2	4	5.5	7.5	10
Available to owners	$2	4	5.5	7.5	10
Percent return on equity	2%	4%	5.5%	7.5%	10%
Hiscompany: Leverage 50%					
Earnings in dollars	$4	8	11	15	20
Less: Interest expense	$4	4	4	4	4
Gross income	$0	4	7	11	16
taxes (50%)°	$0	2	3.5	5.5	8
Available to owners	$0	2	3.5	5.5	8
Percent return on equity	0%	4%	7%	11%	16%
Theircompany: Leverage 75%					
Earnings in dollars	$4	8	11	15	20
Less: Interest expense	$6	6	6	6	6
Gross income	$(2)	2	5	9	14
taxes (50%)°	$(1)	1	2.5	4.5	7
Available to owners	$(1)	1	2.5	4.5	7
Percent return on equity	−4%	4%	10%	18%	28%

° The tax calculation assumes tax credits for losses

Figure 6.2. Economic conditions.

the economy is depressed. When the economy drops from normal to poor, Itscompany's return on equity declines only 27%. Hiscompany, which has a higher leverage, shows a decline in return on equity of 42.9%, and Theircompany, which has the highest leverage, shows a decline in return on equity of a full 60%. In other words, the companies with the highest leverage receive the best return for owner's capital in normal or good times, but the worst return on equity in depressed economic times. The companies with the least leverage (least debt as a percentage of total assets) reap the highest relative return in times of a depressed economy.

Wide variations on the use of financial leverage may be observed among industries and among the individual firms in each industry. Financial institutions use the most leverage. Financial institutions typically have high liabilities. Public utility use of debt stems from a heavy fixed asset investment, coupled with extremely stable sales. Mining and manufacturing firms use relatively less debt because of their exposure to fluctuating sales. Small firms as a group are heavy users of debt.

In the manufacturing industries, wide variations in leverage are observed for individual industries. The lowest debt ratios are found in textile manufacturing because their competitive pressures tend to be great. Low debt ratios are also found in the durable goods industries. The highest reliance on debt is found in consumer nondurable goods industries where demand is relatively insensitive to fluctuations in general business activity.

Sources of Debt Capital

Not counting public debt offerings, there are basically three sources for debt capital: banks, commercial finance companies, and government agencies.

Banks. The advantages of securing a bank loan are:

1. Generally, with the exception of a few government and private programs, borrowing from a bank is the least expensive way to borrow.
2. Borrowing from a bank, as opposed to a government or commercial source, is usually better for your credit rating.
3. Banks have the largest loan breadth; that is, more types of loans, more sources.

4. Banks offer many business services including credit references on customers—or potential customers—of your business; financial, investment, and estate advisory services; discounting services for customers' accounts and notes payable; safe deposit boxes; night depositories.

The disadvantages of dealing with banks include:

1. The financially conservative nature of banks may cause difficulties; that is, bank loans are the most difficult of the loans to obtain.
2. In banks that have a large number of branches, there is a tendency to have a branch manager work at one branch for only a couple of years; therefore it is difficult to set up a long-term relationship with that branch manager.
3. The technical requirements (financial spreads, projected budgets, corporate and ownership information, etc.) of presenting a loan are greater with a bank than with other sources.
4. Because banks are regulated by the federal government and are simultaneously profit-making organizations, they have to be careful their loans do not fail. For most long-term loans, banks demand annual, semi-annual, quarterly, or even monthly income statements and balance sheets so that they can observe your business carefully. Remember, they have the records of every check you have ever written.

What is the best time and the worst time to approach a bank for money? Of course, depending on your personal or company situation, anytime might be a good time or bad time, irrespective of external influences and bank policies. That is, you might fall under what we call the unwritten golden rule of borrowing, which says: "If you don't need money, that's the best time to get a loan."

On an external basis, (i.e., having to do with the bank and the economy only), the following are the best times and situations in which to borrow and the worst time and situations to borrow.

Debt

The Best Environments for Borrowing

1. When interest rates are generally low. This means two things, that the bank has more money to loan than it usually does and that the borrower will get a better deal.
2. When a bank has just opened. New banks, especially independent banks, are looking for business. They love deposit business. Newly opened banks will take more chances with a marginal business because they have to build up their loan portfolio. Sometimes you will find that new banks are conservative, but if you start building a relationship immediately, and you don't ask for a loan at the start, the bank will loan to you when they get to know you. Incidentally, if you have a sizable business, banking with a small independent bank will be good because you might be their biggest depositor. If you are their biggest depositor, they will bend over backwards to give you service.
3. When the economy is in an up-turn. That is, sales all over the economy are increasing, the stock market is up, and disposable consumer income is up. This might be reflected in lower interest rates, but not necessarily.
4. When banks in a particular area are in heavy competition. This might mean that there are too many banks in a new, developing area. One way that you can tell there is a lot of competition is if more than one bank visits your business to start up a relationship (the more, the better for you.) Another sign is if there are a lot of incentives for deposits. That is, the banks are trying to outdo themselves in the premiums (toasters, calculators, etc.) they offer for deposits.
5. When banks are in the process of general expansion. During the 1960s, banks downplayed their traditional conservatism and started expanding their branch systems—including international branches—tremendously. Since there was more competition and a downgrading of traditional restraints, money was easier to obtain. There is a new facet of banking that might spark expansion: electronic banking devices called consumer-bank communication terminals, or CBCT's. These are the electronic devices that banks put outside their branches, or in supermarkets, shopping centers, and so on. These electronic devices

provide money or allow you to deposit without ever going to the bank. If their use becomes widespread, then the banks that get the most deposits will have more money to loan.

6. When there is a special program within the bank, usually a large bank, to take high-risk loans as "the bank's moral obligation." An example of this is loans to minorities and special groups like veterans, the handicapped, and—in some cases—displaced businesses or disaster victims. The large banks sometimes set aside sums for these "special high-risk" loans. But beware: regardless of the bank's good intentions, if the economy is bad or there is a high demand on loan funds, these special loans have a way of being forced out.

The Worst Environments for Borrowing

1. When interest rates are high. This indicates a large demand on bank funds—in many cases, from large, secure "Fortune 500" type firms. Also, at these times, the bank might be up to its loan limit according to the loan-to-deposit ratio (discussed below). High interest rates mean not only that money is more expensive, but that there is less of it to borrow.

2. When the economy is in a recession. In recessionary times, regardless of other influences, banks tend to be more conservative in their lending. There are more chances for a business to go under in a recession. Furthermore, there is usually high demand for money to tide an established business over.

3. When a bank is up to its lending limit, or when the bank has made a decision to decrease their dollars outstanding to make the bank more liquid. When there is an extremely high demand for funds, the bank is tempted to loan at high rates and therefore make a better profit. There is a limit to how much money they can loan out, however, and that limit is their maximum loan-to-deposit ratio. The loan-to-deposit ratio is simply the total loans they have outstanding divided by the total number of deposits they have. During 1974, banks were sometimes up to 75% of their deposits loaned out. This was difficult for the banks because if only 26% of their depositors took out their money, the bank would be in serious trouble, perhaps bankruptcy. Even this 75% loan-to-deposit ratio might be mislead-

ing. Banks have to report their loan-to-deposit ratio to the federal government once a week. They can borrow money from other banks for 24 hours to bring up their deposits to help the ratio. In the early part of the twentieth century, the banks would very seldom go above 33% loan-to-deposit ratio. Thus, 75% is a thin edge to walk on.

In 1975, when money supplies increased, loans did not. The reason was that although more money was available to loan out, the banks wanted to keep the money to build up their loan-to-deposit ratios and make the ratio healthier.

4. When there is very little bank competition for loans and de-deposits. A one bank town is a perfect example. When you need money, you go there and the competition is nil. The best thing to do is go to another town for financing.

5. When the parent bank is in trouble or suffers severe losses. In 1973, when United California Bank had trouble with its Swiss subsidiary, it was very difficult to obtain financing from its branches. If you read the business section of your newspaper, *The Wall Street Journal, Business Week,* or another business publication, you may learn about your bank's various troubles.

Of course, it is not always possible to wait for the right time to get a loan, and chances are good you will need money the most when everyone else needs it.

Commercial Lenders. Commercial lenders, including commercial finance companies (factors, industrial time sales, leases), life insurance companies, foundations, and other private financial companies, are usually more expensive to borrow from than banks, but they make more loans to a broader class of customers than banks.

Commercial lenders, in general, are willing to loan to businesses that are not as strong financially as the businesses that banks would consider. Furthermore, commercial lenders are willing to take as collateral items which banks would be more selective about, such as inventories and receivables. In short, the major advantage of commercial lenders is their flexibility.

The major disadvantage of commercial lenders is that their interest rates are generally higher—and sometimes much higher—than banks.

Life insurance companies, pension funds, and foundations offer money to businesses for real estate, equipment, and sometimes working capital, in amounts that are usually greater than the typical bank loans. Their interest rates are usually only slightly higher than banks. The disadvantage of these companies is that they usually only make large loans (in excess of $1 million) that require the applicant companies to be financially strong. This generally eliminates most small business from consideration.

Government Loans. The largest single lender to business in the United States is the federal government, followed by state and local governments. The federal government lending program is larger than the loan programs of Bank of America, Chase Manhattan, Citibank, Morgan Guaranty & Trust, and the rest of the ten largest banks in America. The United States government loans over $1.852 trillion per year to business.

Without question, the cheapest loans available in this country are those made by the government. Unfortunately, only a few special businesses, under very special circumstances, qualify for these loans. Most businesses, however, do qualify for government loans that have interest at a few points over prime. Although most government loans carry interest rates that are the same as, or a little higher than, bank rates, the government will make loans to higher risk businesses than banks. For instance, a start-up business that requires $100,000 in capital and has only $35,000 would not qualify for a loan at a bank at *any* interest rate. The same business, however, would qualify for a Small Business Administration (SBA) loan at near bank interest rates.

The equity requirements for most government loans are also less than those of a bank. For a start-up business, banks usually require 50% equity, whereas government loans require from 10% to 45% equity. For instance, let us take the example of a person who wants to start a business and has $15,000 in cash. At the bank he would be eligible for a maximum loan of another $15,000, for a total of $30,000. If the same person applied for a government loan, he could receive $18,300 to $150,000, depending on

Debt

the loan program. Starting a business with $45,000 instead of $30,000 can make a big difference in the long-range success of that business.

The repayment period for a government loan is also usually longer than the repayment period for a bank loan. For this reason, your monthly payment as a businessperson is usually lower with a government loan than with a bank loan. For example, if a business borrows $10,000 for 3 years (bank average) at 10.25%, the monthly payments are $323.85. If on the other hand, the same firm borrows the same amount ($10,000) at the same interest rate (10.25%) for 7 years instead of 3 years, the monthly payments are $167.31, or $165.54 less than the 3-year loan.

Along with the advantages to government loans there are some significant disadvantages. Government loans and government guaranteed loans take from 3 months to 3 years to receive approval. The effort required in paperwork and research is four times as great as a bank loan and twice as great as a commercial loan. In short, the greatest disadvantage of a government loan is time required for approval and the paperwork involved.

Types of Loans Available From Banks, Commercial and Government Lenders

The following is a listing of the types of loans that are available to the businessperson and a brief discussion of the type of financing where each is used.

Bank Loans. Loans for periods of 30 to 90 days are called *short-term loans*. Short-term loans are usually employed to finance inventory on which the business person can expect to get a cash return in a short period of time. New businesses very seldom receive short-term loans because most people just getting into business cannot turn their money around during the first few months of operations. However, short-term loans are used extensively for established businesses.

Intermediate term loans are for periods longer than 1 year, but less than 5 years. Equipment loans fall into this category. Most businesses that request bank loans will receive this type of loan unless they are financing property or getting a government guaranteed loan. Someone who plans to buy an existing business and borrow money on a regular bank loan will probably obtain a loan from 3 to 5 years in length.

Long-term loans are for 5 years or more. Government guaranteed loans are usually for more than 5 years. Banks will also make long-term loans on improvements and property.

Besides being named for the term they are for (term loans), loans are further classified into secured and unsecured loans. *Secured loans* require security. That means that the businessperson has to pledge some physical thing of value as security or collateral for the money the bank loans. A loan for buying equipment is a secured loan, because equipment is pledged as security which the bank can repossess if the borrower is unable to make the payments. *Unsecured loans* have no collateral pledged. Unsecured loans are made on "your good name," which means your credit is considered strong by your particular bank.

Only the rare businessperson getting started or attempting extensive expansion will obtain an unsecured loan. Even government guaranteed loans are "partially secured" (not totally supported by collateral, but supported with collateral to a large extent).

Secured loans fall into four categories: loans secured by liquid assets (stocks, bonds, or cash), loans secured by accounts receivable, loans secured by inventory, and loans secured by fixed assets (equipment, improvements, and property).

Liquid asset loans are loans that use savings accounts, stocks, or bonds for collateral. The business leaves its stock, bonds, or savings with the bank and the bank loans an amount equal to (in the case of savings) or less than (in the case of stocks and bonds whose market value fluctuates) the amount of the security. The advantage of this type of loan is that the interest rate charged is low (1%–2% over what you are earning on savings, or near prime in the case of stocks or bonds).

Accounts receivable secured loans include both factoring and accounts receivables financing. They are not available to a business just starting out. Accounts receivable financing and—more especially—factoring—tend to be expensive ways to finance a business. This type of financing is best used in a situation where sales are growing faster than cash flow. In accounts receivable financing (which has lower interest than factoring), the lender loans up to 80% of the value of your receivables (assuming all the accounts are reasonably good). The customer pays the firm and the firm brings the endorsed check to the lender. In factoring, the lender buys the firm's accounts. When a factor buys receivables, the customer pays the factor directly and receives a statement stating that the account is owned by that factor.

Inventory loans are made to businesses where an amount of inventory will be tied up for a long period of time. One example of the type of business that would use inventory loans is a car dealership. It is necessary for the dealership to retain expensive inventory (cars) in the showroom for long periods of time before the cars are sold. In this case the company has physical possession of the inventory (cars), but the bank owns the title. The type of inventory financing used for a new car dealership is called "flooring" (the borrower keeps the merchandise on the floor). Inventory loans are not made for inventory which is made up of numerous items of different prices (grocery, hardware, and most other retail businesses), fast selling items, or work-in-process (the uncompleted goods in manufacturing). You can, however, borrow on this inventory—even though it cannot be financed—if you receive a loan which includes other items like equipment, signs, and additional property.

Fixed Asset secured loans are for large "capital" items like equipment, land and buildings, improvements, and fixtures. Fixed asset loans are usually for the longest period of all the secured loans previously discussed. Real estate loans are a good example of secured fixed asset loans. All fixed assets loans are for terms of at least a couple of years and usually exceed 5 years in length.

Government guaranteed loans are the kind of loans that should interest most businessmen. For the vast majority of small businesses just beginning, the government guaranteed loan which is best is the Small Business Administration (SBA) guaranteed loan. The SBA loan guarantees the bank 90% against loss. That means that if you borrow $100,000 from a bank with an SBA guarantee, and you lose all the money in the first week, the bank will be paid 90% of the loss ($90,000) by the SBA. The SBA guaranteed loan is for high risk types of business—that is, small, and especially new, businesses. The borrower has to meet other requirements; information is available from the local SBA office.

Commercial Finance Companies. Types of loans available from commercial finance companies include inventory loans, equipment and fixture loans (including commercial time financing), accounts receivable loans (including accounts receivable financing), and equipment leasing (leasing companies).

Inventory loans are available to accounts receivable and factoring clients. Such loans are frequently utilized to assist the customer during periods of slow product shipments and inventory build-up, or to facilitate bulk raw material purchases at advantageous prices.

Equipment loans include two basic types: money loaned aginst presently owned equipment, and money loaned to finance new equipment and financed on a time sales financing basis.

On presently owned equipment, commercial finance companies will sometimes make loans. These advances are normally amortized monthly over a period of 1 to 5 years, or even longer. The proceeds from this type of loan may be required by the borrower to increase working capital, discount accounts payable, or simply to purchase new equipment. Very often an equipment loan is accepted in conjunction with accounts receivable or factoring arrangements.

Industrial time sales financing is a process whereby a company buys equipment from an equipment supplier, and the equipment supplier sells the purchase contract to a financier.

The price you pay for buying equipment on installment is usually high; higher, in fact, than the highest interest allowable in your state. How can the additional cost of financing be higher than the maximum allowable interest rate? Because you don't pay "interest" on industrial installment loans—you pay a "time price differential."

This "time price differential" has the following rationale: A seller is presumed to have two prices. One is the cash price; the other price is the "time price," for which the purchaser, who

Debt

wants credit over a period of time, must pay an added charge to compensate the seller for his additional burden. The differential between the cash price and the time is the time price differential. This reasoning assumes that the seller is not a money lender. The price doctrine provides the legal mechanism to remove the time sale from the application of usury laws (the state laws that restrict the maximum interest that can be charged on secured loans) by holding that the transaction is a credit sale and is neither a loan nor a forebearance for money.

Accounts receivable loans are the "bread and butter" of commercial finance companies, and were originally what the commercial finance companies were set up to deal with. Accounts receivable loans fall into two categories: accounts receivable financing and factoring.

Leasing is also a type of financing. It is a way of financing the full amount of the equipment you need. Leasing is the baby of the traditional, popular, funding methods, and there is still a lot of debate as to whether it is a good method for businessmen. To add to the controversy, there is no standard way things can be leased. You can rent a piece of equipment with or without maintenance, or with partial maintenance, and you can lease by the month, year, or several years. You can also obtain leases with the option to purchase.

Advantages of Leasing

1. Leasing offers a tax advantage. When you own something, you have to depreciate it for tax purposes over a lengthy period, so that the cost is recovered slowly. A lot of bookkeeping has to be done to obtain a tax saving. If inflation proceeds at the same pace as in recent years, the tax saving becomes one of the decreasingly valuable dollars as the depreciation table stretches into the future. Despite current efforts to slow inflation, there is little reason to expect that it can be kept under conrol.

   Leasing expenses are operating expenses and do not have to be depreciated, stretched out, held to future years, or back-charged to years gone by.

2. If you choose to have a maintenance contract with the lease (a good example is the maintenance-included lease on a copy machine), your maintenance is done by the company, freeing your company from maintenance problems.
3. You can "walk away" from the lease, return the equipment to the lessor when the equipment becomes outmoded or too slow, without having to finish the payments. In short, leasing is more flexible than ownership.
4. You need not worry about the equipment becoming obsolete, because if the lease can be canceled, you just stop the lease.
5. The cost of the equipment is fixed by the lease agreement, and this makes the cost predictable for projections.
6. Money that might be tied up in expensive fixed assets can be used for other purposes.

Disadvantages of Leasing

1. Down payments from leasing were at one time cheaper than purchases down payments. Now, however, the prepayment on leases is only 2% to 5% less than the down payment required for a purchase contract.
2. The costs for purchasing or buying are about the same, and when the equipment is purchased from the leasing company at the end of the period, the costs of leasing are higher.
3. If your company loses control over maintenance, you are at the mercy of the leasing company as to when the equipment will be fixed and how long the down time is.

In short, leasing requires somewhat less down payment at the start, but is generally more expensive than standard equipment purchase. Leasing is best if you need the flexibility of temporary use of the equipment.

Life Insurance Companies. Because of the striking growth of the industry, the accumulation of assets in life insurance companies has been rapid and substantial. It has been estimated that these companies are accumulating assets at the rate of $6 billion per year. The outflow of their funds can be statistically predicted. Hence, a part of their portfolio is available for long-term financing in the form of mortgages on industrial, commercial, and housing real estate. They also make loans to businesses, but require substantial enterprises with long earnings records dealing in markets not subject to rapid change. The average small or medium-sized business would not qualify because life insurance companies must follow certain loan policies: (1) the borrower has to be a corporation, (2) there is a minimum time for the borrower to be in business, (3) the borrower should have sufficient historical and current earnings to meet obligations, including debt repayments. A life insurance company grants two types of loans: commercial and industrial mortgage loans and unsecured loans. Mortgages by insurance companies cost the same as more orthodox bank loans.

A prevalent type of life insurance company loan is on an unsecured basis to a business in very good financial condition. Life insurance lenders are most interested in long-range financial data demonstrated by projected sales, cash flows, and so on.

Besides the sources mentioned, there are other sources of capital. These include credit unions and pension funds and foundations.

Credit unions. If you are a member of a credit union, you can receive reasonable interest loans for small amounts. Credit union services are offered only to members of credit unions; the credit union law restricts membership in a single credit union to a more or less homogeneous group of members having a common bond of interest. Credit union laws restrict the rate of interest charged and the amount of loan that may be made to a single borrower.

Pension funds and foundations. Because of the pension money coming in, such funds have experienced a rapid and large accumulation of assets and have a predictable outflow. Their standards of investment are similar to those of the life insurance companies, and they charge about the same interest rates.

A good percentage of pension fund money is used for sale-leasehold arrangements. Large foundations make loans in excess of $1 million for periods averaging 10 years. When they evaluate applicants, special emphasis is placed on company management, business background, and realistic projections.

Government Loans. Guidelines for government loans differ with each organization that can grant loans, but generally the government tries to aid business to increase employment when it would otherwise be difficult for the business alone to do so. The government guarantees loans to businesses in financial situations that banks and other financial institutions can not or will not approach.

Government loans are not easy to obtain, yet sometimes the government agencies loan money to extremely high risk businesses, usually at a low interest rate. However, the loan requirements are generally quite complicated.

Applying for government loans demands considerable time and effort to prepare the necessary documentation. The technical requirements—that is, the proposal (analysis of your business, including budgets)—requires much detail and technical work. If you decide to apply for a government loan it is advisable to consult a specialist in this field. Another alternative is to read *Business Loans: A Guide to Money Sources and How to Approach Them Successfully* (2nd edition), by one of the atuhors of this book, Rick Stephan Hayes, published in 1980 by CBI of Boston. This book covers all the procedures and requirements for government loans in detail.

Accounting Implication of Debt

When a lender loans money to a business, the immediate entry is a credit to a note payable account, with an explanation of the terms and length of the loan, as follows:

General Journal

Date	Comment	Debit	Credit
4/7/79	Cash	$17,000	
	Long-term note payable		$17,000
	To record 15%, 120 month note due to Bank of Amerigold, payments are $263.95 per month.		

Debt

An entry is then made in the general ledger as follows:

Bank Of Amerigold Long-Term Note Payable

Date	Comment	Debit	Date	Comment	Credit
			4/7/79	General journal	$17,000

Cash

Date	Comment	Debit			
4/7/79	General journal	$17,000			

Whenever a payment is made to Bank of Amerigold, as in the illustration above, a portion of that payment will be interest, and a portion will be principal. Interest is the amount of money that the lender charges you for using the loan. Principal is that amount of the loan repayment that is applied toward reducing the balance owed the bank. Interest is an expense and should be posted in an expense account. Principal is a reduction of the debt and is posted directly as a debit (a reduction in the amount owed) to the note payable account. Again, interest is an expense, principal is a reduction of a liability.

Each month the lender notifies the borrower how much of the monthly payment ($263.95 in the example) is interest and how much is principal.

Using as our monthly payment $263.95, the interest amount of the loan as 14%, and the amount of the loan as $17,000 as in the example above, we get the following monthly transactions:

General Journal

Date	Comment	Debit	Credit
5/20/79	Interest expense	$198.33	
	Long-term note payable	65.62	
	Cash		$263.95
	To record monthly payment of note to Bank of Amerigold (#12-34789-6)		

Ledgers

Date	Comment	Debit	Date	Comment	Credit

Interest Expense

Date	Comment	Debit	Date	Comment	Credit
5/20/79	General journal	$198.33			

Bank of Amerigold Long-Term Note Payable

Date	Comment	Debit	Date	Comment	Credit
			4/7/79	General journal	$17,000
5/20/79	General journal	$65.62			

Cash—Bank of Amerigold

Date	Comment	Debit	Date	Comment	Credit
			5/20/77	General journal	$263.95

The interest expense can be charged off against income tax in the year of entry (1979 in the example). Principal payments are not an expense that can be charged off, but are a reduction in the balance owed on the loan. After so many payments (120 in this example), the note is paid off and the liability is reduced to zero.

When the firm designs a profit and loss statement and/or a balance sheet for banks, stockholders, government agencies, or other interested parties, a footnote should be included with these financial statements indicating the term and interest amount of the loan and the name of the asset secured by the note, if any.

When he read about the best and worst times to borrow, John Your was unhappy to learn that right now wasn't a good time to borrow. Interest rates were high and the economy was not strong. The only thing that could make it worse would be if his bank, Bank of Amerigold, was in trouble or there wasn't much bank competition in town.

John was in pretty good shape for a loan in terms of his net worth. His leaverage wasn't too high or too low.

Debt

There are three basic sources of money for loans: the bank, commercial financing, and the government. He didn't want to deal with commercial lenders because either his company was too small to get a good deal or interest was too high. Government loans seemed pretty complicated, but he made a mental note to buy Rick Stephan Hayes's bestseller *Business Loans* to see if he could do it himself. It looked like he was going to have to get at least interim money from the bank.

He would probably have to get a secured loan, because John didn't know if his credit was good enough for an unsecured loan. He would like to get an intermediate term loan for more than one year, maybe two, but he would settle for a short term loan of less than a year—maybe a 6-month loan. That would give him time to prepare a government loan.

But what could the bank use as collateral? He had some certificates of deposit and some stock. The bank could loan on these at low interest, but he could only get about $17,000 on these. And that didn't look like enough. He had pretty good accounts receivable, and he would get 80% of that amount loaned to him at high interest rates. That looked like a good shot. He might get inventory loans because his inventory consisted of fairly large, slow moving items. He would check with the bank and see. Most of his present equipment was unsecured, but he didn't know what kind of luck he would have getting the bank to loan him money on these fixed assets.

The absurdity of the whole thing hit him like a bag of wet laundry. Because someone had stolen his money from his company, he was going to have to go to the bank to borrow.

Well, he thought half-heartedly, it could be worse. Martha has only worked for me as bookkeeper for a little over a year. It could have been something I didn't find out about until I was bankrupt. If this was a Fortune 500 firm, I could have lost millions.

John burst out laughing and laughed for a full five minutes, repeating to himself "million, millions . . . millions." He decided to go home early tonight and see his kids.

Chapter Seven
Forms of Business Organizations

John received a call from his insurance man at about 8:30 A.M.

"John, I've checked with the home office and can't go any higher. It looks like my first suspicions were true. Your insurance does not cover embezzlement. The only way it would be covered would be if your money handling people were bonded. I've been telling you this for years. I hate to give you the bad news. I think the only way you can get anything back is to bring charges in court." The insurance man paused, but John didn't answer. There was a long silence. Finally the insurance man asked, "Have you got a new bookkeeper yet?"

"No," was John's short reply.

"When you do, John, please call me. I'll let you go now. Goodbye."

"Goodbye." John put down the phone.

John Your looked at the wall in front of him for several minutes without moving. His mind was completely blank.

Slowly the thoughts came back into his head and he knew he had to borrow money and talk to an attorney. There was going to be no easy way out of this.

John immediately set up an appointment for the next week with his banker. He thought it would be a good idea to wait until he had finished the books before he saw the banker. He called up his attorney and told him the whole story. The attorney told John to continue as he was with the books and to check with the "other" bank to see about the signature card, and so on. He told John to make a special stack of all the documents that looked like they were phony. John told the attorney that this was already being done. The attorney said he would come to the shop to see John next week when the books were finished.

Now John had taken care of all his appointments. But he still didn't feel like getting back to the books. He decided to read the short chapter on business organizations from *Simplified Accounting* to take his mind off what seemed like an uncertain future.

The principal forms of business organizations prevalent in the United States are: 1) sole proprietorships, 2) partnerships and 3) corporations. There are also hybrid forms such as trusts, joint ventures, Subchapter S corporations, and limited partnerships.

SOLE PROPRIETORSHIP

A sole proprietorship is the most basic form of business organization. In essence, you and your business are indistinguishable for legal, accounting, and tax purposes. Your personal assets and your business assets are in effect co-mingled, and your business income and nonbusiness income are reported to the Internal Revenue Service on the same tax form, Form 1040. Business income is simply segregated on Schedule C of Form 1040 (see Figure 7.1). About the only thing you need to acquire as a sole proprietor is a license to do business in the particular locality in which you choose to operate.

If your business is conducted out of your home, the portion of your home that is devoted to business will be considered property used in the business. Furthermore, legitimate pension, profit sharing, and hospital and accident insurance deductions may be available.

One thing to be aware of in owning your own business is miscellaneous taxes such as the self-employment social security tax and the quarterly tax payment that you must make to the federal

SCHEDULE C (Form 1040) Department of the Treasury Internal Revenue Service	**Profit or (Loss) From Business or Profession** (Sole Proprietorship) Partnerships, Joint Ventures, etc., Must File Form 1065. ▶ Attach to Form 1040. ▶ See Instructions for Schedule C (Form 1040).	1978
Name of proprietor		Social security number of proprietor

A Main business activity (see Instructions) ▶ .... ; product ▶ ....
B Business name ▶ ....
C Employer identification number ▶ ....
D Business address (number and street) ▶ ....
 City, State and ZIP code ▶
E Accounting method: (1) ☐ Cash   (2) ☐ Accrual   (3) ☐ Other (specify) ▶
F Method(s) used to value closing inventory:
 (1) ☐ Cost   (2) ☐ Lower of cost or market   (3) ☐ Other (if other, attach explanation)

		Yes	No
G	Was there any major change in determining quantities, costs, or valuations between opening and closing inventory? If "Yes," attach explanation.		
H	Does this business activity involve oil or gas, movies or video tapes, or leasing personal (section 1245) property to others? (See page 25 of the Instructions.)		
I	Did you deduct expenses for an office in your home?		

Part I Income

1 a	Gross receipts or sales	1a	
b	Returns and allowances	1b	
c	Balance (subtract line 1b from line 1a)	1c	
2	Cost of goods sold and/or operations (Schedule C-1, line 8)	2	
3	Gross profit (subtract line 2 from line 1c)	3	
4	Other income (attach schedule)	4	
5	Total income (add lines 3 and 4) ▶	5	

Part II Deductions

6	Advertising		28 Telephone	
7	Amortization		29 Travel and entertainment	
8	Bad debts from sales or services		30 Utilities	
9	Bank charges		31 a Wages	
10	Car and truck expenses		b New Jobs Credit	
11	Commissions		c Subtract line 31b from 31a	
12	Depletion		32 Other expenses (specify):	
13	Depreciation (explain in Schedule C-2)		a	
14	Dues and publications		b	
15	Employee benefit programs		c	
16	Freight (not included on Schedule C-1)		d	
17	Insurance		e	
18	Interest on business indebtedness		f	
19	Laundry and cleaning		g	
20	Legal and professional services		h	
21	Office supplies		i	
22	Pension and profit-sharing plans		j	
23	Postage		k	
24	Rent on business property		l	
25	Repairs		m	
26	Supplies (not included on Schedule C-1)		n	
27	Taxes		o	
			p	
			q	
			r	

33	Total deductions (add amounts in columns for lines 6 through 32r) ▶	33	
34	Net profit or (loss) (subtract line 33 from line 5). Enter here and on Form 1040, line 13. ALSO enter on Schedule SE (Form 1040), line 5a. (For "at risk" provisions, see page 25 of Instructions.) ▶	34	

Figure 7.1. Form 1040.

Schedule C (Form 1040) 1978 Page **2**

SCHEDULE C–1.—Cost of Goods Sold and/or Operations (See Schedule C Instructions for Part I, Line 2)

1 Inventory at beginning of year (if different from last year's closing inventory, attach explanation) .	1
2 a Purchases 2a	
b Cost of items withdrawn for personal use 2b	
c Balance (subtract line 2b from line 2a)	2c
3 Cost of labor (do not include salary paid to yourself)	3
4 Materials and supplies	4
5 Other costs (attach schedule)	5
6 Add lines 1, 2c, and 3 through 5	6
7 Inventory at end of year	7
8 Cost of goods sold and/or operations (subtract line 7 from line 6). Enter here and on Part I, line 2. ▶	8

SCHEDULE C–2.—Depreciation (See Schedule C Instructions for line 13)

If you need more space, please use Form 4562.

Description of property (a)	Date acquired (b)	Cost or other basis (c)	Depreciation allowed or allowable in prior years (d)	Method of computing depreciation (e)	Life or rate (f)	Depreciation for this year (g)
1 Total additional first-year depreciation (do not include in items below)——————————————————————▶						
2 Other depreciation:						
Buildings						
Furniture and fixtures . . .						
Transportation equipment . .						
Machinery and other equipment .						
Other (Specify)						
3 Totals					3	
4 Depreciation claimed in Schedule C–1					4	
5 Balance (subtract line 4 from line 3). Enter here and on Part II, line 13 . . . . ▶					5	

SCHEDULE C–3.—Expense Account Information (See Schedule C Instructions for Schedule C–3)

Enter information for yourself and your five highest paid employees. In determining the five highest paid employees, add expense account allowances to the salaries and wages. However, you don't have to provide the information for any employee for whom the combined amount is less than $25,000, or for yourself if your expense account allowance plus line 34, page 1, is less than $25,000.

Name (a)	Expense account (b)	Salaries and Wages (c)
Owner		
1		
2		
3		
4		
5		

Did you claim a deduction for expenses connected with:	Yes	No
A Entertainment facility (boat, resort, ranch, etc.)?		
B Living accommodations (except employees on business)?		
C Employees' families at conventions or meetings?		
If "Yes," were any of these conventions or meetings outside the U.S. or its possessions? (See page 26 of Instructions.) .		
D Vacations for employees or their families not reported on Form W–2?		

☆ U.S. GOVERNMENT PRINTING OFFICE : 1978—O—263–058   94-0743750

Figure 7.1 (*Continued*)

government. These are made on Schedule SE of Form 1040 and Form 1040-ES respectively.

Proprietorship Accounting

There are two owner's equity accounts that you need to establish in a sole proprietorship: (1) a *proprietor's-capital account,* and (2) a *proprietor's-drawings account.* The proprietor's-drawings account is like salary, but is considered an equity account rather than an expense account.

For a sole proprietorship, the closing entries in the *general ledger* are as follows:

1. If you have a profit, the amount of the profit is entered as a debit in the profit-and-loss summary account and as a credit in the proprietor's-capital account.
2. If you have a loss, the profit-and-loss summary account is credited and the proprietor's-capital account is debited.
3. The total of the proprietor's-drawings account is then credited to that account and debited to the proprietor's-capital account.

These entries reduce the profit-and-loss summary and proprietor's-drawings accounts to zero.

1. Profit-and-loss summary	$20,000	
Proprietor's-capital		$20,000
2. Proprietor's-capital	$18,000	
Proprietor's-drawings		$18,000

PARTNERSHIP

A partnership may be nothing more than two sole proprietors who have agreed to pool their assets and operate a business jointly. There does not have to be a formal agreement between the partners in order for a partnership to exist legally, or for tax purposes. However, most states have partnership laws, and written partnership agreements should be drawn up by a lawyer in conformity with the laws of your particular state. For federal income tax purposes, a partnership includes not only a partnership as it is known in common law, but also a syndicate, group, pool, joint venture, or other unincorporated organization which carries on any business and which is not defined as a trust, an estate, or a corporation.

A partnership is not taxable as such. Only the members of the partnership are taxed in their individual capacities on their share of the partnership taxable income, whether distributed to them or not.

Example: A partnership is composed of two partners sharing profits equally. In the current year, the taxable income of the business is $30,000, none of which is distributed to the partners. The partnership tax return will report the $30,000 and show shares of $15,000 to each of the partners. Each partner will report his share of the partnership taxable income on his own tax return, even though the income has not been distributed to him.

The character of the income earned by a partnership is not altered when the income passes to the partners. For example, if a partnership sells a building and realizes a long-term capital gain on the transaction, the long-term capital gain is passed through to the partners rather than being reflected as part of the partnership income. The types of income, losses, and expenses which are passed to partners include: ordinary income and loss, additional first year depreciation, dividends, interest, short-term capital gains, long term capital gains, and contributions.

Partnership Accounting

If your company is a partnership, separate capital and drawing accounts must be kept for each partner. If no other agreement has been made, the law provides that all partnership earnings are to be shared equally; but the partners may agree in advance to any method of sharing earnings. If they do this, but claim no losses, losses are shared in the same way as earnings.

At the end of every year, your company's profits (or losses) must be distributed to each partner's capital account. Partners, like sole proprietors, cannot actually receive a "salary" from their company. A partner works for partnership profits. You may, however, wish to allocate "salaries" or "interest" payments, or both, to partners as a way of compensating each one fairly for time and capital invested in the business. Two methods of distributing profits are discussed below, but the same principles can be applied to any method you choose.

The easiest way to divide partnership earnings is to assign each partner a fraction, equal or otherwise. For example, two partners could take one half each, one quarter and three quarters, two thirds and one third, and so on.

For example, let us assume Al and Sue have a partnership in which Al contributed $40,000 and Sue $20,000 starting capital. Al is managing the business full time and Sue works for it three quarters of the time. They decide to divide earnings two thirds to Al and one third to Sue.

When $60,000 is invested, the owner's capital accounts will show the following:

Al's Capital		Sue's Capital	
Debit (−)	Credit (+)	Debit (−)	Credit (+)
	40,000		20,000
:	:	:	:
:	:	:	:

(Note: Cash will have been debited with the $60,000.)

At the end of the year, Al and Sue Company has earned $18,000 profit. It will be distributed as follows:

$$\tfrac{2}{3} \times \$18,000 = \$12,000 \text{ to Al}$$
$$\tfrac{1}{3} \times \$18,000 = \$\ 6,000 \text{ to Sue}$$

If no withdrawals were made during the year, the total $18,000 would be credited to Al and Sue capital accounts as follows:

Al's Capital		Sue's Capital	
Debit (−)	Credit (+)	Debit (−)	Credit (+)
:	:	:	:
:	40,000*	:	20,000*
:	:	:	:
:	12,000	:	6,000
:	:	:	:

* Prior entry.

If withdrawals had been made by the partners during the year, they would be debited to owner's drawing accounts and subtracted from net profits at the end of the year:

Net profit: $18,000

Al's share:	$12,000
Less owner's withdrawal:	8,000
	$ 4,000 Al's share

Sue's share:	$ 6,000
Less owner's withdrawal:	5,000
	$ 1,000 Sue's share

Limited Partnership

A limited partnership is a special type of partnership authorized under many state laws. A limited partnership must have at least one general partner, who has unlimited liability for the debts of the partnership, and who is responsible for managing the business. The limited partners are only liable to the extent of their partnership interests, and they must not participate in any way in the management of the business. The advantage of a limited partnership is that it may employ leverage, to earn a high rate of return of the limited partners' invested capital without increasing the risk of the limited partner.

Example: A contractor becomes the general partner in a limited partnership. He agrees to acquire land, construct a building, and sell the building when it is completed. He arranges for five investors to contribute $20,000 each to the project in exchange for limited partnership interests. On the basis of the construction plans and the $100,000 equity, the contractor-general partner is able to arrange a bank loan for $200,000. The loan will be secured by a purchase money mortgage and a performance bond. Considerable leverage would be used, and most of the money contributed by the limited partners—and even that which was borrowed—would be treated as a tax deductible expense.

The leverage aspect of limited partnerships is the reason that a great many tax shelters are constructed as limited partnerships.

Congress felt that the proliferation of tax shelters was not appropriate, and in the Tax Reform Act of 1976 tax shelters were curtailed. Basically, the rule stated that the amount of losses that could be claimed from certain investment activities could not exceed the total amount that the taxpayer had at risk in the partnership. Under the "at risk" rule, loss deductions are limited to the amount of cash contribtued to the partnership by the partner. There is no liability for the limited partners beyond their initial investment. When the building is sold the limited partners will share in the profits. The "at risk" rules apply to all activities other than real estate.

Real estate is still a potential type of investment for a tax shelter limited partnership, even though the rules have been changed. One method of increasing the tax deductible expenses in a real estate limited partnership was to write off interest "points," interest, and taxes during the construction period of a real estate project. The new rules state that points, interest, and taxes during construction must be capitalized and amortized over a 10-year period. This rule applies to all individuals and partnerships as well as Subchapter S corporations.

Subchapter S Corporations

In the eyes of the law, a corporation is a person, and it can sue, be sued, and also pay taxes. Since the individuals who own the corporation also pay taxes on any dividends they receive from the corporation, there is in effect double taxation.

Many people argue that this double taxation should be eliminated. To a certain extent the double taxation has been eliminated by the creation of Small Business Corporations, also referred to as tax option corporations, or Subchapter S corporations.

A Subchapter S corporation is a corporation that has elected, by unanimous consent of its shareholders, not to pay any corporate tax on its income, and, instead, to have the shareholders pay taxes on it, even though it is not distributed. Shareholders of a Subchapter S corporation are entitled to deduct, on their individual returns, their share of any net operating loss sustained by the corporations.

Taxable income is computed at the corporate level in much the same way as it is computed for any other corporation. The shareholders are then taxed directly on this taxable income, whether or not the corporation makes any distributions to them. There is one exception to this "no conduit" rule. The Subchapter S corporation's net capital gains or losses are passed to shareholders and are treated by them as long-term capital gains or losses on their individual returns.

Only a domestic corporation that is not a member of an affiliated group can elect Subchapter S status. A qualifying Subchapter S corporation may not have more than one class of stock or more than 15 shareholders. The shareholders must all be individuals, or estates of deceased individuals who once were shareholders.

The tax aspects of a Subchapter S corporation are somewhat complex. A certified public accountant, or an attorney, should be consulted if you decide that Subchapter S status is an appropriate form of business organization for your particular business.

CORPORATIONS

Most businesses that are not designed strictly for investment purposes eventually decide to incorporate. The reasons for this include: limits on personal liability of owner-managers, financing and growth flexibility, and transferability of interest.

The first decision faced by persons who would like to incorporate a business is where to incorporate. A corporation depends on the legal statutes of a particular state for its permission to exist and for the procedure by which it will come into existence. Some state corporation laws are more attractive to incorporators than others. States such as Delaware have attracted incorporation far out of proportion to the number of corporations actually doing business there. This is because Delaware has had, for many years, a corporation law that offers incorporators certain privileges, advantages, and facilities for incorporation that could not be obtained elsewhere.

Recently, however, differences in corporation laws among the major commercial states have been reduced, and incorporation is often preferred in the state where the major share of the business will be done, unless business will be done throughout the country and internationally.

Although the procedure of incorporation varies in detail from state to state, the pattern is much the same everywhere. Certain steps should be taken before the incorporators draw up a charter. Included among these are: the discovery of a business opportunity, solicitation of pre-incorporation stock subscriptions, and reservation of a corporate name.

Corporate Charters

Corporate charters are required to have certain clauses, and permitted to have others. Usually the first clause of a corporate charter is the corporate name. The name cannot conflict with any other name used in that state. Names of incorporators should not be used because there is a potential of losing the right to use one's own name for business purposes.

A second clause will contain the business purpose. This sets forth the purposes, objects, or general nature of the business. Many states permit a purpose clause to state that the corporation is formed for any lawful purpose.

A third clause of the corporate charter will outline the capital structure. Most corporation laws require a statement of the proposed corporation's capital structure, including the authorized number of shares; the rights, preferences, privileges and restrictions on the various classes and series of shares; whether the shares have a par value; and the voting rights of the shares.

Other provisions appearing in the charter pertain to the location of the principal office, the number of directors, the names and addresses of the original directors, duration of the corporation, existence of preemptive rights, powers of directors, a statement that the corporation may become a partner in a partnership, and other provisions.

The by-laws of a corporation deal with the internal management rules of the corporation. They must be consistent with the charter of the corporation. By-laws usually deal with matters such as the duties and compensation of corporation officers, the qualifications for membership on the board of directors, executive and other director committees, the date and place of annual shareholder meetings, provisions for audits, and other matters.

Common Stockholder Rights

The rights of the holders of common stock in a business corporation are established by the laws of the state in which the corporation is chartered and by the terms of the charters.

Also, collective and specific rights are usually addressed in corporate charters with respect to rights of common stockholders.

Collective Rights. Certain collective rights are usually given to the holders of common stock. Some of the more important rights allow stockholders to amend the charter, to adopt by-laws, to elect directors, to authorize sale of major assets, to enter into mergers, to change the amount of authorized common stock, and to issue preferred stock, debentures, bonds, and other securities.

Specific Rights. Holders of common stock also have specific rights, as do individual owners. They have the right to vote; they may sell their ownership shares; they have the right to inspect the corporate books.

From a legal perspective, the management of a corporation derives its authority from the ownership interests of the corporation. In order to maintain and exercise this authority, a device known as the proxy has developed over time.

For each share of common stock owned, a stockholder has the right to cast one vote at the annual meeting of stockholders. Provision is usually made for a temporary transfer of this right to vote to a proxy. This transfer is limited in duration, typically for a specific occasion such as an annual stockholder's meeting.

The Securities and Exchange Commission (SEC) supervises the use of proxies and issues frequent rules concerning them. If the proxy rules were left solely in the hands of management, there is the possibility that the incumbent management would be self-perpetuated. On the other hand, if it were easy for minority groups of stockholders and opposition stockholder factions to remove incumbent management, it would be possible for small groups of stockholders to gain control of the corporation for their own personal ends. In order to balance these diverse interests, stockholder voting for directors is regulated by law in many states.

Advantages and Disadvantages of Common Stock Financing

There are four principal advantages of using common stock as a source of financing for a corporation:

1. Common stockholders do not receive fixed payments. As a company generates earnings, it may pay common stock dividends. In contrast to bond interest, there is no legal obligation to pay dividends.
2. Common stock carries no fixed maturity date.
3. Since common stock provides a cushion against losses for creditors, the sale of common stock increases the credit worthiness of the firm.
4. Common stock may at times be more easily sold than debt. Common stock may have a higher expected return in periods of inflation because the return may increase whereas the return on debt remains constant.

There are several disadvantages of using common stock as a source of financing for a corporation:

1. The sale of common stock extends voting rights or control to the additional stockholders. For this reason, additional equity financing is often avoided by small and new firms. The owner-managers may be unwilling to share control of their companies with outsiders.
2. Common stock gives more owners the right to share in profits.
3. The costs of underwriting and distributing common stock are usually higher than for underwriting and distributing preferred stock or debt. Underwriting costs for selling common

stock are higher because the costs of investigating an equity security investment are greater than for a comparable debt security.

4. Common stock dividends are not deductible for tax purposes, but bond interest is.

Par and No Par Stock

Either common stock has a par value or it is no par stock. Par value is an arbitrary amount assigned to a share of stock and has no necessary relationship to its market value then or any other time. No par stock, however, is assigned a started value per share for accounting purposes, and this is the basis on which the stock is presented in the balance sheet.

The excess price above either the par or stated value received at the time stock is sold initially is entered in an account entitled "Paid-in Surplus," "Capital Surplus," or "Capital in Excess of Par or Stated Value." This paid-in surplus appears as a separate item in the capital section of the balance sheet (see Figure 7.2).

Assume 9,500 shares sold at $5 per share.
Your Company Stockholder's Equity:
Common stock, $1 par value
  (Authorized: 10,000 shares;
  issued and outstanding: 9,500) $ 9,500
Capital in excess of par value   38,000
  Total stockholder's equity $47,500

Figure 7.2. Stockholder's equity section of balance sheet.

Theoretically, and in the eyes of the law, creditors rely on a company's stated capital (at par or stated value) when granting credit to it. Actually, to the extent that creditors pay attention to financial statements at all, they rely on their appraisal of a company's working capital condition as shown by its balance sheet, and on how well that company is doing judged by their analysis of its income statement.

However, the par or stated value of common stock outstanding may have never been paid for in full. In this case, creditors can require that the stockholders make good the deficiency if the company fails and is unable to pay off its debts.

By selling common stock at a premium above its par or stated value, the danger to a stockholder of a possible later assessment has been avoided. To effect this, the stock has been assigned a low par value, or it has been no par stock with a low stated value. The low par—or low stated—values have also been adopted in order to minimize the fees or taxes involved in the sale of the stock.

In this connection, it should be recognized that corporations are created, carry on their activities, are taxed, and are dissolved under state laws. Thus these statutes have a bearing on how a company reports ownership, as well as how it treats other matters in its balance sheet.

Preferred Stock

Preferred stock has claims or rights ahead of common stock, but behind those of debt securities. The preference may be a prior claim on earnings, or it may take the form of a prior claim on assets in the event of liquidation. It may also take a preferential position with regard to both earnings and assets. The hybrid nature of preferred stock becomes apparent when you try to classify it in relation to debt securities and common stock. The priority feature and the fixed dividend indicate that preferred stock is similar to debt. Payments to preferred stockholders are limited in amount, so that common stockholders receive the advantages or disadvantages of leverage. However, if the preferred dividends are not earned, the company can forego paying them without damage of bankruptcy. In this way, preferred stock is similar to common stock.

The possible characteristics, rights, and obligations of preferred stock vary widely. As economic conditions change, new types of securities are invented. The possibilities are many, limited only by the imagination and ingenuity of the managers formulating the terms of the security issues. It is not surprising, then, that preferred stock can be found in a variety of forms. These are some of the more common features of preferred stock:

- Preference in assets and earning
- Par or liquidation value (dividends as a percentage of par)
- Cumulative dividends (i.e., all dividends in arrears must be paid)
- Convertibility into common stock
- Participation in Earnings
- Call Provision

An important advantage of preferred stock from the viewpoint of the issuer is that, in contrast to bonds, the obligation to make fixed payments is avoided. If a firm's earning power is high, higher earnings for the original owners may be obtained by selling preferred stock with a limited return rather than by selling common stock. By selling preferred stock, a company avoids the equal participation in earnings that the sale of additional common stock would require. Preferred stock also permits a company to avoid sharing control through participation in voting. In contrast to bonds, preferred stock issuance enables the company to leave unencumbered assets that are able to be mortgaged. The lack of maturity date or sinking fund provision typically makes preferred stock a more flexible financing source than bonds.

The disadvantages of preferred stock include the fact that typically it must be sold at a higher yield than bonds. Furthermore, preferred stock dividends are not deductible for tax purposes, which increases their cost relative to bonds even more. Utilities companies, such as telephone, gas, and electric providers, issue the majority of all preferred stocks. For untilities, taxes are an allowable cost for rate-making purposes; that is, higher taxes may be passed on to customers in the form of higher prices. Tax deductibility of preferred dividends is therefore not an issue.

TRANSFORMING THE STRUCTURE OF A BUSINESS

One of the few remaining ways to become a well-to-do person in the United States is to start a business enterprise which then becomes successful, take the company public in a stock offering (retaining a healthy share of the stock yourself), and then see the stock rise significantly in price in the public market. This is, of course, a long shot; but if you win. . . .

Some lawyers, accountants, and investment bankers make a specialty of taking new companies into the public markets. Their goal is to be part of the long shot when it comes through. The tax implications of moving away from proprietorship and partnership towards a corporation are such that generally accepted accounting principles (such as concepts of accrual, depreciation, inventory, etc.) are more frequently brought into play in corporations. The business manager in a corporate setting has to be more aware of his accounting options, and the business's accountant has to be more aware of generally accepted standards of accounting and auditing—not just taxes.

When the corporation decides to go into a public issue of stock, it may want to do many things from an accounting standpoint. For example, in a private company, saving taxes may be paramount; whereas in a public company, reported earnings may be equally important. Therefore, a company moving from private to public status may want to reassess its depreciation and amortization policies along with other accounting treatments, such as bad debt allowances, warranty reserves, inventory valuation, and the like.

Going public may mean that your company will be audited for the first time by a certified public accountant. Many local CPAs are highly competent at tax returns, tax planning, and preparing financial reports from client records, yet are only rarely engaged to perform certified audits. It is generally not possible for a CPA who is closely allied to your business as an advisor and preparer of financial statements to perform a certified audit. Going public often means you have to find a new CPA firm—a costly and somewhat traumatic undertaking. The benefits are obtaining a thorough review of your business, from an objective standpoint, and a general assurance that your financial statements are prepared in conformity with generally accepted accounting principles. Such conformity—together with an unqualified opinion from a respected CPA firm—will enhance the marketability of your company's stock. This means more money if your stock is sold successfully.

A public issue of stock requires several outside consulting persons—notably an accountant and a lawyer with prior experience in public securities offerings, and a securities underwriter or investment banker. Each of these persons will have roles to play in the issuing of public securities. The accountant must prepare a certified audit opinion upon completion of his audit of your business. In most cases, the lawyer will prepare the written parts of any forms and documents that must be filed with the Securities or Franchise Board of the state of incorporation or with the SEC.

Typically, no documents will be required if the total funds raised by the corporation are less than $100,000. If the total funds raised are between $100,000 and $500,000, you may be able to avoid filing many of these documents by complying with Regulation A of the Securities Act of 1933, which specifies an exemption for small offerings. If the total funds raised are over $1,500,000, it will probably be necessary to undergo a complete registration statement procedure. The registration statement will be filed with, and reviewed by, the SEC in Washington, D.C., or a regional field office.

Upon completion of the review, the registration is said to "go effective" and your stock may be legally sold in the public markets. This is where the underwriter plays a role in the issuance and sale. His job is to judge the movement of the market and to estimate the best time to begin selling the stock in the public market. As a fee, the underwriter typically receives a certain percentage of the total amount raised. Alternatively, he will purchase the new stock at a price estimated to be below the market price when the stock is sold publicly. In the latter case, the underwriter must often bear the risk of stock price decline, which is the reason for the name "underwriter."

Most companies who are initially required to file registration statements in conjunction with sales of stock will be compelled to file additional annual, quarterly, and other update reports, and to revise their registration statements, prospectuses, and proxy materials from time to time. This is an added cost in terms of the time involved for management, accountant's and lawyer's fees, and probable printing costs. Such costs should be considered when initially planning a public issue of stock or other securities.

"Yeah, maybe I'll go public," John thought. "The stockholders don't have to worry about being robbed since the company is certifiably robbed already."

Yourcompany was a Subchapter S corporation. It was interesting to note that the company could now have 15 stockholders instead of the old maximum of 10 stockholders. John's company only had seven stockholders. He could sell some of the stock of his company. What were the advantages of equity financing? There would be no fixed payments, it would increase the equity in the company, and it might be easy to sell, now that inflation was high. Preferred stock seemed like a better deal to John than common stock. He decided to ask Pete Popstein about it.

Maybe he could set up a special limited partnership deal for the manufacture of his product. The limited partners could put up cash to manufacture the next series of products that John designed. John would be the general partner. New projects always cost more than they made the first few years. Limited partners could get write-offs and John could get the development of his next product financed. He would ask his attorney and Pete Popstein about it.

John looked at the stack of transaction documents, bills, checks, and other papers, remembered that he had to have the books finished by the following week, and knew he had to get back to work.

John got another cup of coffee, took up his calculator, and began to work. He only had another four months to go.

Chapter Eight
Revenue and Expense

"Well, hello stranger, you're home early tonight," John Your's wife Gin greeted him when he came through the door.

"I called it a day. I'm getting sick of accounting." John answered. "Where are the kids?"

"No you don't. They have to do their homework first. Besides, I want to talk with you. I haven't seen much of you this whole week. Come into the kitchen—I saved some chicken," Gin answered.

"Honey, tell me. How bad is it—this theft?" Gin asked once they were in the kitchen. She stood near the stove as John sat at the table.

"Well, I've found about $50,000 gone. Pete Popstein, you know, the CPA, said it could be $100,000. But I don't know. I think it won't be more than $80,000." John concluded.

"That much."

John sighed, "I'm afraid so. The insurance man called today and said the insurance didn't cover it. I've got a meeting with Riskstein, my attorney, next week. Also with the branch manager of the Chevy branch about the phony account." John answered.

"How's the bookkeeping and reading going?" Gin asked.

"All right. I only have three and a half months to go. I think I'll finish the books by next week. That's why I set up the appointments then. I'm about half finished with the accounting book. It's going faster than I thought," John answered.

"I feel so bad about not being able to help you out with the accounting. I'd like to learn about bookkeeping and accounting so I could help you," Gin told John.

"I thought that you didn't want anything to do with the business."

"That was before I saw what could happen when you have to have other people work for you who don't have your interest at heart." Gin answered.

"How about the kids? You know that we both decided that it was better for you to take care of the kids." John said.

"No. I mean part-time. Once or twice a week. There must be something I could do." Gin insisted.

"Well . . . maybe you could help me with the entries in the books for now. Then maybe you could type out the checks or handle the receipts or something." John thought out loud.

"Good," Gin injected, "I'll do it. I'll start by reading your accounting book to you out loud and then you can explain stuff to me."

"Out loud?" John was hesitant, "That's silly."

"No it isn't. We'll wait until the kids are in bed, then we'll read it together, it might be fun. We don't do too much together lately. Okay?"

"Okay," John agreed.

Later that night Gin began reading "Revenue and Expense . . ."

REVENUE (SALES OR INCOME)

To a salesman, a sale takes place when he receives an order from a customer, but to the accountant it is not a sale until the goods are shipped. A record or order may be kept for management purposes, but a sale is not a sale until the goods are out the door. When goods have been shipped, the accountant will accept the fact that delivery has been made and, accordingly, will record the event as a sale.

Thus, for the majority of companies the word "sales" in an income statement means goods shipped during a given accounting period.

Revenue (Sales or Income)

The term sales may be extended to cover "fees" for services performed as well as other items of income such as commissions, rents, and royalties.

For sales involving the shipment of goods there is normally a passing of legal title, which is evidence that a sale has in fact taken place. In other types of business transactions, however, revenue recognition is not dependent on the passing of title. For example, service industries—such as doctors or hairdressers—do not pass a legal title when they perform a service for their customer.

Other examples of revenue without passing legal title are situations involving long-term contracts. Legal title does not pass until the contract is completed. In the construction of a house, for example, revenue will be recognized each accounting period in accordance with the work performed during that period as measured either by: (a) percentage of completion, or (b) completion of identifiable portions of work. At such times, something less than the full proportion of revenue will be recognized (or a reserve will be established) to make good whatever parts of the work may fail to meet expectations.

Companies selling on the installment payment basis commonly record their sales at the time goods are delivered to the customers. However, these sales are not reported for tax purposes until after their cost of merchandise has been recovered.

Where options are available that permit one type of report to the government and another to the stockholder, the natural tendency is for a company to be most conservative in computing net income for tax purposes.

Sales Discounts and Returns

In many businesses the real price charged to a given buyer is determined by the application of a discount to the list or catalogue price. No buyer is foolish enough to pay full price when he could get a discount. Under these conditions, sales reported for accounting purposes represent revenue net of trade discounts.

The question of whether cash discounts are a financial expense, a selling expense, or a reduction in sales revenue has been debated for many years. Treating the discount as a *financial expense* assumes that it is granted in order to receive payment and to either match or better the offers of competitors. Treating the discount as a *reduction in sales revenue* may also be justified by competition. In any case, these costs are subtracted from gross sales to give a net sales figure.

The value of goods returned is another item subtracted from gross sales to arrive at net sales. The accounting problem caused by returns is that goods returned in the current accounting period may have been sold in the previous period. Treating them as a reduction from current sales is an incorrect matching of revenues and costs.

Unless the returns are unusually large, however, there is no serious distortion of results. The distortion of returns that lag behind sales in one period is similar to distortions happening in the next period or in the previous period. In other words, these distortions will balance out over time.

An allowance for sales returns and adjustments is set as a percentage of sales. This allowance is created to allow for adjustments such as billing errors or other selling price adjustments that occur after the fact. Some companies use an allowance for trade discounts as well.

The sales journal and the accounts receivable ledger discussed in a previous chapter are the primary accounting systems for recording sales and revenue transactions.

Revenues and sales *cannot* be generated without incurring expenses. In order to measure the success of a business, and also to measure its income tax, expenses must be matched against revenues to come up with net income.

EXPENSES

Cost of Goods Sold

Cost of goods sold, sometimes referred to as "cost of sales," is the cost of merchandise that is shipped or sold. It *does not* include the expenses incurred in selling or shipping these goods, or storage, office, or general administrative expenses involved in company operations.

In professional and service businesses there are usually *no costs of sales*. These are companies that receive income from fees, rents, commissions, and royalties and do not have inventories of goods.

In businesses that *do* have inventories—such as retail, wholesale, and manufacturing businesses—there is a cost of sales. Physical inventories are major factors in determining the cost of goods sold and the IRS *requires* that they be taken at the beginning and end of each tax year. Inventory amounts include merchandise to be sold in the normal course of business plus raw materials and supplies that will physically become a part of that merchandise. Companies with inventories are *required* to use the *accrual* method of accounting by the IRS.

Cost of goods sold is established in one of several ways: (1) *directly*, (2) by using a *gross margin* approach, or (3) by a process of *deduction*.

If detailed inventory records are maintained, the cost of goods sold can be established directly as sales take place. A good example of this is the computer cash register system used by large retailers such as Sears. The sales clerk records the inventory number on the cash register as sales are added up. The computer keeps track of all inventory as it is sold. For large manufactured goods, the cost records maintained during production are used as a substitute for cost at the time of shipment. Both these examples illustrate the *direct* method of determining cost of sales.

A shortcut in establishing the cost of goods sold is to classify sales by product groups which have the same percentage mark-up (gross margin) and to multiply the sales in each group by the appropriate percentage. This is called the *gross margin* method of determining cost of sales. For example, if the sales of a product group having a known gross margin of 30% are $100,000 for the period, the cost of goods sold would be established as 70% of this, or $70,000.

Where it is not possible or practical to establish the cost of goods directly or by the gross margin method, it is necessary to determine the cost by *deduction*. An inventory record has four elements:

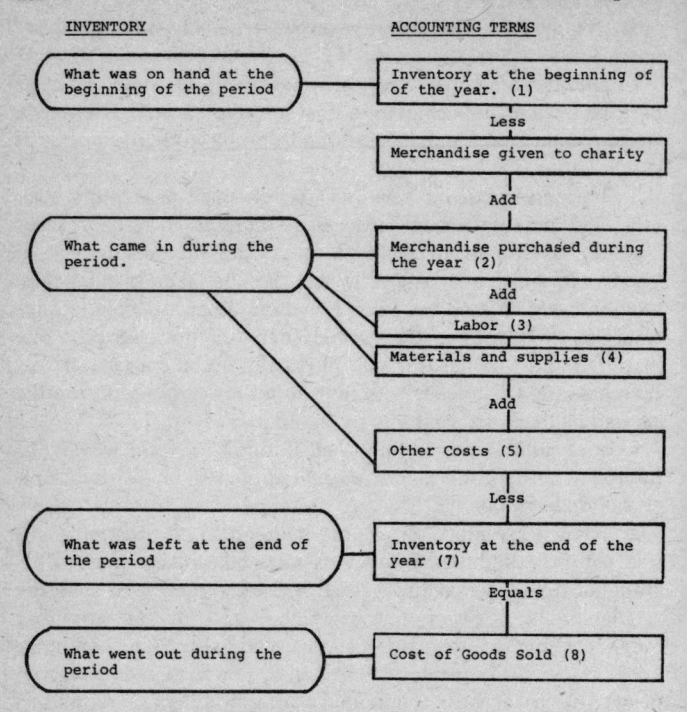

Figure 8.1. Inventory and accounting terms.

INVENTORY	ACCOUNTING TERMS
What was on hand at the beginning of the period	Inventory at the beginning of the year. (1)
	Less: Merchandise given to charity
What came in during the period.	Add: Merchandise purchased during the year (2)
	Add: Labor (3)
	Materials and supplies (4)
	Add: Other Costs (5)
What was left at the end of the period	Less: Inventory at the end of the year (7)
What went out during the period	Equals: Cost of Goods Sold (8)

- What was on hand at the beginning of the period
- What came in during the period
- What went out during the period
- What was left at the end of the period

If any three of these elements are known, it is possible to find the fourth element by deduction. When using this method to determine cost of goods sold, we want to find *what went out during the period*. All companies are required to take inventory at the end of each year, so they should know what their ending inven-

Expenses

tory is and, also, what their beginning inventory was (because it was taken at the end of last year). What came in during the year consists of the purchases of the company.

The following is an illustration of the deductive method of determining cost of goods sold (Figures 8.1 and 8.2).

Inventory at the beginning of the year	$61,400	
Less: Merchandise contributed to charitable organizations	400	$ 61,000
ADD:		
Merchandise (or raw materials) purchased during the year	80,000	
Labor	20,000	
Materials and supplies	4,000	
Other costs	6,000	110,000
Cost of goods available for sale		171,000
SUBTRACT:		
Inventory at the end of the year		35,000
RESULT:		
Cost of goods sold		$136,000

Figure 8.2. Cost of sales by deduction.

The following is an explanation of Figure 8.2.

Inventory at the beginning of the year (opening inventory) for a manufacturer includes the total value of the raw material, work-in-process (goods not finished), finished goods, and materials and supplies used in manufacturing the goods. For retailers and wholesalers it consists of merchandise held for sale. The *ending* inventory for one year is the beginning inventory for the *next* tax year.

Merchandise purchased during the year includes (for manufacturers) the cost of all raw materials or parts purchased for manufacturing finished products. For merchants it includes all the merchandise bought for sale. Merchandise must be reported net of (a) trade discounts, (b) purchase returns and allowances,

(c) merchandise withdrawn for stockholder or owner use, and sometimes (d) cash discounts.*

Labor costs are an element of cost of goods sold *only* in a manufacturing business. Labor includes both direct and indirect labor used in fabricating the raw material into a finished product. Direct labor costs are the wages paid to employees who spend all their time working directly on the product being manufactured. Indirect labor costs are the wages paid to employees who perform a general factory function that does not have any immediate or direct connection with the fabrication of the product, but are a necessary part of the manufacturing process. For example, in an electronic parts factory the indirect laborer would be a janitor in the factory or people in the boxing and shipping department.

Generally, the only kinds of labor costs properly chargeable to cost of goods sold are direct or indirect labor costs, and certain other labor treated as overhead expenses to the manufacturing process.

Materials and supplies, such as hardware and chemicals used in manufacturing goods, are charged to cost of goods sold. Supplies that are *not* consumed in the manufacturing process are *not* deductible as cost of sales.

Other costs are those incurred in connection with a manufacturing or mining process, such as containers and packages; freight-in, express-in and cartage-in; and certain overhead expenses.

If containers and packages are an *integral part* of the product manufactured, they are part of cost of goods sold. If they are *not* an integral part of the manufacturing product, their costs are charged to shipping or selling expenses. Overhead expenses might include rent, heat, light, power, insurance, depreciation, taxes, maintenance labor, and supervision. The overhead expenses in-

---

* Cash discounts can be accounted for in two ways. They can be credited to a separate discount account, or deducted from total purchases for the year. If cash discounts are credited to a separate account, the credit balance in this account at the end of the tax year must be included in the business's income. Whatever method chosen must be used consistently.

curred as direct and necessary expenses of the manufacturing operation are included in costs of goods sold.

Cost of goods available for sale is the total of the first five items representing the cost of goods available for sale during the year.

The *inventory at the end of the year* (closing inventory) should be subtracted from cost of goods available for sale.

Cost of goods sold is reached when the closing inventory is subtracted from the cost of goods available for sale. Gross profit is determined by subtracting cost of goods sold from adjusted total receipts or net sales for the tax year.

Inventory Identification

For the most part inventories determine cost of goods sold. Inventories include all finished or partly finished goods and raw materials and supplies that will physically become part of the business's merchandise intended for sale.

If you have legal title to merchandise you have purchased, you must include it in your inventory, regardless of whether or not the merchandise is physically in your possession. Inventory should also include goods under contract for sale to others and goods out on consignment.

If you sell merchandise by mail and intend that payment and delivery be concurrent (goods sent C.O.D.), the title passes when payment is made. Merchandise shipped C.O.D. is excluded from sales and included in your closing inventory until paid for by the buyer.

Assets such as land, buildings, and equipment used in the business; notes and accounts receivable; and the like, are not to be included in inventory. Real estate dealers are allowed to inventory real estate held for sale. Typically real estate is considered to be inventory in the hands of dealers in real estate. Freight-out, express-out, and cartage-out are shipping or selling expenses and are not part of the cost of goods sold.

Inventory Valuation

If prices of merchandise used in inventory fluctuate in amount, the business faces the problem of deciding how to value the dollar amount of its ending inventory. For example, Z-100 whatchits, an important element in manufacturing your solid-state components, cost ten cents at the beginning of the year and twelve cents at the end of the year. The question arises: Should your ending inventory of Z-100 whatchits be valued at twelve cents or ten cents? The answer depends on the type of inventory accounting you are employing: first-in, first-out (FIFO); last-in, first-out (LIFO); or standard costing.

Standard costs are costs expected under given conditions. In a manufacturing plant, standard costing can provide the *expected* cost of material, labor, and factory overhead on each type of product. One of the uses of such standard costs is to establish the cost of goods sold for a period. Cost of sales may be determined by multiplying the quantity of each type of product sold by its standard costs. Variances between the *actual* and *standard* material, labor, and factory overhead expenses are computed each period. These variances are treated as losses or gains for the period.

When standard costing is used to determine cost of goods sold, the variance (gain or loss) is usually shown as a separate item on the income statement.

Gross Profit (Gross Margin)

Once the cost of goods sold has been established, it is subtracted from net sales to arrive at a figure for the gross margin (gross profit). This figure is the amount of revenue left after paying for the purchase or manufacturing cost of goods sold. It represents the revenue available to cover selling and administrative expenses and to provide an operating profit for the period.

In any business which has no inventory, gross sales (less returns and allowances) *is equivalent to* gross profit. Most professions and businesses that provide personal services determine gross profit as gross sales.

Since gross profit is the money available to pay for all the selling and general and administrative expenses of a corporation or business, it becomes a very important item in finance. The gross profit percentage (gross profit divided by net sales) is also important in determining how a particular company is doing in relation to the industry or historical averages.

OPERATING AND SELLING EXPENSE

Operating expenses and selling expenses are listed in an income statement after the figure for gross margin. They are not included in inventory valuations. Both selling and operating expenses are sometimes listed simply under "operating expenses," "general and administrative expenses," or just "expenses."

Selling Expenses

Practice varies among companies with respect to the specific types of costs that are included under the title of "selling expenses." But in general, selling expenses consist of two major types: order getting (sales) and order handling (shipping). Order-getting expenses are those such as advertising, salesmen's salaries and commissions, and sales office costs. Order-handling costs are those such as order taking and filling expenses, warehousing, and shipping.

The majority of expenses included under the title of selling expenses do not necessarily bear any direct relationship to the sales figure. The shorter the period covered by the statement, the less likely there is any relationship between these figures. This is particularly true of order-getting expenses because realization of sales is more than the sum total of the efforts expended to achieve it, and sales figures only represent the goods shipped.

Operating Expense (General and Administrative Expense)

General and administrative (operating expense) are costs to be deducted from the gross margin (gross profit) to arrive at net profit. From a budgeting and control standpoint, operating expenses are managed costs and in the short run they will be fixed costs. They are regulated over time by management decisions

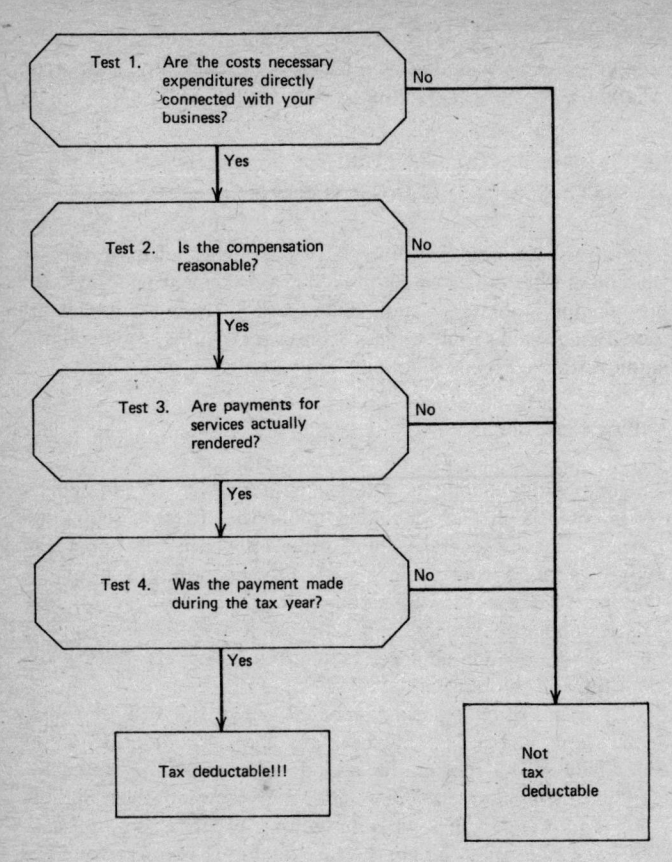

```
┌─────────────────────────────────┐
│ Test 1.  Are the costs necessary│  No
│          expenditures directly  │─────┐
│          connected with your    │     │
│          business?              │     │
└─────────────────────────────────┘     │
              │ Yes                     │
              ▼                         │
┌─────────────────────────────────┐     │
│ Test 2.  Is the compensation    │  No │
│          reasonable?            │─────┤
└─────────────────────────────────┘     │
              │ Yes                     │
              ▼                         │
┌─────────────────────────────────┐     │
│ Test 3.  Are payments for       │  No │
│          services actually      │─────┤
│          rendered?              │     │
└─────────────────────────────────┘     │
              │ Yes                     │
              ▼                         │
┌─────────────────────────────────┐     │
│ Test 4.  Was the payment made   │  No │
│          during the tax year?   │─────┤
└─────────────────────────────────┘     │
              │ Yes                     │
              ▼                         ▼
     ┌──────────────────┐      ┌──────────────┐
     │ Tax deductable!!!│      │ Not          │
     └──────────────────┘      │ tax          │
                               │ deductible   │
                               └──────────────┘
```

Figure 8.3. What is a tax deductible salary cost?

Operating and Selling Expense

and do not necessarily bear any direct relationship to production or sales volume.

Items Included in Operating and Selling Expense

There are certain expenses that are tax deductible and others that are not. So for the purposes of this chapter, we will group these items into: wages and salaries; rental expense; repairs, replacements, and improvements; travel and transportation; business entertainment; interest; insurance; taxes; and other business expense. Each of these groups will be discussed in turn.

Wages and Salaries. Salaries, wages, and other forms of compensation paid to employees are deductible business expenses for tax purposes if they meet the following four tests (see Figure 8.3):

Test 1: You must be able to show that salaries, wages, and other compensation are, according to the IRS, "ordinary and necessary expenditures directly connected with carrying on (your) business or trade." The fact that you pay your employees reasonable compensation for legitimate business purposes is not enough, by itself, to qualify the expense as deductible. Remunerations of services can be deducted only if the payment is an ordinary and necessary expense of carrying on your trade or business.

Test 2: The IRS states that reasonable compensation is determined by the amount that "ordinarily would be paid for like services, by like enterprises, under like circumstances." The following factors are considered in determining reasonableness of compensation:

- Duties performed by the employee
- Volume of business handled
- Character and amount of responsibility
- Complexities of the business
- Amount of time required

- General cost of living in the locality
- Ability and achievements of the individual performing the service
- Comparison of the compensation with the amount of gross and net income of the business

As a practical matter, however, most compensation deducted is never questioned. If the amount of compensation is questioned, the foregoing factors serve as a basis for determining reasonableness.

Test 3: You must be able to prove that the payments were made for services actually rendered. You must, also, reasonably expect your business to benefit from the service performed.

Test 4: You must have paid the compensation or incurred the expense during the tax year. Using the cash accounting method, only the salaries actually paid during the year are deductible. If you use the accrual method of accounting, the deduction for salaries and wages is allowable when the obligation to pay the compensation is established.

Bonuses you pay to employees are allowable deductions if they are intended as additional compensation, not gifts, and are paid for services actually rendered.

If, to promote employee goodwill, you distribute turkeys, hams, or other merchandise of nominal value at holiday times and on other special occasions, the value of these gifts is not considered salary or wages to your employees. You can deduct the cost of these gifts as a business expense, however, under the gift category. These gifts are limited to a $25 value per person. If, however, you distribute cash, gift certificates, or similar items of readily convertible cash value, the value of such gifts is considered additional wages or salary, regardless of amount.

Compensation need not be paid in cash. It may be in the form of meals, lodging, capital assets, or shares of stock in the business.

If you give stock in your company to your employees as compensation, you are entitled to deduct the fair market value of that stock as of the date given. If you transfer a capital asset or an asset used in your business to one of your employees in payment for services, its fair market value on the date of the transfer is deductible. Both of these forms of compensation are taxable income of the employee.

The cost of meals and lodging furnished to the employees as part of their compensation is deductible by the employer. In some cases meals and lodging are not taxable to the employee as income. To enable the employees to exclude from their gross income the value of meals and lodging furnished them without charge by the employer, the following tests must be met: (1) The meals or lodging must be furnished on the employer's business premises; (2) the meals or lodging must be furnished for the employer's convenience; and (3) in the case of lodging (but not meals), employees must be required to accept it as a condition of employment. This means that acceptance of the lodging is required to enable them to properly perform the duties of their employment (if, for example, they must be available for duty at all times).

Fringe benefits such as premiums on insurance, hospitalization, and medical care for employees are deductible by the employer. This does not include life insurance premiums except under special circumstances (there is a $25,000 term insurance limit).

Contributions made for deferred compensation—such as supplemental unemployment benefits, pension plans, annuity plans, profit-sharing plans, bond-purchase plans, and stock bonus plans—are deductible if made by the employer, up to certain limits.

Rental. You may ordinarily deduct, as current expenses, rent paid or accrued for property used in your trade or business. If you allocate rental expenses to the cost of goods sold, however, you cannot include such costs again as operating expenses.

Rent paid in property is deductible as rent to the extent of the fair market value of that property or service.

Rent paid in advance, sums paid to acquire a lease, and commissions, bonuses, fees, or other expenses you pay to obtain possession of property under a lease must be deducted over the term of the lease or the period covered by the advance.

Repairs, Replacements, and Improvements. Any expenditure for property or equipment may be deducted as an expense or not, depending on whether it only maintains the property or actually adds to the value and life of the property.

Repairs, including labor, supplies, and certain other items, are deductible expenses. This is because repairs generally just maintain property. The value of your own labor expended in this repair, however, is not deductible as an expense. Examples of repairs include patching and repairing floors, repainting the inside and outside of a building, repairing roofs and gutters, and mending leaks.

Replacements that arrest deterioration and appreciably prolong the life of the property are *not* deductible as expense. They should be capitalized and depreciated. Expenditures for replacement parts of a machine to maintain it in operable condition *are* deductible business expenses. Major overhauls of machinery also require capitalization and depreciation.

Travel and Transportation. Travel expenses are the expenses incurred traveling away from home overnight in pursuit of your trade or business. Transportation expenses, on the other hand, include only the costs of travel (not meals and lodging) directly attributable to the actual conduct of your business while you are *not* away from home overnight.

Travel expenses include:

- Meals and lodging (both en route and at your destination)
- Air, rail, and bus fares
- Baggage charges
- The cost of transporting sample cases or display materials
- The cost of maintaining and operating your automobile
- The cost of operating and maintaining your house trailer
- Reasonable cleaning and laundry expenses
- Telephone and telegraph expenses
- The cost of a public stenographer
- The cost of transportation from the airport or station to your

hotel, from your hotel to the airport or station, from one customer or place of work to another
- Reasonable transportation costs from where you obtain meals and lodging to where you are working while away from home overnight
- Other similar expenses incidental to qualifying travel
- Reasonable tips incidental to any of the expenses

You can deduct travel expenses you incur for yourself—but not for your family—in attending a convention. Incidental personal expenses incurred for your entertainment, sightseeing, social visiting, and so on are not deductible.

Transportation expenses (sometimes referred to as local travel expenses) include such items as air, train, bus, and cab fares, and the expenses of operating and maintaining your business vehicle. Commuting expenses between your residence and usual place of business are not deductible regardless of the distance involved.

If you use your automobile entirely for business purposes, you can deduct all of your actual expenses for its operation, including depreciation. However, if your automobile is used only partly for business, you must apportion its expense and a reasonable allowance for depreciation between business and personal usage.

If you lease a car that you use in your business, you can deduct your lease payments to the extent that they are directly attributable to your business. You cannot deduct any portion of the lease payments for commuting or other personal use of the car.

Instead of using actual expenses and depreciation to determine deductible costs of operating an automobile (including pick-up or panel truck) for business purposes, you can use a standard mileage rate of 17 cents a mile for the first 15,000 miles of business usage per year, and 10 cents a mile for each additional business mile in that year. To use the standard mileage rate, you must:

- Own your car
- Not use more than one car simultaneously in your business or profession

- Not use the car for hire, such as taxi
- Not operate a fleet of cars of which two or more are used simultaneously
- Not claim depreciation using any method other than the straight-line method
- Not claim additional first-year depreciation on the car

If the car is fully depreciated you can only deduct 10 cents a mile for all miles of business usage. Parking fees and tolls incurred during business use are deductible in addition to the standard mileage rate.

Business Entertainment. This includes any activity generally considered entertainment, amusement, or recreation. It usually covers entertaining guests at restaurants, theaters, sporting events, and on yachts, on hunting or fishing vacations, or similar trips. It may also include satisfying the person or family needs of any individuals, the cost of which would otherwise be a business expense to you, such as furnishing food and beverages, or providing a hotel suite or automobile to business customers or their families.

Costs are considered business deductible entertainment expenses only if they are ordinary and necessary expenses directly related to or associated with the active conduct of your trade or business.

Interest. Interest is defined as, according to the IRS publications, "the compensation allowed by law or fixed by the parties for the use (or forebearance) of money." A business can deduct all interest paid or accrued in the tax year on a business debt. This debt is generally referred to as a liability.

The liability must be *your* liability or you cannot deduct the interest paid. An individual, for instance, cannot deduct interest paid on the debt of a corporation. In the special case when you purchase property and pay interest owed by the seller, you *cannot* deduct the interest but must capitalize it (make it part of the cost of the property).

Operating and Selling Expense

Insurance. If you carry business insurance to protect your company against losses by fire or other hazards, the premiums paid are deductible as business expenses. The following are sample deductible expenses:

- Premiums on fire, theft, flood or other casualty insurance
- Merchandise and inventory insurance
- Credit insurance
- Employee's group hospitalization and medical insurance
- Premiums on employer's liability insurance
- Malpractice insurance
- Public liability insurance
- Workman's compensation insurance
- Overhead insurance
- Use and occupancy insurance and business interruption
- Employee performance bonds
- Expenses for bonds the business is required to furnish either by law or by contract
- Automobile and other vehicle insurance (unless you use the standard mileage rate to compute auto expense).

Taxes. Various taxes, imposed by federal, state, local, and foreign governments, incurred in the ordinary course of business or trade are deductible.

Taxes that are deductible as business expenses are broken down into broad categories:

- Real property taxes
- Income tax
- Other taxes
- Employment taxes (payroll, social security, etc.)

Next to income tax, the greatest tax paid by business people is *real property tax*. Ordinarily, a business can deduct all taxes imposed on real property that the business owns. Sometimes the business can elect to capitalize expenditures for taxes as a cost of the property. Those taxes that are *not* deductible include federal income, estate, and gift taxes; state inheritance, legacy, and succession taxes; and assessments for local benefits.

"Well, that's it." Gin finished reading and closed the book. "I don't know if I understood it all. Could you go over it?"

"Okay," John began. He was used to the names of expenses and the other jargon. "Sales, or revenue, is not sales until the goods are shipped. In other words, if someone orders a Your-company computer system, that's not sales. When they pay us cash, that's not sales. It is considered sales when the system is shipped.

"The cost of goods sold is the cost of manufacturing my systems. It includes the cost of the components, the assembly labor —both assemblers and janitors—the incoming freight costs, and some overhead costs. The formula for determining the amount of inventory that went out during the year is what you have at the beginning of the year plus what you purchased and what your labor and other costs were, minus what you have on hand at the end of the year.

"The gross profit which is also called the gross margin is sales minus the cost of goods.

"Operating expenses include salaries, selling expenses, shipping expenses, rent, repairs, travel, entertainment, depreciation, taxes, insurance, and interest."

"How about advertising and office supplies?" Gin asked.

"Yeah, now you're gettin' it." John answered.

"Tell me more about the wages. That seems complicated," Gin said.

"Well, let's see if I can remember. . . . It has to be payment for some business service—that's obvious. It has to be reasonable. It seems like 'reasonableness' could be a real loophole. It has to be paid during the year. Gifts are not part of salaries. Each person—employee—can only get $25 in gifts from me per year. Martha took over $50,000. I hope I'm not breaking the law. Maybe there's an exception for bookkeepers." Gin laughed at John's joke.

"What about travel expenses?" Gin asked. "When you go to a

convention, can you pay for me and the kids and deduct that?"

"No. I can only deduct expenses for myself or some client and/or employee. Now, if you were an employee I might be able to deduct you; I don't know. I'll ask Pete. Travel includes transportation, hotel, exhibit cost, cleaning and laundry, secretarial.

"Local transportation expenses are my car at 18½ cents a mile up to 15,000 miles. But I can only do that if I use only one car for business. . . . Hey, that's enough. Let's go to bed."

"You want me to come to work with you tomorrow and help you with the books?" Gin asked.

"Ahhh . . . yeah, okay, after you take the kids to school."

John now had reliable help. But he didn't know if it was such a good idea to have Gin involved in the business finances. Well, he'd worry about that tomorrow. Tonight he was going to get some sleep.

Chapter Nine
The Second Transformation— the Work Papers and Closing the Books

John Your, together with his wife Gin, worked through the weekend and had the books finished by the next Monday—one week to the day after John discovered the loss.

John and Gin thought that the loss for the previous year was $81,316. Since this was 3 months into the current year, it was possible that even more losses would be recorded.

John had called to ask his CPA Pete Popstein to come to the shop on Monday and show him how to close the books for the year.

Pete Popstein arrived early Monday morning, and Gin was there along with John to receive instruction.

"Before you tell how to close the books, I'd like to ask you a question," Gin asked Pete.

"Okay," Pete responded.

"If I was an employee of the company, could the company write off my expenses if I traveled to a convention?" Gin asked.

"With John? . . . Well, legally the company can pay the expenses of an employee at a convention. But you would have to be an employee for more than just the time you spent at the convention."

"Well. I'm gonna help John with the books. Work part-time all year," Gin responded.

"I guess it would be deductible. But you have to be real careful with being married to the company president and all."

"You mean, it's all right?" Gin smiled. John didn't quite know what to think. "Okay, now go ahead with the closing of the books instruction."

Pete began. . . .

An accounting period can be a maximum of 1 year and usually not less than 1 month. Large corporations traded in the public market usually end their accounting period every 3 months and then obtain final totals at the end of a year. Smaller businesses and closely-held corporations like Yourcompany usually end their accounting period at the end of a year.

At the end of a period, all of the accounts that a business has (assets, liabilities, equity, income, expenses, and costs of sales) have to be totaled and summarized. This is the second transformation. The first transformation was posting from original documents to ledgers and journals.

The summarizing process performed on a bussiness's books is called "closing the books." You transfer all the totals of all the accounts for one year to a summary sheet.

THE ASSUMPTIONS OF ACCOUNTING FOR BUSINESS

To understand the process of "closing the books" you must understand the primary assumptions of accounting. These asumptions are:

1. Businesses are ongoing entities with unlimited life.
2. Although businesses have unlimited lifetimes, they require an "accounting" of their actions at least once a year.
3. There is a part of a business's acounts that lives forever and another part that "dies" each time an accounting is made. That is, it will have "permanent" and "cyclical accounts."

First, let's discuss the proposition that a business's life is unlimited. In the early days af accounting there was usually no reason for closing the books. The accountant simply kept track of the transactions as they happened. Few people were interested in what the cummulative total was until the business was dissolved.

Every business is expected to continue until the owner sells or retires, and it is in this spirit that the accounting period records are kept.

A business may in fact exist on a monent-to-moment basis with an unpredictable future. But this line of thinking is not in accord with a logical system. And accounting is *above all* a logical system.

For instance, to prepare a depreciation schedule for the business and for tax purposes, an accountant must assume that the business will last long enough for the business equipment (cash-register or forklift) to lose its value. The equipment will be part of the business long enough for the equipment to become completely "depreciated."

The second assumption, that businesses with an unlimited lifetime require periodic "accountings," is fairly recent. In the early days, there was really no reason to summarize the accounts at the end of a period because transactions were relatively few and simple. As the number of accounts grew, the importance of periodically summarizing the transactions became important for two reasons: (1) Summarizing provides "milestones" to compare how the business did in the past, with how it is doing now. The periodic accountings (closing of the books) of a business are the measure of the business's past performance against their present performance. (2) In most countries (such as the United States), a periodic accounting is required by law.

Governments that tax businesses require every business to prepare a summary of their performance (sales, expenses, profit, etc.). The businesses are then taxed on the basis of these "summaries." The summaries that the United States government requires of a business are called "income statements" (profit and loss) and, in some cases, a "statement of financial condition" (balance sheet). If the company is publicly traded it must provide annual reports and financial statements quarterly.

These summaries that business provides to the government are for a period no longer than one year by law.*

The third assumption, that some business accounts have only limited (cyclical) lives and others are permanent, is a result of the periodic accounting assumption. Some account information is only needed for one period.

For the given period summary, the old information from the previous period is not needed. For example, sales for last year are not needed to calculate this year's sales. Expenses and cost of sales that you incurred last year should not be added to this year's expense and cost of sales. Sales, expenses, and cost of sales records need only exist for the single period that they are used to calculate profit or loss. These are "cyclical" accounts.

Some accounts continue as the business does. These accounts are never closed, but are summarized and brought forward each year. These "permanent accounts" are assets, liabilities, and equity. Obviously, if you owe someone money at the end of one period (a liability) that obligation will continue into the next period. If someone owes you money (accounts receivable—an asset), this obligation will also continue into the next year. Your company's equipment, buildings, cash, inventory, and other assets also have a permanent nature. They are not lost at the end of the period, but retain their value from one period to the next.

THE TRIAL BALANCE AND THE ACCOUNTING WORKSHEET

Format of the Trial Balance

Figure 9.1 shows the format of a trial balance sheet and company worksheet. Notice that the illustration has one column for the account number (usually taken in numerical order) and another column for the name of the account. The third and fourth

---

* There are some exceptions to this one-year rule in the tax codes. One exception would be when a company can show that its business cycle requires a longer period (up to 13 months).

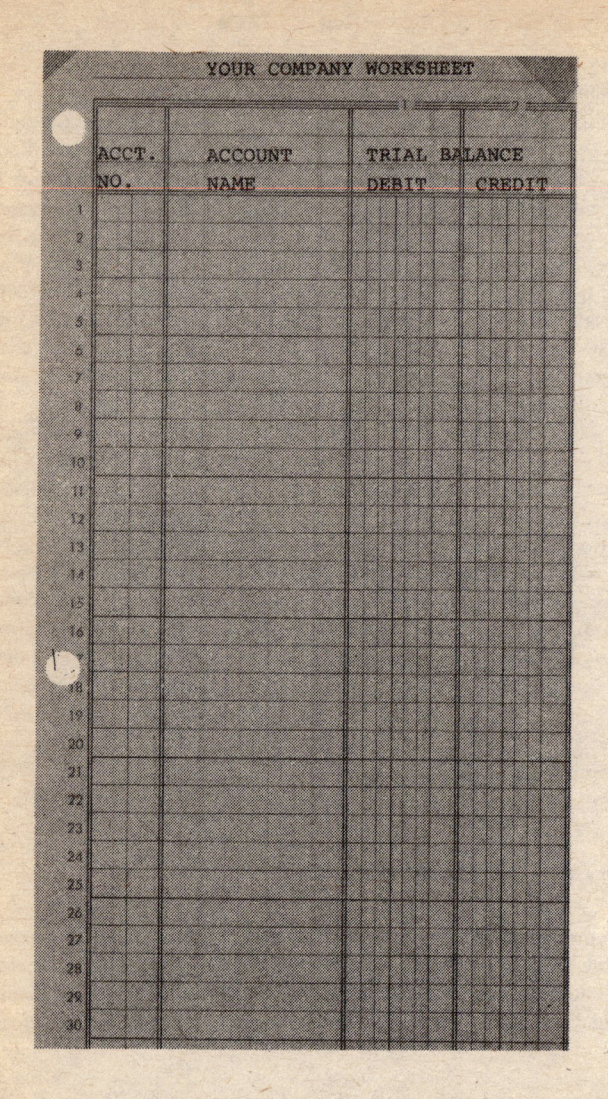

Figure 9.1. Yourcompany worksheet.

The Trial Balance and the Accounting Worksheet

columns are for recording the totals from each account in the general ledger.

Making Entries—Yourcompany Examples

The trial balance is made to test if the accounts properly balance. The total debits should equal the total credits. The equality of debits and credits is determined by (1) the total balance in each account in the general ledger, and (2) adding debit and credit balances separately to see if the totals are equal.

The balance of an account is computed by first adding the figures on each side, and then subtracting the smaller total from the larger total to obtain the difference.

Using the cash account (account number 101) of Yourcompany (Figure 9.2), first the debit side is added, then the credit side. The total of each column is usually entered in pencil at the bottom of the column. These totals are called *footings*.

Adding up the debit column you see that the total cash taken in by Yourcompany adds up to $30,429. The total cash spent by the company (total cash credits) adds up to $41,520. The company spent more than it took in. Subtracting the smaller total (cash you took in—the debit total) from the larger total (cash spent—the credit total), you get $11,091. Since the credit total is larger than the debit total by $11,091, the cash account is said to have a credit balance of $11,091.

"I don't understand," John said. "If we had a negative balance in January like you said, I would have been bouncing checks. I would have been $11,091 overdrawn."

"Well, not necessarily," Pete commented. "These books start at the first of the year. You probably had cash in the bank at the beginning of the year that isn't taken into consideration here because we have no book record of it. When we finish this closing of the books, we'll find out what your balances were in all the permanent asset, liability, and equity accounts. We'll do that by looking at your income tax returns, and the records of your bank balances. Right now we are more interested in what happened during last year."

"Okay," John said, "I understand. Go ahead and continue."

214 The Second Transformation—the Work Papers and Closing the Books

\multicolumn{4}{l	}{CASH}	\multicolumn{4}{r	}{ACCOUNT NO. 101}
							SHEET NO. 1
DATE	ITEMS	folio ✓	DEBITS	DATE	ITEMS	folio ✓	CREDITS
1980				1980			
1/2	BANK LOAN	GJI-1	25000 —	1/3	TEST EQUIP	GJI-2	5000 —
1/12	TOTAL 1/1–1/12	CRJ-1	5429 —	1/4	INVENTORY-PARTS	GJI-3	15000 —
				1/5	ACCTS. PAYABLE	GJI-4	13500 —
				1/5	RENT EXPENSE	GJI-5	1200 —
				1/7	TOTAL 1/1–1/7	CDJ-1	6820 —
			30429				41520
					BALANCE $11,091		

Figure 9.2

"When we total the account columns, we write the amount of the totals and the balance ($11,091 in this case) in pencil. Since the balance is a credit balance, we write 'Balance $11,091' on the credit side.

"No footings are required if the account has only one entry on either or both sides of the ledger.

"After the balance in each account has been established, they are listed in numerical order on the trial balance. The totals from the accounts are placed in the proper column: debit balances are shown in the left column and credit balances are shown in the right column.

"Since we don't have time today to go through all the accounts for every month, we'll just use the January Yourcompany accounts that I went over with you last week and fill out the trial balance with them" (Figure 9.3).

Notice that the 100 (with the exception of cash), 500, and 600 accounts (assets, expenses, and cost of sales) are all entered in

The Trial Balance and the Accounting Worksheet

Acct.	Account Name	Trial Balance	
		Debit	Credit
101	CASH		11091
111	ACCOUNTS RECEIVABLE	1980	
120	DEPOSITS	130	
130	PARTS INVENTORY	30000	
150.1	TEST EQUIPMENT	10000	
201	ACCOUNTS PAYABLE		3720
211.1	NOTES PAYABLE - BANK AMERIGOLD		25000
211.2	NOTES PAYABLE - ZARKOFF EQUIPMENT		5000
410	SYSTEM INCOME		3280
420	COMPONENT SALES		3429
430	RENTAL		700
508	RENTAL EXPENSE	1200	
510	TELEPHONE EXPENSE	300	
560	OFFICE SUPPLIES	150	
591	BUSINESS LICENSE	40	
601	INVENTORY PURCHASE	7220	
610	SUB-CONTRACT	1200	
	TOTALS	52220	52220

Figure 9.3

the debit column because they all have debit balances. The 200, 300, and 400 accounts (liabilities, equity, and sales) are all entered in the credit columns because they all have credit balances.

The total of the debit column is $52,220. The total of the credit column is also $52,220 and thus both columns balance. This shows that the original journal entries were made correctly.

If the debit and credit columns do not equal each other, an error has been made.

Common Errors

1. Errors in addition
2. Recording only half an entry (the credit without the debit, or vice versa)

3. Recording both halves of the entry on the same side (two debit or two credit entries rather than one debit and one credit)
4. Recording one or more accounts incorrectly
5. Arithmetic errors in the journal entry
6. Arithmetic errors in balancing the accounts
7. Errors made by putting an entry in the wrong account

One technique used by long-time bookkeepers to find out where the errors have occurred is to divide the difference between the debit side and the credit side by 9. If the amount of the difference is evenly divisible by 9, the discrepancy may either be a transposition ($432 for $423) or a slide ($423 for $42.30). Dividing the difference by 2 may suggest that a credit was posted as a debit or vice versa.

TRIAL INCOME STATEMENT AND BALANCE SHEET

After you have posted the trial balance and it is accurate, you can change the trial balance summary into the more usable form of an income statement and a balance sheet.

The Income Statement and Balance Sheet Workpaper Format

The trial balance extended for four more columns becomes the total workpaper. Notice (Figure 9.4) that a debit and credit column is added for the income statement and a debit and credit column is added for the balance sheet.

The columns marked "income statement" and "balance sheet" are used to organize the figures needed for these financial reports. Each of these headings has two columns, one for debits and one for credits.

Accounts 100, 200, and 300 (the asset, liability, and equity accounts) are carried over to the balance sheet columns. Accounts 400, 500, and 600 (the income, expense, and cost of sales accounts) are carried over to the income statement columns. Ac-

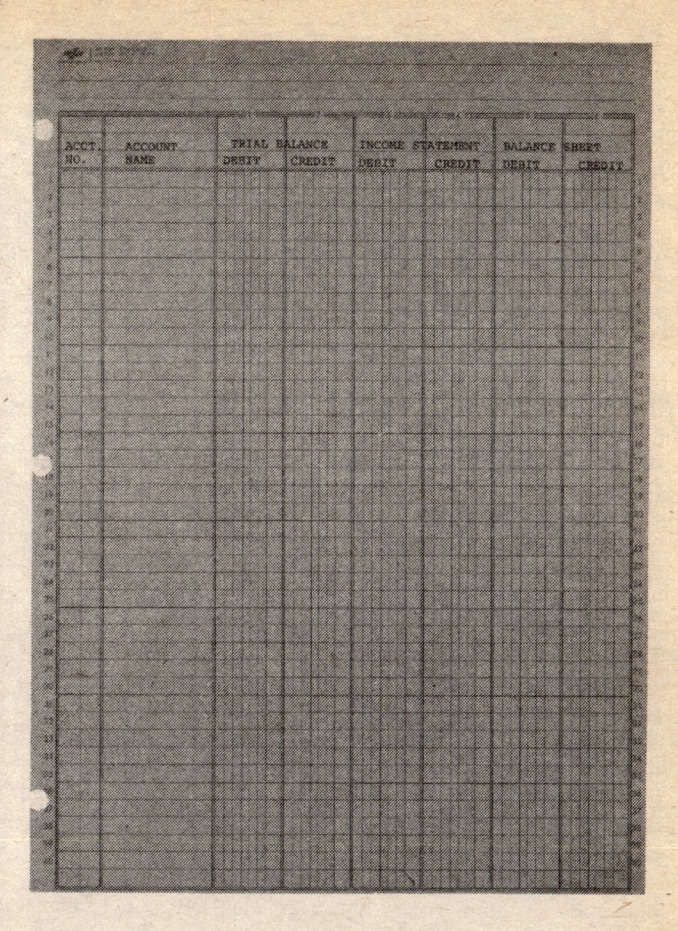

Figure 9.4. Sample worksheet.

counts that had *debit* amounts in the trial balance will continue to be recorded as *debits* when transferred to the income statement or balance sheet columns. Accounts that are listed as *credits* in the trial balance will continue to be listed as *credits* in either the balance sheet or the income statement columns.

Yourcompany Balance Sheet and Income Statement Example

Figure 9.5 shows the trial balance from Figure 9.3 expanded into the balance sheet and income statement columns.

Income Statement. The three income accounts—system sales (410), component sales (420), and rental income (430)—are moved to the credit side of the income statement. All the expense accounts are moved to the debit side of the income statement. This includes rental expense, rental commission, telephone expense, office supplies, and business licenses. All of the cost of sales accounts—inventory purchases (601) and subcontract work (610)—are moved to the debit side of the income statement.

As the next step, both columns (debit and credit) are totaled. You will notice from the example that the income statement totals do not balance. The total of the credit column (which is only the total of sales) is $7,409; $2,701 less than the debit total. The debit side total of the income statement is $10,110. This means that the expense and cost of sales exceeded the sales. That is, the company has a net operating loss. Since expense and cost of sales (the debit side) exceed sales (the credit side) the company has a net loss for the difference (a $2,701 loss).

This is somewhat misleading because (1) Yourcompany may have some of the inventory they purchased left over, (2) total expense does not include depreciation, and (3) no allowance was made for bad debt. These are "adjustments" that will be discussed later.

Balance Sheet. All assets from the trial balance are transferred from the trial balance debit column to the balance sheet debit column. These include cash (101), accounts receivable (111), deposits (120), parts inventory (130), and test equipment

YOURCOMPANY WORKSHEET 307

Acct. No.	Account Name	Trial Balance Debit	Trial Balance Credit	Income Statement Debit	Income Statement Credit	Balance Sheet Debit	Balance Sheet Credit
101	CASH		11091			⟨11091⟩	
111	ACCTS. REC.	1980				1980	
120	DEPOSITS	130				130	
130	PARTS INVENT.	30000				30000	
150.1	TEST EQUIP.	10000				10000	
201	ACCTS. PAY.		3720				3720
211.1	NOTES PAY.- B.A.		25000				25000
211.2	NOTES PAY.- Z.E.		5000				5000
410	SYSTEM INCOME		3280		3280		
420	COMPONENT SALES		3429		3429		
430	RENTAL INCOME		700		700		
508	RENTAL EXPENSE	1200		1200			
510	TELEPHONE	300		300			
560	OFFICE SUPP.	150		150			
591	BUS. LICENSE	40		40			
601	INVENT. PURCH.	7220		7220			
610	SUB-CONTRACT	1200		1200			
	TOTALS	52220	52220	10110	7409	31019	33720
	NET LOSS				2701		⟨2701⟩
				10110	10110	31019	31019

Figure 9.5

(150.1). All liabilities and equity accounts are transferred from the credit column of the trial balance to the credit column of the balance sheet. The liabilities that are transferred are accounts payable (201), notes payable—Bank of Amerigold (211.1), and notes payable—Zarkoff Equipment (211.2).

It is important to note that the cash balance of minus $11,091 (credit) is placed in the debit column as a negative entry. The reason is that it indicates the assets total more accurately than if the cash balance were put as a credit.

If you add up the debit column and the credit column of the balance sheet workpaper, you see that the liability and equity column (credit) exceeds the asset (debit) column. This is because there is a net loss of $2,701 which will be deducted from the company equity to make the balance sheet in balance. If the company had a profit, the two columns would also have different totals, but the asset column would be a larger number. Equity would have to be increased by the amount of the net profit to bring the totals into balance.

The balance sheet debit (asset) total is $31,019 and the credit column (liabilities and equity) total is $33,720. Subtract the amount of the net loss carried from the income statement ($2,701) from the credit side, and the totals come into balance at $31,019 each.

Again, this is not totally accurate. The ending inventory might be higher or lower than the beginning inventory (the $30,000 that Yourcompany started with), and equipment should be depreciated.

ADJUSTMENTS TO ACCOUNTS

Before you add up the accounts and summarize them, some expenses have to be calculated that only occur at the end of an accounting period. Depreciation and bad debt expense must be calculated. Furthermore, in all businesses that do not have a "perpetual" inventory system, a physical count of inventory must be made.

At the end of the period, the following is usually true:

1. Equipment and fixtures are carried in their accounts at their original cost, without regard for the usual wear and tear during the period or for what their salvage value will be if they are sold after a number of years.
2. The amount in the accounts receivable account might include some money that will not be collected in the future.
3. There is no recognition of merchandise held in inventory that has not been sold by the end of the period.

If Yourcompany's test equipment will last 5 years, it will also have a value at the end of that 5 years. This is the value that the equipment will bring if it is sold—called the "salvage value."

Depreciation

Note the adjustments format (Figure 9.6). Two adjustments columns are added to the trial balance format. The general ledger of Yourcompany shows that the company has $10,000 worth of test equipment (account 150.1).

In reality, of course, this test equipment experiences wear and tear. Both accounting logic and the tax authorities allow this wear and tear to be taken into consideration and listed as an expense. This expense is called "depreciation." Depreciation is unusual in that it is not a cash expense. It is an allowance for the decline in value of the equipment.

Because most equipment does not lose all of its value in one period, the loss in value is apportioned over a longer period—the useful life of the asset. The useful life of an asset (equipment) is a period of years after which the asset will be useless to the company and therefore, sold. The IRS has certain guidelines for different types of equipment and other assets in its *Publication 534*.

Bad Debt Expense

In any business there is always the probability that some accounts receivable will *not* be collected.

There are two methods for determining bad debt loss. One

	ACCT. NO.	ACCOUNT NAME	TRIAL BALANCE		ADJUSTMENTS	
			DEBIT	CREDIT	DEBIT	CREDIT
1						
2						
3						
4						
5						
6						
7						
8						
9						
10						
11						
12						
13						
14						
15						
16						
17						
18						
19						
20						
21						
22						
23						
24						
25						
26						
27						
28						
29						
30						
31						
32						

Figure 9.6. Sample adjusted and trial balance.

method is to wait until the company is sure that the account of a specific customer is uncollectible before the expense is recorded. An entry is made debiting a bad debt expense account and crediting the asset account, accounts receivable.

Another way to allow for bad debt expense is to anticipate bad debt losses and provide for them ahead of time. This is called setting up an allowance for bad debt.

	ACCT. NO.	ACCOUNT NAME	TRIAL BALANCE		ADJUSTMENTS	
			DEBIT	CREDIT	DEBIT	CREDIT
1	101	Cash		11091 —		
2	111	Accounts Receivable	1980			
3	111A	Allowance for Bad Debt				(B) 6165
4	120	Deposits	130			
5	130	Parts Inventory	30000			
6	150.1	Test Equipment	10000			
7	150.1A	Allowance for Depreciation				(A) 15833
8						
9	201	Accounts Payable		3720 —		
10	211.1	Notes Payable - BA		25000 —		
11	211.2	" " - Z. Equip		5000 —		
12						
13	410	System Income		3280 —		
14	420	Component Sales		3429 —		
15	430	Rental Income		700 —		
16						
17	508	Rental Expense	1200 —			
18	510	Telephone	300 —			
19	560	Office Supplies	150 —			
20	591	Business License	40 —			
21	595	Depreciation			(A) 15833	
22	599	Bad Debt			(B) 6165	
23						
24	611	Inventory	7220 —			
25	610	Sub-Contract	1200 —			
26						
27		Totals	52220	52220	21998	21998

Figure 9.7. Yourcompany worksheet.

224 The Second Transformation—the Work Papers and Closing the Books

Bad debt losses are estimated as a percentage of total credit sales. In some industries bad debt loss might be 10%; in others it might run 1% of credit sales.

Using the industry experience or your past experience you can set up a bad debt account.

Yourcompany's industry generally experiences 3% loss on credit sales, so we'll use that figure:

Credit sales for the month	$2,055
Less: Sales returns and allowances	-0-
Net credit sales	$2,055
Times: Estimated percentage bad debt loss	× .03
Estimated bad debts on January sales	$61.65

Yourcompany's expected bad debt loss for January sales is $61.65, 3% of total credit sales ($2,055).

In Figure 9.7 bad debt allowance and expense is added to the adjustments column. The amount of bad debt for that month is debited to bad debt expense (599) and credited to allowance for bad debts (111A). The allowance for bad debt (111A) is a reduction in accounts receivable expected.

Note that the two entries are marked with a "(B)" for later identification.

At this point, all the adjustments for the adjustments column next to the trial balance columns have been made. We can now total the columns. Next we add three more sets of columns: the adjusted trial balance, income statement, and balance sheet (see Figure 9.8). The adjusted trial balance columns can now be filled in by adding the debit and credit columns of the trial balance with the adjustments. All the entries of the trial balance are now combined with the entries from adjustments (see Figure 9.9).

There is still one more adjustment to be made to the working papers, but this will be made when the worksheet is extended to an income statement and balance sheet. The adjustment that will have to be made is in the inventory asset and the cost of sales figure.

Adjustments to Accounts

Inventory and Cost of Sales Adjustments

Before finishing the worksheet, you must recognize that some of the purchased merchandise has not yet been sold and is still on hand. For this reason the following steps must be taken: (1) the value of the merchandise that is unsold at the end of the period must be recorded as an addition to the asset inventory; (2) the cost of the merchandise sold *only* should be recorded as part of the cost of sales.

Before any recording can be done, you must first determine how much inventory you have on hand at the end of the period. That is, you must take inventory. This almost always requires a physical count of the inventory. The result of this count is recorded on an "inventory sheet" that shows the type of item (description), the amount of that item (quantity), the unit cost, and the total. Luckily, Yourcompany took a physical inventory last January. Figure 9.10 shows the result of that physical inventory that was taken at the end of January 1980.

Before we can go any further, we have to look at what Yourcompany's ending inventory was at the end of the year before last (1979). In order to get an accurate picture of what the inventory was at the end of January 1980, you need to know what it was at the beginning of January 1980. This information is on Yourcompany's income tax for 1979. The income tax shows closing inventory of $5000.

The amount of inventory used during January is calculated as follows:

Total Merchandise Purchases (601)		$ 7,220
Plus:	Subcontract work (610)	1,200
Plus:	Parts inventory purchased (130)	30,000
Plus:	Beginning inventory	5,000
Less:	Ending inventory	39,620
Cost of Goods Sold		$ 3,800

	ACCT. NO.	ACCOUNT NAME	TRIAL BALANCE		ADJUSTMENTS	
			DEBIT	CREDIT	DEBIT	CREDIT
1						
2						
3						
4						
5						
6						
7						
8						
9						
10						
11						
12						
13						
14						
15						
16						
17						
18						
19						
20						
21						
22						
23						
24						
25						
26						
27						
28						
29						
30						
31						
32						
33						
34						

Figure 9.8

Sample worksheet.

Your Company Worksheet
Month Ending January 1980

	ACCT. NO.	ACCOUNT NAME	TRIAL BALANCE DEBIT	TRIAL BALANCE CREDIT	ADJUSTMENTS DEBIT	ADJUSTMENTS CREDIT
1	101	Cash		11091		
2	111	Accounts Receivable	1980			
3	111A	Allowance for Bad Debt				(B) 6
4	120	Deposits	130			
5	130	Parts Inventory	30000			
6	150.1	Test Equipment	10000			
7	150.1A	Allowance for Depreciation				(A) 158
8						
9	201	Accounts Payable		3720		
10	211.1	Notes Payable - B.A.		25000		
11	211.2	" " - Z.Equip.		5000		
12						
13	410	System Income		3280		
14	420	Component Sales		3429		
15	430	Rental Income		700		
16						
17	508	Rental Expense	1200			
18	510	Telephone	300			
19	560	Office Supplies	150			
20	591	Business License	40			
21	595	Depreciation			(A) 158 33	
22	599	Bad Debt			(B) 61 65	
23						
24	601	Inventory	7220			
25	610	Sub-Contract	1200			
26						
27		Totals	52220	52220	21998	21

Figure 9.9

ADJUSTED TRIAL BALANCE		INCOME STATEMENT		BALANCE SHEET		
DEBIT	CREDIT	DEBIT	CREDIT	DEBIT	CREDIT	
	11091					1
1980						2
	6165					3
130						4
30000			(C) 39620	(C) 39620		5
10000						6
	15833					7
						8
	3720					9
	25000					10
	5000					11
						12
	3280					13
	3429					14
	700					15
						16
1200						17
300						18
150						19
40						20
15833						21
6165						22
						23
						24
						25
						26
5243998	5243998					27

Recording Inventory Adjustments on the Worksheet

The adjustments to inventory are recorded directly on the income statement and balance sheet areas of the worksheet (see Figure 9.9). The value of the closing inventory ($39,620) in the example is recorded on the inventory line in the *debit* column of the balance sheet. The entry is marked "C" for identification.

The other part of the entry is a little more difficult to see. It will be a *credit* entry of $39,620 (the amount of the ending inventory) to the income statement. Also the beginning inventory of $35,000 (the $30,000 purchase plus beginning inventory of $5000) is entered, but as a debit of the income statement. These entries will have the effect of reducing the cost of sales by the amount of inventory that was not sold. There is already an entry for the amount of inventory purchased (inventory purchases—601) of $7200. The credit entry of $39,620 and debit entry of $30,000 will reduce the effective cost of merchandise sold. This is also marked with a "(C)" for identification.

The entry of the inventory purchased but not sold in the credit column has the same effect as the cost of goods sold calculation:

Merchandise purchases (601)	$ 7,220
Plus: Subcontract	1,200
Inventory Purchases (120)	30,000
Beginning Inventory	5,000
Less: Ending Inventory	39,620
Cost of Goods Sold	$ 3,800

Completing the Worksheet

The following steps are now taken to complete the worksheet (see Figure 9.11). First, carry over the balances from assets, liabilities, and equity (100, 200, and 300 accounts) to the balance sheet.

Second, carry over the balances from income, expenses, and cost of sales (accounts 400, 500, and 600) to the income statement.

Then add up all the columns. The income statement and the balance sheet will have different amounts in the debit and in the

YOURCOMPANY
Inventory Sheet
January 31, 1980

Quantity	Description	Unit Cost	Total
100	Z-90 chips	$100/ea	$10,000
200	breadboards	$3/ea	600
89	misc. I.C.'s	$25/ea	2,225
70 boxes	screws	.50/ea	35
60 cases	X-198 I.C.'s	$30/ea	18,000
310	V-916-X12 assemblies	$28.26/ea	8,760
			$39,620

Counted by: R.S. Harris   Checked by: D.B.Smith

Figure 9.10. Yourcompany inventory sheet.

credit column. This difference represents Yourcompany's net profit. On the income statement the debit column (expenses and cost of sales) adds up to $45,329.98 and the credit column (income and inventory adjustments to cost of sales) adds up to $47,029. The difference between $47,029 (the credit total) and $45,329.98 (the debit total) is $1699.02. This amount represents the *net profit* and is added to the debit side to bring the columns in balance. Similarly, the balance sheet debit and credit columns do not balance when they are first added up, but if the $1699.02 net profit from the income statement is carried over and entered in the credit column, the totals will both add up to $1730. This is because net profit is actually an addition to Owner's Equity.

You may notice that the $5000 beginning Yourcompany inventory is listed as owner's equity because Yourcompany had this much in the beginning of the year.

Your Company Worksheet
Month Ending January 1980

	ACCT. NO.	ACCOUNT NAME	TRIAL BALANCE DEBIT	TRIAL BALANCE CREDIT	ADJUSTMENTS DEBIT	ADJUSTMENTS CREDIT
1	101	Cash		1109.1		
2	111	Accounts Receivable	19.80			
3	111A	Allowance for Bad Debt				(B) 61.6
4	120	Deposits	1.30			
5	130	Parts Inventory	300.00			
6	150.1	Test Equipment	100.00			
7	150.11	Allowance for Depreciation				(A) 15.83
8						
9	201	Accounts Payable		37.20		
10	211.1	Notes Payable - B.A.		250.00		
11	211.2	" " - T Equipment		50.00		
12	300	Equity				
13	410	System Income		32.80		
14	420	Component Sales		34.29		
15	430	Rental Income		7.00		
16						
17	508	Rental Expense	12.00			
18	510	Telephone	3.00			
19	560	Office Supplies	1.50			
20	591	Business License	.40			
21	595	Depreciation			(A) 15.833	
22	599	Bad Debt			(B) 6.165	
23						
24	601	Inventory	72.20			
25	610	Sub-Contract	12.00			
26						
27		TOTALS	522.20	522.20	21.998	21.998
28		NET PROFIT FOR MONTH				
29		TOTAL				

Figure 9.11

ADJUSTED TRIAL BALANCE		INCOME STATEMENT		BALANCE SHEET		
DEBIT	CREDIT	DEBIT	CREDIT	DEBIT	CREDIT	
	1109 1				1109 1	1
19 80				19 80		2
	61 65				61 65	3
1 30				1 30		4
300 00		350 00	(c) 396 20	(c) 396 20		5
100 00				100 00		6
	158 33				158 33	7
						8
	37 20				37 20	9
	250 00				250 00	10
	50 00				50 00	11
					50 00	12
	32 80		32 80			13
	34 29		34 29			14
	7 00		7 00			15
						16
12 00		12 00				17
3 00		3 00				18
1 50		1 50				19
40		40				20
158 33		158 33				21
61 65		61 65				22
						23
		72 20				24
		12 00				25
						26
5243 98	5243 98	4532 98	470 29	517 30	5003 98	27
		1699 02			1699 02	28
		470 29	470 29	517 30	519 30	29

233

STEP	ACTION
1	TOTAL DEBIT AND CREDIT BALANCES IN ALL ACCOUNTS
2	ENTER ACCOUNT BALANCES IN TRIAL BALANCES
3	ADJUST FOR DEPRECIATION AND BAD DEBT ON ADJUSTED TRIAL BALANCE
4	EXTEND TRIAL BALANCE FIGURES TO ADJUSTED TRIAL BALANCE
5	MAKE INVENTORY ADJUSTMENTS TO INCOME STATEMENT AND BALANCE SHEET COLUMNS OF WORKSHEET
6	EXTEND TOTALS FROM ADJUSTED TRIAL BALANCE COLUMNS TO INCOME STATEMENT AND BALANCE SHEET COLUMNS
7	MAKE ALL CLOSING ENTRIES IN GENERAL JOURNAL AND LEDGERS

Figure 9.12. Step-by-step closing the books.

Flow Diagram of Closing Procedures

Closing the books, the end of the second transformation, is not difficult but it does require several steps. The diagram in Figure 9.12 describes the procedure step by step.

Step 1 is to determine the debit or credit balances in each of the ledger accounts. This is done by adding both columns in each account and finding the difference (subtracting one from the other). The column which has the highest total will have this difference written in the explanation space (see Figure 9.2).

Step 2 requires the balance in each account to be entered in either the debit or credit column of a trial balance worksheet, depending on whether it is a debit or credit balance in the ledger account (see Figure 9.3).

Step 3 is to adjust for depreciation and bad debt in the adjusted trial balance columns in the worksheet (see Figure 3.7 and Figure 9.7).

Step 4 is to extend the trial balance figures over to the adjusted trial balance (see Figure 9.9).

Step 5 is to make the inventory adjustments to the income statement and balance sheet columns of the worksheet (see Figure 9.9).

Step 6 extends all the totals from the adjusted trial balance to the income statement and balance sheet columns (see Figure 9.10).

Step 7 is to make all the closing entries in the general journal and the ledgers.

"This is how you will close out the books of the company," Pete Popstein suggested, "Now, what you need to do is to get to it, so I'll leave you alone. When you finish with the year-end books, I'll come back when you are finished and pull an income statement and a balance sheet."

"We're going to take off this next weekend." John looked at Gin. "So why don't we just set up an appointment for Tuesday. Everything should be in order by then."

That weekend John and Gin went to their favorite lake resort and rented a cabin. They didn't even talk about books.

Chapter Ten
Business Financial Statements

Pete Popstein arrived early Tuesday morning. Both John Your and his wife Gin were there.

Pete sat down, looked up at the two, and asked, "Wanna start right away on what financial statements are?"

"Okay," John answered.

"You saw what items go on the income statement and what accounts are for a balance sheet from doing the trial balance." Pete began. "Now let's get more specific. . . ."

Business financial statements include:

- The income statement (profit and loss statement)
- The statement of financial condition (balance sheet)
- Statement of retained earnings and funds flow statement

The financial statements are the culmination of the accounting process. They are also the beginning for finance. The financial statements are the summary of all the activity that has happened in the business during the period.

The most used of the financial statements is the *income statement*—the IRS requires an income statement for all businesses. The income statement is a summary of money that came into the business (revenue or income), money that was spent (cost of sales and expenses), and how much money remained after costs were paid (net profit).

The next most widely used financial statement is the *balance sheet*. The IRS does not require that partnerships and proprietorships file a balance sheet with their income tax returns. Because it is not required, many small businesses do not understand or use the balance sheet. The balance sheet is a summary of what the business owns (assets), what it owes (liabilities) and how much of the owner's money is in the business (equity).

To explain the difference between balance sheet and income statement, the analogy of a moving train is often used.

Let's assume that two photographers are assigned to document the last trip of the Wabash Cannonball. One photographer chooses to use a 35mm. still camera. The other will use a movie camera.

The Wabash Cannonball heads through the countryside while the still photographer waits at the Copper Canyon Bridge. When the Wabash arrives at the bridge, the still photographer takes a snapshot of the train. This is a picture of the Wabash at one moment in time.

The movie photographer, on the other hand, travels alongside the train and films it from the time it leaves the station until it arrives at the Copper Canyon Bridge. This is a picture of the train over a period of time.

The still photo that was taken at the bridge—of the Wabash at one moment in time—is similar to a balance sheet. The balance sheet is a picture of a business at one moment in time—at the end of a period. It shows how many assets the business has, how much it owes, and how much investment the owners have in the business at a certain date.

The movie of the Wabash Cannonball from the station to the Copper Canyon Bridge is like an income statement, which measures costs and expenses against sales revenues over a period of time. The income statement shows the operation of the business and the profit over an *entire period*.

Since the balance sheet is a statement of one moment in time, it is headed with the date. For example:

Yourcompany
Statement of Financial Condition
January 31, 1980

The income statement, on the other hand, shows a continuous period ending on the date of the financial statement. Therefore, the income statement date is prefaced with the words "for the period ending . . ." For example:

Yourcompany
Income Statement
For the One Month Period Ending Jan. 31, 1980

The statement of retained earnings and the funds flow statement are not used as much as the balance sheet and income statement. The IRS does *not* require the statement of retained earnings or funds flow statement to be included in any business's income tax. However, for an audited statement, generally accepted accounting principles require that these financial statements be included.

Retained earnings are the amount of money that is *retained* from net profit to be put back into the business. Retained earnings are what is left over after net profit after tax, dividends, owner's draw, principal loan repayment, and other items are taken out. Funds are defined as either the amount of working capital (current assets minus current liabilities) or cash.

By stretching the Wabash Cannonball example you can get an idea of what the statement of retained earnings and the funds flow statement measure in a business. Assume that the Wabash crew has a certain amount of coal to stoke the engine when they start, and every so often along the track they pick up more coal as they get low. The coal is constantly burned up and has to be replaced. Besides using the coal for running the engine, the engineer may use the coal to heat the train, or he may carve statues out of the coal for the tourist trade.

At the beginning of the train trip, the Wabash has a certain amount of coal and along the route they picked up some more. During the trip they used coal and at the end of the trip they will have a certain amount of coal left over. The engineer keeps an account book summarizing all the sources and uses of coal.

The statement of retained earnings and the funds flow statement are like the engineer's account book. Instead of coal, a business uses cash, working capital, and long term capital. The

THE INCOME STATEMENT

An income statement, commonly called a "profit and loss statement" consists of income, cost of sales, and expense accounts. *Gross margin* (the difference between income and cost of sales) and *net profit* (the difference between gross profit and operating expenses) are income statement amounts that are calculated.

Two graphic presentations of income statements are shown in Figures 10.1 and 10.2. The accounts used (income, cost of sales, and operating expense) have amounts that come directly from the company's books. By subtracting cost of sales from income, the result is the gross margin (gross profit). If you subtract the operating expense from the gross margin the result is net profit. An income statement is usually presented in the following format:

	Income
Less:	Cost of Sales
Equals:	Gross Margin
Less:	Operating Expense
Equals:	Net Profit

Example: Zip Tips Company has $100,000 in sales for the year. Zip has $60,000 in cost of sales and $30,000 in operating expense. Their income statement would be calculated as follows:

Sales	$100,000
Cost of sales	60,000
Gross margin	$ 40,000
Operating expense	30,000
Net profit	$ 10,000

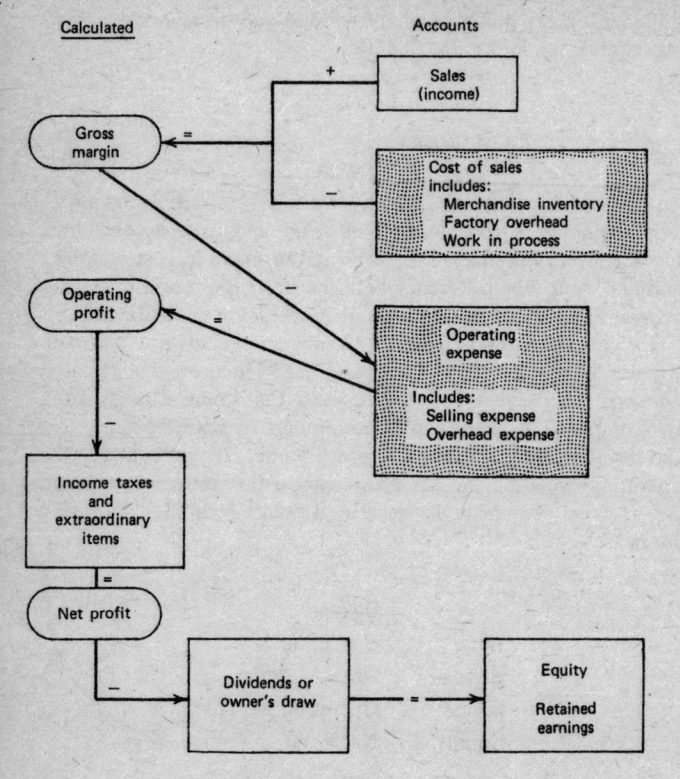

Figure 10.1. Income statement.

You can also see (Figure 10.2) that some costs, such as taxes, principal loan repayment, and owner's salary or dividends, come out of net profit. Whatever is left after these costs are deducted from net profit becomes *retained earnings,* which is part of the owner's equity on the balance sheet.

Figures 10.3, 10.4, 10.5, and 10.6 show a cross section of income statements from various industries. Notice that the Monar Company (Figure 10.3) is a retail store whose income statement has

THE ACCOUNTS CIRCLE

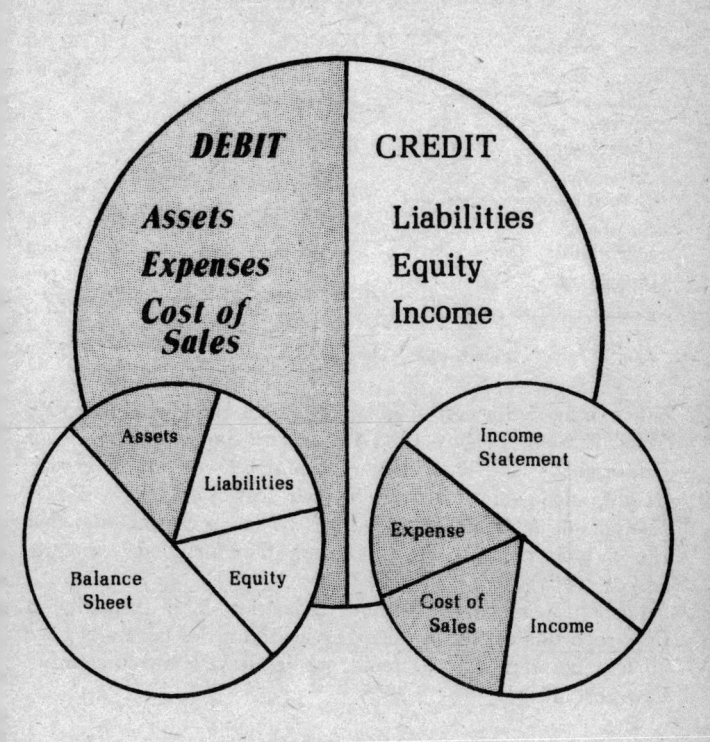

Figure 10.2. The accounts circle.

Profit-and-Loss Statement
For the Year Ended December 31, 19—

Sales		$120,000
Cost of goods sold		70,000
Gross margin		$50,000
Selling expenses:		
Salaries	$15,000	
Commission	5,000	
Advertising	5,000	
Total selling expenses		25,000
Selling margin		$25,000
Administrative expenses		10,000
Net profit		$15,000

Figure 10.3. The MONAR Company.

only one figure for cost of sales. The Wald Wholesale Company (a wholesaler) (Figure 10.4) has a more complex statement of cost of goods sold. They include beginning inventory, purchases, freight, and ending inventory in their cost of sales. The Hayes Manufacturing Company (Figure 10.5) has a cost of sales that is even more complex. For this reason, they included a separate cost of goods schedule (Figure 10.6).

Income statements of various industries differ primarily in their reporting of cost of sales. Service industries generally have *no* cost of sales whereas retail, wholesale, and manufacturing have cost of sales.

THE BALANCE SHEET

A balance sheet (statement of financial condition) is a summary of what a business owns (assets) and what claims there are against those assets (liabilities — creditor's claim; — and equity — the owner's claim).

The balance sheet is the financial summary in the form of the basic accounting equation:

$$\text{Assets} = \text{liabilities} + \text{equity}$$

Profit-and-Loss Statement
For the Year Ended December 31, 19—

Net sales		$666,720
Cost of goods sold:		
Beginning inventory, January 1, 19—		$184,350
Merchandise purchases	$454,920	
Freight and drayage	30,210	485,130
Cost of goods available for sale		$669,480
Less ending inventory, December 31, 19—		193,710
Cost of goods sold		475,770
Gross margin		$190,950
Selling, administrative, and general expenses:		
Salaries and wages	$88,170	
Rent	24,390	
Light, heat, and power	8,840	
Other expenses	21,300	
State and local taxes and licenses	5,130	
Depreciation and amortization on leasehold improvements	4,140	
Repairs	2,110	
Total selling, administrative, and general expenses		154,080
Profit from operations		$ 36,870
Other income	$7,550	
Other expense	1,740	5,810
Net profit before taxes		$ 42,680
Provision for income tax		15,120
Net profit after income tax		$ 27,560

Figure 10.4. Wald Wholesale Company.

The balance sheet is based on historical costs. Assets are stated on the balance sheet at their original cost less any depreciation. Common and preferred stock is recorded at the original amount received for the stock. Liabilities are recorded at the amount

Profit-and-Loss Statement
For the Year Ended December 31, 19—

Net sales			$669,100
Cost of goods sold:			
Finished goods inventory, January 1, 19—		$ 69,200	
Cost of goods manufactured (exhibit 6)		569,700	
Total cost of goods available for sale		$638,900	
Less finished goods inventory, Dec. 31, 19—		66,400	
Cost of goods sold			572,500
Gross margin			$ 96,600
Selling and administrative expenses:			
Selling expenses:			
Sales salaries and commissions	$26,700		
Advertising expense	12,900		
Miscellaneous selling expense	2,100		
Total selling expenses		$ 41,700	
Administrative expenses:			
Salaries	$27,400		
Miscellaneous administrative expense	4,800		
Total administrative expenses		32,200	
Total selling and administrative expenses			73,900
Net operating profit			$ 22,700
Other revenue			15,300
Net profit before taxes			$ 38,000
Estimated income tax			12,640
Net profit after income tax			$ 25,360

Figure 10.5. Hayes Manufacturing Company.

Statement of Cost of Goods Manufactured
For the Year Ended December 31, 19—

Work-in-process inventory, January 1, 19—			$ 18,800
Raw materials:			
Inventory, January 1, 19—		$154,300	
Purchases		263,520	
Freight In		9,400	
Cost of materials available for use		$427,220	
Less inventory, December 31, 19—		163,120	
Cost of materials used		$264,100	
Direct labor		150,650	
Manufacturing overhead:			
Indirect labor	$23,750		
Factory heat, light, and power	89,500		
Factory supplies used	22,100		
Insurance and taxes	8,100		
Depreciation of plant and equipment	35,300		
Total manufacturing overhead		178,750	
Total manufacturing costs			593,500
Total work in process during period			$612,300
Less work-in-process inventory, December 31, 19—			42,600
Cost of goods manufactured			$569,700

Figure 10.6. Hayes Manufacturing Company.

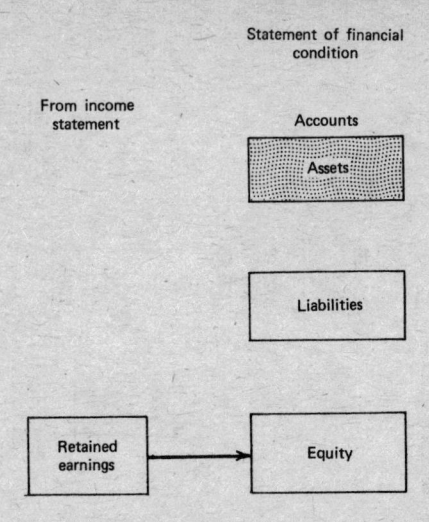

Figure 10.7. Statement of financial condition.

currently (at the end of that accounting period) owed. The reason for using historical cost is that it reduces to a minimum the extent to which the accounts are affected by the personal opinions of the owners.

Balance Sheet Examples

Figure 10.7 shows the three account groups that make up the balance sheet: assets, liabilities, and equity. Notice that there is no computation required in a balance sheet unlike an income statement. The statement is fully represented by the accounts on the books. Notice from the illustration that "retained earnings" from the income statement is incorporated into the equity position.

Figure 10.8 is a sample balance sheet of Fatcat, Inc. This illustration shows the typical categories and items of a balance sheet. Assets are presented first and liabilities and equity are presented last. The first items of assets are the current assets. The

The Balance Sheet

Assets:		
Current Assets		
Cash	$ 12,000	
Accounts receivable	119,000	
Notes receivable	7,800	
Inventories at cost (LIFO)	235,200	
Prepaid Assets	26,000	
Total Current Assets		$ 400,000
Fixed Assets		
Land	$ 45,000	
Buildings and improvements	230,000	
Equipment and vehicles	497,000	
Furniture and fixtures	31,456	
Less: Accumulated depreciation	(212,456)	
Total Fixed Assets		$ 591,000
Other Assets		
Investment in subsidiaries	$ 49,000	
Goodwill	76,000	
Research and development	82,000	
Less: R&D amortization	(51,000)	
Total Other Assets		$ 156,000
Total Assets		$1,147,000
Liabilities:		
Current Liabilities		
Accounts payable	$ 98,500	
Notes payable	7,340	
Accrued taxes	103,182	
Accrued salaries	10,340	
Provision for pensions	56,300	
Total Current Liabilities		$ 275,662
Long-Term Liabilities:		
Notes payable	$ 28,503	
Bonds (8-½% due 1985)	310,635	
Total Long-Term Liabilities		$ 339,138
Total Liabilities		$ 611,800
Equity		
Capital stock	$100,000	
Paid-in surplus	120,000	
Retained earnings	315,200	
Total Equity		$ 535,200
Total Liabilities and Equity		$1,147,000

Figure 10.8. Balance sheet of Fatcat, Inc., December 31, 198X.

first items presented in liabilities are the current liabilities. Current assets are assets that can be converted to cash within one year. Current liabilities also reflect a one year period, but they are debts which must be repaid within the next year.

Current assets are followed by a group of assets called "fixed assets" and by another group called "other assets." "Fixed assets" will remain for more than one year and generally (with the exception of land) are depreciable or amortized assets. "Other assets" are not owned by every company. They are assets that can not be converted to cash within one year and are usually not depreciable or amortizable. "Other assets" include patents and intangibles which are amortized.

Following current liabilities are "long-term liabilities." These are debts that will take more than one year to pay off. In accounting, more than one year is considered "long-term."

The equity (or capital) portion of the balance sheet shows the basic components of the owners' investment and retention of capital in the business: stock, paid-in surplus, and retained earnings. In proprietorships and partnerships this section may contain only the owners' cumulative equity in the business (owners' equity) and the retained earnings for that period (sometimes just stated as "net profit").

STATEMENT OF RETAINED EARNINGS AND FUNDS FLOW STATEMENT

The major difference between a statement of retained earnings and funds flow statement is that the first is only concerned with determining retained earnings at the *end of a period*. The funds flow statement includes the results of the statement of retained earnings, but it *also* goes further by tracking down every movement of funds *during* the period.

The statement of retained earnings shows the retained earnings at the beginning of a period, the adjustments to retained earnings during the period, and the retained earnings calculated for the end of the period.

Statement of Retained Earnings and Funds Flow Statement

The purpose of the funds flow statement is to trace the flow of working capital during the accounting period.

Neither the statement of retained earnings nor the funds flow statement is required for income tax purposes, but both are required by "generally accepted accounting principles."

Statement of Retained Earnings

Most corporations are required to show their retained earnings in a "Statement of Retained Earnings." This financial statement shows the retained earnings at the beginning of the period (the end of the *last* period), adjustments made during the accounting period, and what the retained earnings are at the end of the present period.

Adjustments made during the period include:

1. Profit or loss from period after taxes
2. Dividends or owner's draw
3. Adjustments or charges or credits resulting from transactions in the company's own capital stock (buying treasury stock or selling stock)
4. Transfers to and from accounts properly designated as appropriated retained earnings such as contingency reserves or provisions for replacement costs of fixed assets, or
5. Adjustments made pursuant to a quasi-reorganization.

Statement of Retained Earnings Design and Examples

Figure 10.9 shows the general design of the statement of retained earnings. The illustration is divided into three parts, labeled "from income statement," cash costs ($-$) or inflow ($+$)," and "from balance sheet." From the balance sheet comes the (1) retained earnings for the last period (the beginning of this period), and (2) the calculated retained earnings from this period (circle in illustration). All adjustments to retained earnings except "net income after tax" are from cash funds and do not appear either on the income statement or the balance sheet

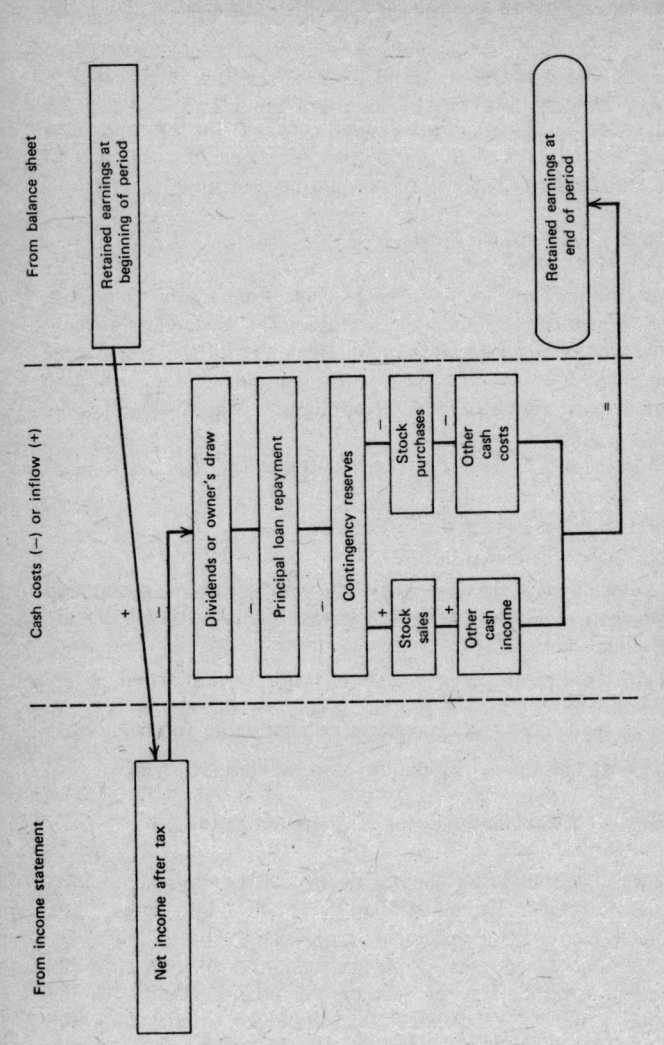

Figure 10.9. Statement of retained earnings.

(except as a decrease or increase to the cash asset). In the illustration, a plus sign (+) indicates that that item is added to retained earnings from the beginning of the period, and a minus sign (−) indicates that items are subtracted.

	For the Years Ending	
	Dec. 31, 1979	Dec. 31, 1980
Retained Earnings at beginning of the period	$100,320	$212,431
Net Income for Period	112,111	157,900
Common stock dividend - 5% (4320 shares and $435 cash for partial shares)	-0-	$ 43,645
Retained earnings at end of period	$212,431	$326,686

The Funds Flow Statement

Publicly held companies are required to have a funds flow statement along with their income statement and balance sheet. The funds flow statement traces the flow of working capital during the accounting period. Working capital is the excess of current assets over current liabilities.

The funds flow statement answers some of the following questions.

1. Where did profits go?
2. Why were dividends not larger in view of the profits made?
3. How was it possible to distribute dividends when the company had a net operating loss?
4. How was the expansion in plant and equipment financed?
5. What happened to the sale of additional stock and the proceeds from the sale of fixed assets?
6. How was the retirement of debt accomplished?
7. What brought about the increase or decrease in working capital?

Sources of Funds	Application of Funds

Increase in liabilities
  Loans
  Mortgages
	Decrease in liabilities
	  Pay-off loans
	  Pay-off mortgages

Increases in owner's equity:
  Owner cash injection
  Stock sales
  Increase in retained earnings
	Decrease in owner's equity
	  Withdrawals by owners
	  Decrease in retained earnings
	  Net loss

Decreases in fixed assets
  Sale of fixed assets
  Depreciation
	Increase in fixed assets
	  Purchase equipment, furniture
	  and fixtures, land and
	  building and leasehold
	  improvements

Figure 10.10. Funds flow statement.

Figure 10.10 shows how the funds flow statement can be divided into sources of funds (working capital) and application (uses) of funds. Notice that working capital is a *source* of funds when there is (1) an *increase* in liabilities or owner's equity, or (2) a *decrease* in fixed assets. Funds are used (applied) when there is (1) a *decrease* in liabilities or owner's equity, or (2) an *increase* in fixed assets.

Examples of sources of funds are loans and mortgages, injection of ownership cash into the business (stock or owner's injection), or increase in retained earnings from the previous year (from statement of retained earnings). Sources of funds also include a decrease in fixed assets (sales of equipment and other fixed assets) and the ongoing depreciation expense.

Funds are used (applied) by paying off loans and mortgages (decreasing liabilities), withdrawals by owners through dividends or owner's draw, or by decreases in retained earnings resulting from net losses or large nonoperating cash expenditures. Funds are also used by increasing fixed assets such as purchase of equipment, buildings, and so on.

The following funds flow statement is an example:

Acme Mousetraps, Inc.
Funds Statement
For the Period Ending Dec. 31, 197X

Source of Funds:

Operations: Net income	$25,316	
Add depreciation	5,720	$31,036
Sale of stock		10,000
Total sources		$41,036

Use of Funds:

Purchase of fixed assets	$ 4,750	
Cash dividends paid	10,000	
Retirement of long-term debt	17,812	$32,562
Net increase in working capital		$ 8,474

"Well," Pete said smiling, "Now you know everything that you need to know about accounting. Anything more that I could tell you would be special tax stuff, auditing control, finance, law, or something else. What you've learned yourself, what I've taught you, and what you've read in the last couple of weeks have given you almost everything you need to know."

"All I need to find out now is how to get my $80,000 back from the theft." John said, "But I guess Riskstein, my attorney, will help me with that. Thanks a lot, Pete. I appreciate this."

"Before you go, Pete," Gin said to Pete as he was getting his examples together, "I want to ask you a question. Is there anything else that we could do to get a handle on accounting. Like how to determine if we have enough inventory, if we are collecting right, if the business is getting better or worse."

"What you're talking about," Pete said, "is finance. Finance is taking the accounting numbers and diagnosing the business. Accounting is keeping track of business costs, assets, debt, equity, and income in a reliable and accurate manner. Finance is the process of making predictions from these figures."

"Well, where do I read about finance?" Gin asked.

"I think the last chapter of *Simplified Accounting* is on finance. You can read that."

Chapter Eleven
Business Finance and Ratios

John Your's attorney, Ed Riskstein, told John that in order to press charges against his bookkeeper, John would have to produce all the documents and original records showing how the thefts were perpetrated. John knew enough about accounting to give Riskstein the right documents.

John wanted to take this thing to court as soon as possible so that he might still recover some of Yourcompany's cash. Riskstein had found that the signature on the "other bank account" belonged to a person who was identified as being the bookkeeper's boyfriend. The addresses for the Softfare and Thermafac companies were phony, as John had expected.

It was now a matter of letting the court and the wheels of justice run their course.

Martha had another job as a bookkeeper and John couldn't help but wonder how much she would take that company for, and how much that company's president knew about accounting.

While John was talking to Riskstein, Gin was sitting in the waiting room reading *Simplified Accounting*. . . .

Accounting information is the basic data of business. It shows how much you make, what you spend, what you own, what you owe, and what investment the owners have in the business. But by itself accounting information has no predictive or deductive qualities. It does not show you how to control operating expenses, to grant credit intelligently, to understand basic inventory relationship, and to manage cash flow. Finance is the art of gathering accounting information and making predictions and deductions from it as to how your business can improve and what the problem areas are. Taking the raw accounting data and making judgments about how this compares to a typical situation and how it compares to the history of the business is what finance is all about.

FINANCIAL STATEMENTS AND FINANCE

Of themselves, a balance sheet and income statement are a collection of inanimate figures. But when the assorted financial symbols are interpreted and evaluated, they begin to talk.

A single balance sheet is like the opening chapters of a book —it gives the initial setting. Thus, one balance sheet will show how the capital is distributed, how much is in the various accounts, and how much surplus of assets over liabilities exists. A lone income statement indicates the sales volume for a given period, the amount of costs incurred, and the amount earned after allowing for all costs.

When a series of balance sheets for related intervals, such as years, months, and so forth, is arranged in vertical columns, the changes in related items may be compared. The comparative balance sheets no longer resemble individual snapshots, but are converted into x-rays, penetrating outward tissue and outlining skeletal structure of all basic management actions and decisions.

Did sales go up? If so, what about expenses? Did they remain proportionate? Was more money spent on office help? Where did the money come from? How about fixed overhead? Was it controlled? It is only by comparing operating income and cost account items from one period to another that revealing answers are found.

Types of Financial Uses

The areas where most businesspeople use finance are:

1. To control and predict collections of accounts receivable
2. To control and predict inventory movement and depletion

3. To control operations
4. To manage finances, including borrowing money and selling business ownership.

The type of financial tools that a businessperson uses depends on which of these four areas needs to be analyzed. For instance, if the business is having cash flow problems because it is *not* collecting on receivables, collection financial tools are the most important.

In order to make this chapter more practical for the average reader who is a businessperson, we will cover the ratios in general, and then cover the specially applicable ratios for each general use: collections, inventory, operations, and financial management.

BASIC INFORMATION ON RATIOS

All ratios are based on the balance sheet and income statement. Ratios either: (1) use only balance sheet numbers to show relations between the various balance sheet items (2) use only income statement numbers to show their relationships, or (3) use both the balance sheet and the income statement to show the relationship between an item on the income statement and on the balance sheet.

When you calculate ratios all you need is 11 numbers: seven from the balance sheet, two from the income statement, and one that is calculated by subtracting two balance sheet figures from each other. The figures you need are:

From the Balance Sheet

1. Total current assets
2. Accounts receivable
3. Inventory
4. Total fixed assets
5. Total current liabilities
6. Total all liabilities
7. Net worth

From the Income Statement

1. Net sales
2. Net profit after taxes

Basic Information on Ratios

Calculated from Two Balance Sheet Items
  Working capital (current assets minus current liabilities)

Eleven Key Ratios

The following 11 ratios, organized by their applicable area of management, are the most practical for business:

Collections:
  1. Average collection period of receivables

Operations:
  2. Net profit on net sales
  3. Net fixed assets to tangible net worth

Inventory:
  4. Net sales to inventory
  5. Inventory to net working capital

Financial Management:
  6. Current assets to current liabilities
  7. Current liabilities to tangible net worth
  8. Net sales to tangible net worth
  9. Net sales to net working capital
  10. Net profits to tangible net worth
  11. Total debt to tangible net worth

Looking at Figure 11.1 we can see what the different ratios are and what financial statements (balance sheet or income statement) are used. Note that there is a middle column for the ratios that have figures from both the balance sheet and the income statement. The figures from the balance sheet are marked "(B)" and income statement figures are marked "(I)."

Industry Ratio Studies

It is important to note that the ratios by themselves, based on your company alone, are not as significant as your ratios compared to those of other companies in your industry.

Income Statement	Both Income Statement (I) and Balance Sheet (B)	Balance Sheet
(2) $\dfrac{\text{Net profit}}{\text{Net sales}}$	(1) $\dfrac{\text{Credit sales (I)}}{\text{Days in period}} = \text{S/D}$	(3) $\dfrac{\text{Fixed assets}}{\text{Net worth}}$
	$\dfrac{\text{Accounts receivable (B)}}{\text{S/D}}$	(5) $\dfrac{\text{Inventory}}{\text{Working capital}}$
	(4) $\dfrac{\text{Net sales (I)}}{\text{Inventory (B)}}$	(6) $\dfrac{\text{Current assets}}{\text{Current liabilities}}$
	(8) $\dfrac{\text{Net sales (I)}}{\text{Net worth (B)}}$	(7) $\dfrac{\text{Current liabilities}}{\text{Working capital}}$
	(9) $\dfrac{\text{Net sales (I)}}{\text{Working capital (B)}}$	(11) $\dfrac{\text{Total debt}}{\text{Net worth}}$
	(10) $\dfrac{\text{Net profit (I)}}{\text{Net worth (B)}}$	

Figure 11.1. Table of ratios and their financial statements.

For instance, your company's average collection period of 45 days might be good or bad depending on your industry. In the computer industry receivables sometimes run as high as 60 days under normal circumstances, but in the food industry any receivable over 15 days is considered too long.

The most important *specialized industry sources* for ratio data are trade associations. In addition, however, accounting firms, trade magazines, universities, and some large companies publish ratio studies. The National Credit Office, an affiliate of Dun and Bradstreet, Inc., also publishes a number of intermittent reports on the industries in which it specializes.

For this reason it is a good idea not only to compute your company's ratios, but also compare them to your industry. Several industry ratio studies are available to the public. The following is a discussion of the different sources:

Basic Information on Ratios

Ratio sources may be classified into two groups: those agencies which compile data for a number of individual industries and those which confine their work to a particular industry or a group of related industries. The best known of the former are Dun and Bradstreet, Inc., Robert Morris Associates, and The Accounting Corporation of America. The latter group is composed of trade associations, publishers of trade magazines, specialized accounting firms, industrial companies (e.g. National Cash Register), and colleges and universities.

Dun and Bradstreet, Inc., has been publishing its "Key Business Ratios" annually since 1932 in *Dun's Review and Modern Industry*, a monthly magazine. They also appear in separate pamphlet form. The data are essentially by-products of Dun and Bradstreet's very extensive financial and reporting services. The report covers 125 lines of business activity consisting of 71 manufacturing and construction industries, 32 wholesaling industries, and 22 lines of retailing.

In addition to the annual reports, Dun and Bradstreet, Inc. publishes *Cost of Doing Business* studies covering a number of industries.

The National Cash Register Company publishes an annual "Expenses in Retailing." This booklet examines the cost of operation in over 50 lines of business. The ratios are obtained from primary sources, most of which are trade associations. For some lines of business, the expense percentages are broken down into "controllable expense" and "fixed expense."

Robert Morris Associates has developed ratio studies for over 225 lines of business. Owners and managers of small concerns wishing further information on the availability of this material may address inquiries to the Executive Manager, Robert Morris Associates, Philadelphia National Bank Building, Philadelphia, PA 19107.

Federal government publications provide a wealth of data covering somewhat broader industry classifications in most cases than the private sources.

The most current and completely developed ratio data are published jointly by the Federal Trade Commission and the Securities and Exchange Commission in the form of the *Quar-*

	Hero Manufacturing		Rotten Distribution	
	Present Year 12/30/19X2	Previous Year 12/30/19X1	Present Year 12/30/19X2	Previous Year 12/30/19X1
Assets				
Current assets:				
Cash	200,000	353,400	(5,000)	50,000
Securities	900,000	623,483	-0-	-0-
Accounts receivable	580,000	528,367	690,410	712,300
Allowance for uncollectibles	(30,000)	(27,300)	(60,000)	(61,000)
Inventory	330,300	386,000	583,310	551,300
Prepaid expense	69,500	69,500	-0-	-0-
Total current assets	2,049,800	1,933,450	1,208,720	1,252,600
Fixed assets				
Furniture and fixtures	75,000	75,000	12,000	12,000
Equipment	520,500	303,503	195,000	195,000
Vehicles	90,000	85,000	55,000	45,000
Buildings and leasehold improvements	350,000	350,000	200,000	200,000
Less: Accumulated depreciation	(302,000)	(191,453)	(52,000)	(43,000)
Land	100,000	100,000	30,000	30,000
Total fixed assets	833,500	722,050	420,000	439,000
Other assets				
Investment in subsidiary	-0-	-0-	271,280	238,000
Organizational expense	40,000	40,000	50,000	50,000
Less: Amortization	(35,000)	(32,000)	(20,000)	(17,000)
Trademarks			40,000	40,000
Notes receivable from officers			200,000	178,000
Total other assets	5,000	8,000	541,280	489,000
Total assets	2,888,300	2,663,500	2,170,000	2,180,600

Liabilities						
Current liabilities:						
Accounts payable	209,490		129,950		512,000	507,800
Payroll taxes payable	57,010		48,000		35,000	39,000
Provision for income tax	60,300		42,250		12,600	52,800
Notes payable	162,900		156,500		510,000	469,582
Accrued wages	10,062		10,000		10,062	9,518
Other accruals	-0-		153,400		11,458	10,000
Total current liabilities		499,762		543,700	1,091,120	1,088,700
Mortgages payable	320,338		331,000		160,000	173,000
Notes payable	339,000		285,000		218,880	208,300
Total long-term liabilities		659,338		616,000	378,880	281,300
Total liabilities		1,159,100		1,159,100	1,470,000	1,870,000
Net worth:						
Common stock	300,000		30,000		810,600	801,400
Preferred stock	50,000		50,000		N/A	N/A
Paid-in surplus	150,000		150,000		N/A	N/A
Retained earnings	1,229,200		1,004,400		29,400	79,200
Less: Owner's draw	N/A		N/A		75,000	50,000
Principal debt repay	N/A		N/A		65,000	20,000
Total net worth		1,729,200		1,504,400	700,000	810,600
Total liabilities and net worth		2,888,300		2,663,500	2,170,000	2,180,600

Figure 11.2. Statement of financial condition—12/30/78.

	Hero Manufacturing		Rotten Distribution	
	Present Year 12/30/19X2	Previous Year 12/30/19X1	Present Year 12/30/19X2	Previous Year 12/30/19X1
Sales and Revenue				
Net sales of product	5,620,000	4,323,000	4,200,000	4,620,000
Interest income	51,750	40,100	-0-	-0-
Total income	5,671,750	4,363,100	4,200,000	4,620,000
Less: Cost of sales				
Merchandise	1,067,800	767,333	2,940,000	3,194,083
Wages	2,135,600	1,534,665	185,000	201,062
Factory overhead	640,680	460,399	65,000	70,594
Selling costs	427,120	306,933	212,000	230,261
Total cost of sales	4,271,200	3,069,330	3,402,000	3,696,000
Gross profit	1,400,550	1,293,770	798,000	924,000
Operating expense:				
Wages general	400,000	380,000	400,000	420,000
	80,000	70,000	N/A	N/A
Payroll tax	43,200	40,500	43,200	48,700
Insurance	90,000	82,000	45,300	47,000
Accounting and legal	42,000	36,000	25,000	27,000
Administrative costs	85,000	81,000	10,446	22,200
Supplies and postage	3,500	3,200	5,000	6,100
Rent for premises	65,000	55,000	26,000	26,000
Utilities and phone	7,200	6,900	12,010	11,600
Travel and entertainment	41,700	40,900	63,000	74,200
Leases	28,000	24,000	12,200	10,900
Tax and license	3,800	3,200	2,600	2,700
Dues and subscriptions	4,500	4,600	3,100	3,700
Depreciation and amortization	3,000	2,900	1,700	1,700
Interest	65,779	71,460	176,444	90,200
Commissions	39,140	30,110	-0-	-0-
Total Operating expense	991,823	921,770	756,000	792,000

Cost of Sales Schedule

Merchandise:				
Furnished goods inv.—beginning	176,000	145,320	551,300	550,200
Work in process inv.—beginning	95,000	78,311	N/A	N/A
Raw material inv.—beginning	115,000	94,503	N/A	N/A
Material purchases	991,000	817,829	2,875,890	3,153,583
Freight-in	21,000	17,300	32,100	41,600
Less:	90,000	115,000	N/A	N/A
Less: Finished goods ending	150,000	176,000	583,310	551,300
Less: Work-in process	90,300	95,000	N/A	N/A
Total cost of materials	1,067,800	767,333	2,940,000	3,194,083
Direct labor costs				
Factory salaries	1,312,260	939,216	107,000	119,000
Shipping salaries	498,000	356,042	55,000	59,000
Payroll tax and benefits	161,113	118,169	16,200	17,800
Bonus and vacation	164,227	121,238	6,800	5,262
Total direct labor costs	2,135,600	1,534,665	185,000	201,062
Factory overhead:				
Rent and equipment leases	320,000	280,000	25,800	25,800
Utilities	93,133	39,399	1,200	1,300
Supplies	60,000	56,000	4,000	6,000
Repairs and maintenance	57,000	43,000	5,000	11,494
Equipment depreciation	110,547	42,000	29,000	26,000
Total factory overhead	640,680	460,399	65,000	70,594
Selling expense	265,000	201,200	129,000	129,000
Payroll tax payable	26,500	20,120	12,000	12,900
Travel and transportation	35,620	10,613	26,000	29,000
Bad debt losses	80,000	75,000	40,000	47,800
Advertising	20,000	—0—	14,000	11,561
Total selling expense	427,120	306,933	212,000	230,261
Total cost of sales	2,271,200	3,069,330	3,402,000	3,696,000

Figure 11.3. Income statement.

Line of Business (and number of concerns reporting)	Current assets to current debt	Net profits on net sales	Net profits on tangible net worth	Net profits on net working capital	Net sales to tangible net worth	Net sales to net working capital	Collection period	Net sales to inventory	Fixed assets to tangible net worth	Current debt to tangible net worth	Total debt to tangible net worth	Inventory to net working capital	Current debt to net working capital	Funded debts to net working capital
	Times	Per cent	Per cent	Per cent	Times	Times	Days	Times	Per cent	Per cent	Per cent	Per cent	Per cent	Per cent
3821–22 Instruments, Measuring & Controlling (53)	4.32 2.83 2.28	5.71 4.00 1.41	15.30 8.26 3.79	18.03 11.80 4.80	3.14 2.29 1.71	3.81 3.05 2.37	51 64 83	5.8 4.1 3.1	28.4 40.4 57.9	21.3 44.3 71.8	47.5 90.3 100.4	56.1 74.1 89.4	45.6 69.6 92.9	23.7 30.1 64.5
3321–22–23 Iron & Steel Foundries (56)	3.45 2.37 2.07	4.86 3.10 2.07	15.92 9.30 5.55	33.38 15.40 12.08	3.59 2.71 2.09	8.13 8.30 3.72	40 48 60	21.6 10.3 5.9	47.9 83.4 79.0	22.6 30.7 53.8	33.1 58.8 80.5	37.5 63.1 89.1	77.3 115.4 177.6	16.8 39.2 75.1
2253 Knit Outerwear Mills (56)	2.94 2.01 1.55	3.57 2.83 1.35	19.97 11.71 5.77	27.82 16.33 9.18	6.46 4.04 2.84	8.73 6.40 4.18	30 49 68	9.9 6.8 4.7	13.2 28.4 54.8	35.8 60.6 126.9	58.4 89.0 163.1	58.3 86.8 147.2	80.0 114.9 154.9	12.8 33.0 61.7
2082 Malt Liquors (30)	2.92 2.31 1.74	5.08 1.65 (0.55)	9.84 4.97 (1.61)	32.80 12.64 (6.23)	4.16 2.49 2.07	12.75 8.93 5.69	11 16 25	18.3 15.1 11.6	53.7 70.7 103.8	17.8 24.9 44.0	40.0 58.2 91.4	34.1 55.8 77.9	129.5 137.4 210.0	39.8 94.4 138.8
2515 Mattresses & Bedsprings (46)	3.36 2.58 1.69	3.03 1.38 0.55	12.24 5.12 3.39	15.35 8.18 4.17	6.05 3.76 2.36	8.18 5.70 4.09	41 50 61	11.3 7.7 6.4	14.4 29.1 50.0	24.6 48.2 92.3	65.6 95.2 131.8	55.8 76.7 103.9	65.8 101.1 140.4	13.0 30.9 16.5
2011 Meat Packing Plants (92)	3.70 2.00 1.47	1.33 0.67 0.20	14.79 8.57 2.59	25.89 17.96 5.73	19.05 10.45 7.00	34.13 19.79 12.57	12 15 20	55.1 30.1 21.2	42.9 63.2 90.0	23.9 52.7 100.6	58.2 95.9 184.5	34.1 69.0 111.4	87.3 143.3 227.7	16.5 47.6 88.4
3461 Metal Stampings (104)	4.35 2.55 1.67	4.90 2.84 0.72	12.16 7.83 2.59	21.75 13.33 6.72	4.39 3.11 1.94	8.16 5.98 4.18	34 48 58	11.1 6.3 5.2	30.9 54.1 82.2	17.4 34.6 72.0	44.0 71.8 153.5	44.4 71.8 102.4	64.5 105.7 167.4	26.4 59.2 65.6
3541–42–44–45–48 Metalworking Machinery & Equipment (124)	4.36 2.83 1.96	5.93 3.08 0.62	12.76 6.94 0.93	20.02 11.21 1.75	3.23 2.13 1.49	5.54 3.46 2.29	46 61 76	13.4 5.9 3.2	34.8 48.3 65.6	18.9 29.8 62.0	38.8 71.4 114.8	36.2 66.2 92.5	56.4 91.1 161.0	15.0 43.1 76.8
2431 Millwork (55)	4.14 2.27 1.75	4.25 2.61 1.37	21.08 10.08 5.40	29.04 16.83 6.08	6.25 4.10 2.92	8.56 5.74 4.09	34 48 59	10.9 8.1 5.5	23.7 39.0 61.8	26.0 51.3 87.8	58.9 106.0 204.9	52.6 73.9 118.2	72.0 94.5 164.6	17.1 44.2 23.7
3599 Miscellaneous Machinery, except Electrical (90)	4.45 2.71 1.84	5.75 3.20 1.23	14.65 6.07 3.89	28.54 12.70 7.49	4.03 2.78 1.83	7.14 4.67 3.44	33 46 61	23.8 9.4 5.0	32.7 51.1 70.8	19.0 32.8 65.4	29.7 59.1 113.3	22.5 54.2 87.3	61.8 103.1 154.7	7.9 27.5 70.1
3714 Motor Vehicle Parts & Accessories (89)	3.70 2.77 2.19	5.72 4.28 2.96	16.23 11.53 8.22	26.74 19.20 13.21	4.60 2.68 2.16	5.91 3.93 2.87	35 44 54	9.0 5.8 4.1	27.2 44.5 62.5	25.6 37.1 45.4	55.2 78.4 117.9	55.2 72.3 96.0	54.8 80.3 116.7	27.8 47.4 9.1
3361–62–69 Nonferrous Foundries (47)	4.03 2.75 1.59	5.65 2.74 1.08	14.63 8.63 3.41	29.96 13.46 5.79	4.05 3.01 2.15	8.71 5.28 4.00	42 47 53	18.9 13.4 6.7	33.3 54.6 77.8	16.0 24.5 73.1	34.2 84.9 175.3	27.6 44.5 83.7	74.2 130.4 260.4	12.5 30.0 122.5
2541–42 Office & Store Fixtures (60)	3.54 2.22 1.59	5.66 2.45 0.48	16.00 8.58 2.21	26.81 12.85 2.34	4.80 3.52 2.23	9.50 4.86 3.32	36 56 70	12.2 7.2 4.5	20.2 42.8 70.6	30.8 59.3 91.2	39.2 114.3 155.5	45.1 75.8 123.7	74.6 116.4 174.4	25.4 46.9 109.0
2361–63–69 Outerwear, Children's & Infants' (58)	2.70 1.89 1.46	2.46 1.40 0.49	15.29 8.31 2.54	18.50 10.16 2.72	8.83 5.88 3.60	12.11 7.84 4.50	10 42 60	12.9 7.5 5.9	6.8 11.2 24.2	46.9 92.1 175.5	55.7 116.9 315.8	51.1 89.9 146.5	81.1 126.8 208.7	7.4 18.7 37.5
2851 Paints, Varnishes, Lacquers & Enamels (112)	3.81 2.92 2.13	3.96 2.61 1.50	17.91 8.87 5.59	20.55 13.50 6.87	6.60 3.40 2.51	6.80 4.85 3.43	35 48 59	25.4 16.4 5.0	23.3 40.0 55.4	44.4 72.6 106.8	58.1 73.3 89.3	53.3 81.3 109.7	15.6 33.1 56.1
2621 Paper Mills, except Building Paper (55)	3.52 2.82 2.17	4.91 3.28 1.56	10.01 6.27 3.27	28.19 14.02 6.85	2.56 1.97 1.67	6.22 4.30 3.78	34 43 54	11.4 7.8 6.2	67.8 87.4 117.5	19.0 22.1 40.5	50.5 75.4 121.4	46.7 60.6 82.7	68.0 98.0 172.3	39.9 117.4 156.7
2651–52–53–54–55 Paperboard Containers & Boxes (61)	4.17 2.22 1.64	3.87 2.63 1.35	19.66 7.38 4.28	30.20 14.28 7.95	4.37 3.06 2.06	10.80 6.45 4.76	33 46 64	11.7 8.0 6.2	46.7 70.5 101.2	17.1 38.3 64.1	59.1 75.2 129.1	54.3 80.8 140.9	64.4 82.8 162.7	40.3 67.5 124.5
3712–13 Passenger Car, Truck & Bus Bodies (46)	3.54 2.07 1.49	3.14 1.82 1.16	14.02 8.48 4.21	19.64 18.11 6.14	6.78 4.21 2.46	7.67 9.35 3.92	29 41 56	9.0 6.1 4.3	18.5 30.5 66.3	25.6 69.2 128.5	47.6 116.0 218.6	59.4 88.8 141.1	64.1 90.8 151.9	17.3 31.3 48.1

( ) Indicates Less

Figure 11.4

Line of business (and number of concerns reporting)	Current assets to current debt	Net profits on net sales	Net profits on tangible net worth	Net profits on net working capital	Net sales to tangible net worth	Net sales to net working capital	Collection period	Net sales to inventory	Fixed assets to tangible net worth	Current debt to tangible net worth	Total debt to tangible net worth	Inventory to net working capital	Current debt to inventory	Funded debts to net working capital
	Times	Per cent	Per cent	Per cent	Times	Times	Days	Times	Per cent	Per cent	Per cent	Per cent	Per cent	Per cent
5097 Furniture & Home Furnishings (81)	2.98 / 2.10 / 1.67	3.40 / 1.56 / 0.94	14.42 / 8.42 / 4.17	20.14 / 10.09 / 5.94	6.85 / 4.83 / 3.24	7.82 / 5.50 / 4.33	40 / 49 / 70	9.5 / 6.8 / 4.6	6.8 / 13.5 / 30.7	42.3 / 75.4 / 138.3	74.1 / 140.2 / 198.4	58.0 / 88.1 / 117.8	66.6 / 108.7 / 138.3	16.0 / 31.7 / 43.9
5041 Groceries, General Line (196)	3.15 / 2.00 / 1.51	1.21 / 0.57 / 0.23	13.86 / 7.77 / 3.49	16.81 / 8.79 / 4.30	20.27 / 12.43 / 7.69	25.58 / 15.06 / 9.45	8 / 12 / 17	18.0 / 12.5 / 8.7	11.7 / 32.3 / 67.7	39.7 / 80.2 / 139.7	83.1 / 138.1 / 224.8	86.9 / 123.8 / 172.8	49.7 / 76.6 / 108.6	20.9 / 37.4 / 83.2
5072 Hardware (174)	4.08 / 2.62 / 1.81	2.62 / 1.76 / 0.80	10.81 / 7.82 / 3.64	13.08 / 8.34 / 4.07	5.71 / 3.80 / 2.73	7.20 / 4.61 / 3.31	32 / 43 / 52	6.6 / 4.9 / 3.7	6.3 / 13.8 / 25.1	26.3 / 50.9 / 79.2	55.5 / 98.7 / 152.9	75.2 / 87.1 / 130.0	38.4 / 67.0 / 100.6	6.5 / 19.0 / 36.2
5084 Industrial Machinery & Equipment (97)	3.27 / 2.12 / 1.59	3.78 / 2.83 / 0.75	17.24 / 9.50 / 4.11	23.65 / 11.03 / 4.76	7.90 / 4.73 / 3.24	8.80 / 5.50 / 4.04	34 / 43 / 59	11.2 / 6.6 / 4.0	8.4 / 18.8 / 46.6	35.5 / 80.5 / 139.7	79.6 / 134.0 / 216.8	62.5 / 92.1 / 125.1	65.4 / 103.0 / 150.3	13.5 / 41.7 / 67.9
5098 Lumber & Construction Materials (146)	3.60 / 2.20 / 1.64	3.05 / 1.85 / 0.94	16.67 / 11.00 / 6.18	23.17 / 13.02 / 7.00	8.64 / 5.73 / 3.38	11.36 / 6.18 / 4.01	36 / 47 / 58	11.3 / 8.0 / 5.8	8.8 / 21.8 / 39.5	32.5 / 88.5 / 124.6	75.3 / 125.0 / 247.4	52.5 / 83.7 / 118.4	60.3 / 104.4 / 173.2	14.0 / 33.0 / 64.7
5047 Meats & Meat Products (48)	2.93 / 2.03 / 1.45	1.33 / 0.74 / 0.23	21.62 / 12.13 / 3.54	22.58 / 13.75 / 4.72	25.28 / 16.94 / 9.36	29.41 / 20.44 / 14.67	15 / 22 / 30	76.4 / 42.0 / 24.2	9.6 / 29.0 / 50.0	37.2 / 79.2 / 175.3	65.9 / 114.5 / 256.6	33.5 / 50.3 / 104.1	133.5 / 197.1 / 378.0	12.8 / 36.7 / 71.3
5091 Metals & Minerals (76)	4.03 / 2.36 / 1.51	3.54 / 2.07 / 1.21	14.13 / 8.44 / 5.11	21.01 / 10.51 / 6.57	6.34 / 4.04 / 2.38	7.46 / 4.96 / 3.45	39 / 47 / 60	7.9 / 5.3 / 3.7	11.2 / 22.2 / 43.5	28.9 / 66.2 / 134.7	54.1 / 110.5 / 172.7	57.8 / 93.3 / 141.1	54.1 / 85.9 / 130.5	11.5 / 27.3 / 59.4
5028 Paints & Varnishes (38)	6.13 / 3.50 / 2.00	3.56 / 2.55 / 1.43	12.92 / 9.52 / 3.10	19.35 / 8.09 / 4.76	4.74 / 3.29 / 2.52	6.29 / 4.26 / 3.27	33 / 41 / 48	8.0 / 6.4 / 5.4	6.1 / 16.1 / 27.7	17.7 / 25.8 / 70.9	33.8 / 68.1 / 93.7	45.0 / 89.4 / 93.0	42.4 / 60.4 / 99.9	7.0 / 18.1 / 40.3
5096 Paper & Its Products (121)	3.88 / 2.34 / 1.70	2.33 / 1.23 / 0.60	11.31 / 7.00 / 3.43	14.92 / 8.79 / 4.26	8.06 / 5.39 / 3.63	10.73 / 6.68 / 4.61	31 / 40 / 51	11.8 / 8.1 / 6.1	7.8 / 14.5 / 35.7	30.4 / 59.8 / 104.2	67.6 / 107.4 / 177.6	57.1 / 83.2 / 102.2	57.5 / 95.9 / 146.6	12.2 / 23.1 / 53.8
5092 Petroleum & Petroleum Products (66)	3.45 / 2.07 / 1.50	3.21 / 1.31 / 0.69	14.52 / 9.09 / 3.53	37.55 / 10.02 / 8.79	7.70 / 4.80 / 3.08	15.38 / 8.40 / 5.59	25 / 34 / 52	35.4 / 24.2 / 13.7	26.6 / 48.3 / 86.7	20.7 / 38.0 / 86.5	42.3 / 90.3 / 189.1	23.1 / 47.9 / 84.3	112.7 / 174.0 / 287.5	18.9 / 62.3 / 130.0
5033 Piece Goods (128)	3.17 / 2.10 / 1.64	2.39 / 1.36 / 0.67	11.04 / 6.35 / 3.68	13.84 / 7.22 / 3.89	8.13 / 4.74 / 3.25	8.91 / 5.96 / 3.51	29 / 47 / 68	9.1 / 8.1 / 4.6	2.1 / 5.0 / 15.2	43.9 / 64.1 / 132.8	61.1 / 122.2 / 176.8	62.5 / 91.2 / 124.3	59.4 / 100.8 / 146.5	8.7 / 17.4 / 41.2
5074 Plumbing & Heating Equipment & Supplies (179)	3.66 / 2.63 / 1.94	3.13 / 1.77 / 0.99	13.04 / 7.76 / 4.28	16.30 / 9.72 / 5.39	6.58 / 4.50 / 3.32	7.62 / 5.24 / 3.70	36 / 45 / 58	8.4 / 6.8 / 4.8	6.9 / 13.2 / 28.4	31.4 / 53.3 / 99.2	59.8 / 97.9 / 158.6	65.4 / 82.5 / 106.1	53.0 / 79.9 / 120.0	9.8 / 20.4 / 44.1
5044 Poultry & Poultry Products (45)	3.39 / 2.09 / 1.39	2.21 / 0.83 / 0.26	15.79 / 8.11 / 2.55	31.97 / 10.77 / 3.50	14.44 / 10.52 / 6.47	25.90 / 16.16 / 8.17	14 / 21 / 31	66.7 / 31.1 / 15.0	12.1 / 26.5 / 80.8	27.1 / 59.3 / 108.7	61.0 / 104.2 / 263.0	24.7 / 49.4 / 100.0	111.9 / 157.8 / 248.2	19.4 / 85.4 / 187.0
5093 Scrap & Waste Materials (61)	4.10 / 2.41 / 1.54	3.37 / 1.90 / 0.80	12.11 / 8.99 / 4.72	24.18 / 12.57 / 9.09	7.32 / 3.74 / 2.67	10.61 / 7.91 / 4.39	20 / 30 / 48	30.0 / 11.5 / 7.1	19.3 / 36.8 / 59.4	21.3 / 57.3 / 86.3	36.1 / 103.1 / 182.0	20.5 / 63.0 / 103.6	58.1 / 127.3 / 275.5	15.9 / 47.0 / 107.7
5014 Tires & Tubes (44)	2.58 / 1.93 / 1.58	3.09 / 1.80 / 0.93	14.15 / 7.69 / 3.67	17.50 / 10.00 / 6.21	6.11 / 4.51 / 3.43	8.26 / 5.07 / 4.33	32 / 42 / 63	9.7 / 6.0 / 4.4	13.8 / 24.9 / 45.1	50.1 / 87.3 / 125.7	101.2 / 122.3 / 251.6	60.7 / 94.8 / 137.0	84.6 / 116.7 / 150.0	8.9 / 30.4 / 66.7
5094 Tobacco & Its Products (97)	2.71 / 1.97 / 1.43	1.04 / 0.73 / 0.40	13.94 / 9.65 / 5.40	23.78 / 13.12 / 7.02	21.35 / 12.40 / 7.48	27.49 / 17.29 / 10.42	13 / 16 / 24	25.6 / 18.9 / 12.3	9.4 / 17.3 / 31.9	46.2 / 80.5 / 152.0	81.0 / 118.2 / 170.1	60.7 / 93.0 / 141.5	81.2 / 114.1 / 164.0	9.8 / 20.9 / 40.9

Figure 11.5

terly *Financial Report for Manufacturing Corporations*. These reports are available, however, only for broadly defined industry groups. The data cover all manufacturing corporations, except newspapers and related subgroups.

The Internal Revenue Service of the U.S. Treasury Department publishes annually, with an approximately 3-year lag at present, the Statistics of Income, Corporation Income Tax Returns. The reports represent selected income statement, balance sheet, and tax items obtained from Federal Income Tax returns. It is possible to utilize the basic dollar data presented to derive valuable ratio information.

FINANCIAL RATIOS FOR COLLECTIONS, OPERATIONS, INVENTORY, AND FINANCIAL MANAGEMENT

Figures 11.2 and 11.3 are the income statements and balance sheet for two hypothetical companies: Hero Manufacturing and Rotten Distribution. Hero Manufacturing Company is a well managed company and all of their ratios look good. Rotten Distribution, on the other hand, is a mismanaged company, so the illustrations of their ratios will reflect this.

Hero Manufacturing is an iron and steel foundry, so we will use the Dun and Bradstreet *Key Business Ratios* for this industry so that we might compare Hero's performance to that of the industry. Figure 11.4 is the *Key Business Ratios* for Iron and Steel Foundries.

Rotten Distribution is a scrap and waste materials wholesaler. This industry's ratios are shown in Figure 11.5, from Dun and Bradstreet *Key Business Ratios*.

Collection Ratios

Of all the ratios, the most important may be the one which indicates how long many businesses, especially small businesses, run into cash flow problems. In about 70% of the cases, this cash flow problem is caused by not collecting receivables in a timely manner. Since customers will very seldom pay their invoices until they are reminded, and some companies won't pay unless you

Financial Ratios

"stand on them," an effective collection policy is of the utmost importance to a business.

The collection period ratio will tell you if your customers are generally paying in the time they are allocated. If they are not paying, corrective action must be taken.

(1) Collection Period. As any top manager can tell you, a company's credit and collections program and terms exert a direct influence on sales attainment, profits, and the need for borrowing capital. This ratio helps analyze the collectibility of receivables. The average collection period should not exceed the net maturity indicated by selling terms by more than 10 to 15 days. This ratio is especially important today when accounts receivable is an increasingly major asset.

The collection period in days is determined by a two-step formula. The first step is to divide the annual *credit* sales by 365 days to obtain the average daily credit sales. If all the company's sales are on credit, the credit sales equal the total net sales. But if the company does a large portion of its business on a cash basis, the cash sales must be subtracted from net sales to get credit sales. The second step in the formula is to divide accounts and notes receivable by the average daily credit sales (the result of the first step calculation) to get the average collection period in days.

$$\text{Step 1:} \quad \text{Average daily credit sales} = \frac{\text{total annual credit sales}}{365 \text{ days}}$$

$$\text{Step 2:} \quad \text{Collection period in days} = \frac{\text{notes and accounts receivable}}{\text{average daily credit sales (above)}}$$

Example   Hero Mfg.   Rotten Dist.

Step 1: $\dfrac{\$5,620,000°}{365 \text{ days}} = \$15,397 \qquad \dfrac{\$4,200,000°}{365 \text{ days}} = \$11,507$

Step 2: $\dfrac{\$\ 580,000}{\$\ 15,397} = 37 \text{ days} \qquad \dfrac{\$\ 690,000}{\$\ 11,507} = 60 \text{ days}$

° Note: All of Hero Mfg. and Rotten Dist.'s sales are on credit.

Hero Manufacturing collects its receivables faster than anyone in the industry (industry best: 40 days; average: 48 days). The faster a company collects their receivables, the less likely the need for additional working capital. Rotten Distribution collects its receivables slower than anyone in the industry (48 days) and much slower than the average (36 days). This means that Rotten is going to require more working capital than any one else in the industry and, since they have precious little working capital now, they will have to borrow or go slow on their trade obligations.

Note. If the figures you have from your business are not annual figures but interim figures, you must divide credit sales by the number of days in the period (183 days for two quarters, 90 days for one quarter, etc.). Dividing by 365 days is done only if you are using annual figures.

Operations Ratios

Operating ratios help you determine how well the operation of your business is. One ratio tells you how profitable your company is, the other ratio helps you determine if you have enough (or too much) invested in fixed assets.

(2) *Net Profit on Net Sales.* The net profit to sales ratio is important for measuring the profitability of your business. This ratio represents the net profit margin as a percentage of sales. It explains what percentage of sales the actual net profit is after taxes. Too small a profit margin may indicate ineffective management or other internal problems. Every company has as its goal the maximum realization of profit from each dollar of sales. This ratio measures a company's success in achieving that goal. The net profit to sales ratio is calculated by dividing the net profit after taxes by the net (after returns and allowances) sales:

$$\text{Net profit on net sales} = \frac{\text{net profit after tax}}{\text{net sales}}$$

Example Hero Mfg. Rotten Dist.

$$\frac{\$\ 224{,}800}{\$5{,}620{,}000} = 4.0\% \qquad \frac{\$\ 29{,}400}{\$4{,}200{,}000} = 0.7\%$$

Four percent of Hero Manufacturing sales go to profit after tax, whereas Rotten Distribution is making about a half of a percent, 0.7%, net profit margin. For Hero, the industry average is 3.19% and the best in the industry is 4.85%. Hero is better than the industry average, and almost as good as the best. Rotten's industry average is 1.59%, and the worst is 0.8%. Rotten does worse than the worst.

(3) *Fixed Assets to Tangible Net Worth.* This ratio indicates what percentage of your company's net worth is invested in fixed assets. Ordinarily, this ratio should not exceed 100% for a manufacturer, and 75% for a wholesaler or retailer; but industries differ widely on this ratio, and it is necessary to check the industry ratio. A percentage beyond the maximum limits of the industry indicates that a disproportionate amount of capital is frozen in machinery and the building itself. This will limit the amount of operating funds for carrying inventories, receivables, and maintaining day-to-day cash outlays. It also means that the business will be unprepared for the hazards of unexpected developments (and every business gets its share of those) and will drain income into heavy debt payment and maintenance charges. But remember, a high percentage for this ratio does not automatically prove that fixed assets are excessive. The ratio may be distorted by inadequate net worth or recent investment in modernizing an out of date plant.

The fixed assets to tangible net worth ratio is computed by dividing fixed assets by net worth and is expressed as a percentage.

$$\text{Fixed assets to tangible net worth} = \frac{\text{total fixed assets}}{\text{tangible net worth}}$$

Example   Hero Mfg.   Rotten Dist.

$$\frac{\$833,500}{\$1,724,200} = 48.3\% \qquad \frac{\$420,000}{\$630,000} = 66.7\%$$

Hero Manufacturing does not have excessive fixed assets. Fixed assets are a smaller percentage of net worth than the industry average (63.4%). Rotten's fixed assets are much too large a percentage of net worth, a higher percentage than the industry average (37.2%) and almost the industry worst (88.3%). This indicates that Rotten has too many, probably unproductive, fixed assets, which limits the amount they have for day-to-day operations.

Inventory Ratios

The two inventory ratios show how inventory is managed and how future inventory will be purchased. The net sales to inventory ratio shows how fast the inventory is "turned," helping you determine if the company has obsolete inventory. The inventory to net working capital ratio shows if your company is able to easily finance new inventory.

(4) *Net Sales to Inventory*. This ratio determines the number of times your business turns its inventory in one period. If the ratio is less than the industry average, it would indicate obsolete merchandise, poor buying, or conservative buying. A ratio higher than the industry average might indicate overtrading using the supplier's money to buy and sell merchandise. This ratio does not indicate an actual physical turnover of inventory, but it provides a yardstick for comparing stock-to-sales ratios of one firm to another. Higher than average ratios also will indicate a chronically understocked condition in which sales are being lost because of lack of adequate inventories. Lower than average ratios may mean obsolete or stagnant inventories. This could indicate that a write-off of inventory is in store for the future.

The net sales to inventory ratio is computed by dividing sales for the period by the book value of the inventory, expressed as "times."

$$\text{Net sales to inventory} = \frac{\text{net sales}}{\text{inventory}}$$

Example   Hero Mfg.   Rotten Dist.

$$\frac{\$5,620,000}{\$\ 330,300} = 17 \text{ times} \qquad \frac{\$4,200,000}{\$\ 583,310} = 7.2 \text{ times}$$

Financial Ratios

Hero Manufacturing again demonstrates that it is one of the best credit risks in the industry. Hero is turning inventory neither too fast nor too slow (fastest: 21.6; average: 10.3). They do well in managing their inventory and should have plenty of money for inventory in the foreseeable future. Rotten Distribution has too much inventory, as this ratio again shows. Rotten shows a poorer percentage than the worst in the industry (103.6%). Rotten's high percentage shows that the company has too much inventory or too little working capital, or—more likely—both.

Financial Management Ratios

Financial management ratios are a general group of ratios which are perhaps the most widely used in finance. Financial lenders such as banks and private sources will generally compute the current asset to current liability and debt to net worth ratio as a first step to evaluating any business.

These ratios give the general financial picture of a business including its debt load, how well owner's equity is providing returns from investors, how sales are doing in relation to the money invested in the business, and so on.

These ratios show general financial performance and trends for each business.

It is good for the businessperson to remember that these ratios are almost always calculated when financing is sought from outside (banks, bonding, etc.). Therefore, it would be wise to calculate these ratios before going to a lender to see if your company is strong enough or if it might have some problems securing loans.

These ratios are the "financial facade" that a company shows to the public. It may pay to heed what these ratios show about your company.

(6) *Current Ratio (Current Assets to Current Liabilities).* The current ratio measures a company's liquidity and the extent of protection for short-term creditors. It gives a general picture of the adequacy of the company's working capital and its ability to meet day-to-day payment obligations. It measures the margin of

safety provided for paying current debts in the event of a reduction in the value of current assets. If receivables and inventory are valid, the current ratio is important as a specific measure of the capacity of a company to meet daily financing requirements.

To calculate the ratio, divide the total current assets by the total current liabilities as follows:

$$\text{Current ratio} = \frac{\text{total current assets}}{\text{total current liabilities}}$$

Example Hero Mfg. Rotten Dist.

$$\frac{\$2,049,800}{\$\ 499,762} = 4.1 \text{ times} \qquad \frac{\$1,208,720}{\$1,091,120} = 1.11 \text{ times}$$

In the example, Hero Manufacturing has enough current assets to cover their current liabilities approximately four times. If they were forced to liquidate their current assets to pay their current liabilities they would have much more than they needed to pay off obligations. If you look at the industry ratios for iron and steel foundries (Figure 10.4) you can see that the lowest times assets cover liabilities is 2.02; the average 2.37 times; and the highest 3.45 times. With a ratio of 4.1 times Hero is not only above the industry average, it is higher than the highest ratio recorded for the industry.

Rotten Distribution, on the other hand, had a very poor ratio. With only 1.11 times coverage, if nip came to tuck they would barely be able to cover their current liabilities with the liquidation of their current assets. Rotten has a ratio that is lower than the lowest in the industry, just the opposite of Hero. For the scrap and waste materials wholesale industry (Figure 10.5), the highest current ratio is 4.1 times; average, 2.41 times; and lowest, 1.54 times.

(7) *Current Debt to Tangible Net Worth*. This ratio is infrequently used. [The more frequently used ratio—total liabilities (total debt) to net worth—follows.] This ratio of current debt to worth should not exceed 80%, and generally the higher the percentage, the more the company depends on current financing to meet operation capital requirements. The current debt to tangible net worth ratio is computed by dividing current liabilities by tangible net worth and is expressed as a percentage:

$$\text{Current debt to tangible net worth} = \frac{\text{current liabilities}}{\text{tangible net worth}}$$

Example   Hero Mfg.   Rotten Dist.

$$\frac{\$499{,}762}{\$1{,}724{,}200} = 29\% \qquad \frac{\$1{,}091{,}120}{\$630{,}000} = 173.4\%$$

Hero Manufacturing has current liabilities as a percentage of tangible net worth at pretty close to the industry average (30.7%), which indicates that they use current liabilities no more than the industry in general. Rotten Distribution is very dependent on short-term (current liability) financing. As a matter of fact, they are more dependent on current liability financing than anyone in the industry (highest percentage: 88.3%).

(8) *Net Sales to Tangible Net Worth.* The net sales to net worth ratio is sometimes known as the trading ratio. It indicates that the extent to which a company's sales volume is supported by invested capital (net worth). A substantially higher than average ratio indicates that the company is an overtrader, that is, a company that is attempting to stretch the invested dollar to its maximum capacity. The overtrader's financial statement shows heavy debt. When someone has heavy debt their survival will hinge on the long-term continuation of optimum internal and external conditions. The undertrader, on the other hand, has either large capital reserves or inadequate sales to support the business. The most pressing need of the undertrader is generally to bring sales up to a profitable level. The net sales to net worth ratio measures the degree to which a company has attained a balance between the extremes of undertrading and overtrading.

In other words, the ratio is a measure of the relative turnover of capital. If capital is turned over too rapidly, liabilities build up excessively. If capital is turned over too slowly, funds become stagnant and profitability suffers. The net sales to net worth ratio is calculated as net sales divided by tangible net worth (net worth minus intangibles):

$$\text{Net sales to tangible net worth} = \frac{\text{net sales}}{\text{tangible net worth}}$$

Example Hero Mfg.   Rotten Dist.

$$\frac{\$5,620,000}{\$1,724,200} = 3.25 \text{ times} \qquad \frac{\$4,200,000}{\$\ 630,000} = 6.67 \text{ times}$$

Hero Manufacturing turned over its capital a little more than the industry average of 2.71 times. Yet they can not be considered as overtrading because they came in well below the industry's greatest overtraders who turned over capital 3.59 times. A quick look at Hero's large cash and security amounts and at the current ratio indicates that they have more than enough working capital to pay any foreseeable short-term obligation. Rotten Distribution turns over its capital twice as much as Hero, but they still have to go some distance before they can equal the worst in the industry at 7.32 times. The industry average is 3.74 times, higher than the average in Hero's industry.

(9) *Net Sales to Net Working Capital*. This ratio indicates the demands made upon working capital to support the sales volume of the company. It is much like the ratio above except that it measures the turnover of working capital. If the ratio is too high, the business has a tendency to owe too much money. Turning working capital very fast necessitates dependence upon credit granted by suppliers, banks, and others to provide operating funds. In cases where this ratio is disproportionately high, there is a good indication of working capital deficiencies.

The net sales to net working capital ratio is calculated by dividing net sales by net working capital:

$$\text{Net sales to working capital} = \frac{\text{net sales}}{\text{working capital}}$$

Example Hero Mfg.   Rotten Dist.

$$\frac{\$5,620,000}{\$1,550,000} = 3.63 \text{ times} \qquad \frac{\$4,200,000}{\$\ 117,600} = 35.7 \text{ times}$$

Financial Ratios

Hero Manufacturing obviously has plenty of working capital because it turns over so slowly. As a matter of fact, Hero turns over its working capital slower than the best in the industry (3.72 times); the industry average is 5.3 times. Rotten Distribution is 180 degrees in the opposite direction. Rotten turns over its working capital more than three times faster than the worst in its industry (10.61 times). Rotten turns over its working capital five times more than the industry average (7.51 times).

(10) *Net Profit on Tangible Net Worth.* This ratio measures the return on invested capital and gauges the possibilities of future growth. The tendency today is to look more and more to this ratio, rather than the profit to sales ratio above, as a criterion of profitability. Generally, a profits to worth relationship of at least 10% is regarded as necessary for providing draw or dividends plus funds for future growth. Tangible net worth is net worth *minus* such intangibles as goodwill, patents, copyrights, trademarks, organization expense, and treasury stock. To arrive at Hero Manufacturing's tangible net worth we have to subtract $5000 amortized value of the organization expense from $1,729,200 net worth, leaving $1,724,200. In the case of Rotten Distribution, we must subtract $40,000 in trademarks, and $30,000 amortized value of organization expense from a net worth of $700,000, leaving $620,000. The net profit to net worth is calculated by dividing net profit by net worth:

$$\text{Net profit to net worth} = \frac{\text{net profit after tax}}{\text{tangible net worth}}$$

Example Hero Mfg.   Rotten Dist.

$$\frac{\$\ 224{,}800}{\$1{,}724{,}200} = 13.0\% \qquad \frac{\$\ 29{,}400}{\$630{,}000} = 4.67\%$$

Hero is returning 13% on net worth (investment) to its owners. This is a good return for the industry, better than the average return of 9.39%, and almost as good as the top industry return of 15.92%. Rotten Distribution's return to its owners isn't as good as the industry average of 6.95% (the scrap industry has a lower average return than the iron and steel foundries). Rotten (again) did worse than the worst company recorded at 4.72%. How does Rotten Distribution survive!

(11) *Total Debt (Total Liabilities) to Tangible Net Worth*. Sometimes simply called the debt to worth ratio, this ratio measures the proportion of the owner's investment in the business compared to the creditors' investment. If the total debt exceeds the net worth, it means that the suppliers and the banks have invested more than the owner. The management of top-heavy liabilities entails strains and hazards that can become a threat to business survival. They expose the business to unexpected risks such as a sudden downturn in sales, changes in customer preferences, strikes, fires, rapid rises in business costs, and other factors. Companies that have a lower than average ratio indicate a strong ownership interest. Although this total debt to worth ratio is more frequently used than the current debt to worth ratio, the current ratio is more immediate. On the other hand, long-term debt has its own peril in that it is generally more exactly fixed as to maturity and more enforceable because almost all long-term debt is supported by specifically pledged collateral.

The total debt to tangible net worth ratio is calculated by dividing total liabilities by tangible net worth, expressed as a percentage:

$$\text{Total debt to tangible net worth} = \frac{\text{total liabilities}}{\text{tangible net worth}}$$

Example   Hero Mfg.   Rotten Dist.

$$\frac{\$1,470,000}{\$1,724,200} = 85.3\% \qquad \frac{\$1,470,000}{\$\ 630,000} = 233\%$$

Hero Manufacturing has a weak percentage of total liabilities compared to the net worth, though slightly more than the industry average percentage (58.8%). Hero's percentage is slightly more than the highest in the industry (80%). Rotten Distribution exceeds the worst percentage in its industry (182.8%) which again points up Rotten's strong dependence on outside financing to the tune of twice its net worth.

It was dark outside. John had just finished his conference with the attorney Riskstein. Gin had just finished reading *Simplified Accounting*.

"Well, I've learned quite a lot since the company books were stolen," Gin told John, "How about you?" she asked.

"Yeah I learned a lot," John said opening the car door, "but I still hate accounting."

GLOSSARY

Accelerated depreciation. A method of depreciation that charges off more of the original cost of the fixed assets in the earlier years than in the later years of the asset's service life.

Account. A recording unit used to reflect the changes in assets, liabilities, or owners' equity.

Account receivable. An amount that is owed to the business, usually by one of its customers, as a result of the ordinary extension of credit.

Accounting period. The period of time over which an income statement summarizes the changes in owners' equity; usually the period is one year.

Accrual basis. The measurement of revenues and expenses, as contrasted with receipts and expenditures.

Accrued expense. A liability arising because an expense occurs in a period prior to the related expenditure.

Accumulated depreciation. An account showing the total amount of depreciation of an asset that has been accumulated to date.

Acid-test ratio. The ratio obtained by dividing quick assets by current liabilities.

Allowance for doubtful accounts. The amount of estimated bad debts that is subtracted from accounts receivable on the balance sheet.

Amortization. The process of writing off the cost of intangible assets; similar to depreciation.

Asset. An item which is owned by the business and has a value that can be measured objectively.

Auditing. A review of accounting records by independent, outside public accountants.

Bad debts. The estimated amount of credit sales that will not be collected.

Balance. The difference between the totals of the two sides of an account.

Balance sheet. A financial statement which reports the assets and equities of a company at one point in time. Assets are listed on the left and equities on the right.

Bond. A written promise to repay money furnished the business, with interest, at some future date, usually five or more years hence.

Capital stock. A balance sheet account showing the amount that was assigned to the shares of stock at the time they were originally issued.

Capital turnover. A ratio obtained by dividing annual sales by investment.

Cash basis accounting. An accounting system that does not use the accrual basis.

Closing. The transfer of the balance from one account to another acount.

Common stock. Stock whose owners are not entitled to preferential treatment with regard to dividends or to the distribution of assets in the event of liquidation; usually, common stockholders control the company.

Cost accounting. The process of identifying manufacturing costs and assigning them to inventory in the manufacturing process.

Cost concept. Assets are ordinarily valued at the price paid to acquire them.

Cost of goods sold. The cost of the merchandise sold to customers.

Credit. The right-hand side of an account or an amount entered on the right-hand side of an account.

Creditor. A person who lends money or extends credit to a business.

Current assets. Assets which are either currently in the form of cash or are expected to be converted into cash within a short period of time (usually one year).

Current liabilities. Obligations which become due within a short period of time (usually one year).

Current ratio. The ratio obtained by dividing the total of the current assets by the total of the current liabilities.

Days' receivables. The number of days of sales that are tied up in accounts reveivable.

Debt. The left-hand side of an account or an amount entered on the left-hand side of an account.

Debt capital. The capital raised by the issuance of bonds.

Debt ratio. The ratio obtained by dividing debt capital by total capital.

Deferred revenue. The liability that arises when a customer pays a business in advance for a service or product. It is a liability because the business has an obligation to render the service or deliver the product.

Depletion. The process of writing off the cost of a wasting asset.

Depreciation. The process of recognizing a portion of the cost of an asset as an expense during each year of its estimated service life.

Direct labor or material. The labor or material that is used directly on a product.

Dividend. The funds generated by profitable operations that are distributed to the shareholders.

Double-declining balance method. An accelerated method of depreciation.

Double-entry system. A characteristic of accounting in which each recorded transaction causes at least two changes in the accounts.

Dual-aspect concept. The accounting concept which assumes that the total assets of a company always equal the total equities.

Earnings. Another term for net income.

Earnings per share. A ratio obtained by dividing the total earnings for a given period by the number of shares of common stock outstanding.

Entity concept. The accounting concept which assumes that accounts are kept for business entities, rather than for the persons who own, operate, or are otherwise associated with the business.

Entry. The accounting record made for a single transaction.

Equities. Claims against assets that are held by owners or by creditors.

Equity capital. The capital raised from owners.

Expenditure. An amount arising from the acquisition of an asset.

Expense. A decrease in owners' equity resulting from operations.

FIFO. The first-in, first-out inventory method which assumes that the goods that enter the inventory first are the first to be sold.

Fixed assets. The tangible properties of relatively long life that are generally used in the production of goods and services, rather than being held for resale.

Going-concern concept. The accounting concept which assumes that a business will continue to operate indefinitely.

Goodwill. An intangible asset; an amount paid for a favorable location or reputation.

Gross margin. The difference between sales revenue and cost of goods sold.

Income statement. A statement of revenues and expenses for a given period.

Interim statements. Financial statements prepared for a period of less than one year.

Inventories. Goods being held for sale, and material and partially finished products which will be sold upon completion.

Inventory turnover. Tells how many times inventory was totally replaced during the year; calculated by dividing the average inventory into cost of goods sold.

Investments. Securities that are held for a relatively long period-of-time and are purchased for reasons other than the temporary use of excess cash. They are noncurrent assets.

Journal. A record in which entries are recorded in chronological order.

Lease. An agreement under which the owner of property permits someone else to use it.

Ledger. A group of accounts.

Liability. The equity or claim of a creditor.

LIFO. The last-in, first-out inventory method which assumes that the last goods purchased are the first to be sold.

Liquid assets. Cash and assets which are easily converted into cash.

Liquidity ratios. The relationship of obligations soon coming due to assets which should provide the cash for meeting these obligations.

Manufacturing overhead. All manufacturing costs that are not direct material or direct labor.

Market value. The amount for which an asset can be sold in the marketplace.

Marketable securities. Securities that are expected to be converted into cash within a year; a current asset.

Matching concept. Costs are matched against the revenue of a period.

Materiality concept. Disregard trivial matters; disclose all important matters.

Money measurement concept. Accounting records show only facts that can be expressed in monetary terms.

Mortgage. A pledge of real estate as security for a loan.

Net book value. The difference between the cost of a fixed asset and its accumulated depreciation.

Net income. The amount by which total revenues exceed total expenses for a given period.

Net loss. The amount by which total expenses exceed total revenues for a given period.

Nominal account. An income statement account that is closed at the end of the period to a balance sheet account.

Noncurrent liability. A claim which does not fall due within one year.

Note receivable. An amount owed that is evidenced by a promissory note.

Obsolescence. A loss in the usefulness of an asset because of the development of improved equipment, changes in style, or other causes not related to the physical condition of the asset.

Operating expenses. Costs associated with sales and administrative activities, as distinct from those associated with production of goods or services.

Overhead rate. A rate used to allocate overhead costs to products.

Owners' equity. The claims of owners against the assets of a business.

Paid in capital. An amount in excess of the par or stated value of stock that is paid by investors.

Par value. The specific amount printed on the face of a stock certificate.

Partnership. An unincorporated business with two or more owners.

Period costs. Costs associated with general sales and administrative activities.

Permanent capital. Debt and equity capital.

Perpetual inventory. An individual record of the cost of each item in inventory.

Physical inventory. The counting of all merchandise currently on hand.

Posting. The process of transferring transactions from the journal to the ledger.

Preferred stock. Stock whose owners receive preferential treatment with regard to dividends or with regard to the distribution of assets in the event of liquidation.

Prepaid expenses. Services and certain intangibles purchased prior to the period during which their benefits are received; treated as assets until they are consumed.

Price-earnings ratio. A ratio obtained by dividing the average market price of the stock by the earnings per share.

Product costs. Costs associated with the manufacture of products.

Profit. See net income.

Profit margin. Net income expressed as a percentage of net sales.

Proprietorship. An unincorporated business with a single owner.

Glossary

Quick assets. Current assets other than inventory and prepaid expenses.

Real account. An account with a balance after the closing process has been completed; it appears on the balance sheet.

Realization concept. An accounting concept which assumes that revenue is recognized when goods are delivered or services are performed, in an amount that is reasonably certain to be realized.

Recognize. The act of recording a revenue or expense item in a given accounting period.

Residual value. The amount for which a company expects to be able to sell a fixed asset at the end of its service life.

Retained earnings. The increase in the shareholders' equity as a result of profitable company operations.

Return. The amount earned on invested funds during a period.

Return on shareholders' investment. A ratio obtained by dividing the return by the average amount of shareholders' investment for the period.

Revenue. An increase in owners' equity resulting from operations.

Security. An instrument such as a stock or bond.

Service life. The period of time over which an asset is estimated to be of service to the company.

Shareholders. The owners of an incorporated business.

Solvency. The ability to meet long-term obligations.

Stated value. The amount that the directors decide is the value of no-par stock.

Statement of changes in financial position. A financial statement explaining the changes that have occurred in asset, liability, and owners' equity items in an accounting period.

Stock split. An exchange of the number of shares of stock outstanding for a larger number.

Straight-line method. A depreciation method which charges off an equal fraction of the cost of a fixed asset over each year of its service life.

Taxable income. The amount of income subject to income tax, computed according to the rules of the Internal Revenue Service.

Transaction. A business event that is recorded in the accounting records.

Treasury stock. Previously issued stock that has been bought back by the company.

Write down. To reduce the cost of an item, especially inventory, to its market value.

Years'-digit method. An accelerated method of depreciation.

Index

Account groups, 27–34, 38–39, 40
Account transactions, 41–43
   sequence, 50
Accounting assumptions, 209–211
Accounting Handbook for Non-Accountants, 31
Accounting Principles Board (APB), 112
   Opinion No. 21, 112
Accounts payable ledger, 88–89, 93–95
Accounts receivable, 111–122
   aging, 115–116
   financing, 121
   ledger, 88–89, 93–95
Allowance for bad debts, 112
American Institute of Certified Public Accountants (AICPA), 27
   bulletins, 27
Amortization, 135
Asset valuation, 135–137
   cash purchase, 135
   credit purchase, 135–136
   exchange for other assets, 136–137
   exchange for stocks and bonds, 136
   gains and losses on sale of fixed assets, 144
Assets, 22, 27–28, 38–39, 40, 43–45, 51, 53, 99–100
   current, 28, 99, 100
   fixed, 28, 99–100, 134
   noncurrent, 134
   other, 28, 100
"At risk" rule, 176

Bad debts
   business, 119
   expense, 114–116, 221–224
   and the IRS, 119–120
   as percentage of credit sales, 114
   as percentage of outstanding receivables, 115
   personal, 119
   reserve for, 119–120
   trial balance adjustments, 221–224
   uncollectible accounts, 112
Balance sheet, 43, 236–238, 242–248
Bank documents, 9–14
Basic accounting equation, 43–47, 242
Book of final entry, 77
Borrowing environments, 153–155
Business bad debts, 119
Business entertainment expense, 204
Business financial statements, 236–255
Business organizations, 169–185

Capital, 29, 33
Capital stock, 29–30, 33
   paid-in surplus, 30, 33
   par value, 30, 181–182
   stated value, 30
Cash, 101–111

Cash controls, 107–109
  on disbursements, 108
  on receipts, 108
  separation of duties, 108–109
  stewardship controls, 107–109
Cash disbursements journal, 46, 62–64
Cash forecasts, 106–107, 109
  long-term, 106–107
  short-term, 106
Cash management, 105–111
Cash payments, 103–105
Cash: Planning, Forecasting, and Control, 105
Cash receipts, 101–102
Cash receipts journal, 64–68
Cash register receipts, 6
Cash summary form, 9, 10
Cash tank method, 104, 105–106
Cash transactions, 102–103
Charge sales, 8
Chart of accounts, 51–54
Check register, 11, 13
Check stub, 11
Checking account reconciliation, 12, 13
Checks, 9, 11
Collection period, 267–268
Collection ratios, 266–268
Common stock financing, 180–185
  no-par stock, 181
  par value, 181–182
Common stockholder rights, 179–180
  collective, 179
  specific, 179
Corporate charters, 178–179
Corporations, 176–185
Cost of sales, 32–33, 34, 38–39, 40, 43–45, 54, 190–197
  by deduction, 191–195
  by direct calculation, 191
  by gross margin, 191
  trial balance adjustments, 225, 230
Credit application, 8
Credit information system, 117

Credit policy, 116–117
  payment stimulation techniques, 118–120
Credit sales, 8
Credit scores, 117–118
Credit scoring system, 117
Credits, 39–40

Debits, 39–40
Debt, 148–166
Debt capital, 151–164
Debt capital available, 157–161
  accounts receivable loans, 161
    secured, 158–159
  bank loans, 157–160
  equipment loans, 160–161
  fixed asset secured loans, 159
  government guaranteed loans, 159–160
  industrial sales time financing, 160
  intermediate term loans, 157–158
  inventory loans, 159, 160
  leasing, 161–162
  liquid asset loans, 158
  long-term loans, 158
  partially secured loan, 158
  secured loans, 158
  short-term loans, 157
  unsecured loans, 158
Debt capital sources, 151–157
  banks, 151–155
  commercial finance companies, 160
  commercial lenders, 155–156
  credit unions, 163
  government loans, 164
  life insurance companies, 162–163
  pension funds and foundations, 163
Deferring tax, 120–121
Depletion, 135
Deposit slip, 9, 12, 14
Depreciation, 134–135, 140–143
  salvage value, 141–142

Index

trial balance adjustments, 221
useful life, 141
Depreciation methods, 141
　declining balance, 141–143
　straight line, 141–142
　sum-of-years'-digits, 141–142
Depreciation periods, 144
Detailed audit strips, 6
Discounting, 112–113
Double-entry bookkeeping, 35–39

Embezzlement, 107–109
"Employers Tax Guide," 20–22
Entertainment expense, 18, 19
Equity, 29–30, 33, 38–39, 40, 43–45, 52, 53
Expenses, 190–206; *see also* Operating expenses

Factoring, 121, 122, 123
　to improve financial ratios, 122, 123
Federal payroll taxes, 20
Federal unemployment tax, 22
Finance, 255–256
Financial leverage, 148–151
Financial management ratios, 271–277
　current debt to tangible net worth, 272–273
　current ratio (current assets to current liabilities), 271–272
　net profit on tangible net worth, 275–276
　net sales to net working capital, 274–275
　net sales to tangible net worth, 273–274
　total liabilities to tangible net worth, 276–277
Financial ratios, 256–276
　key ratios, 257
Float; *see* Money float
Flooring, 159

Funds flow statement, 251–253

General and administrative expense, 197–199
General journal, 46, 54–62
General ledger, 77, 81–88
Gross margin, 239; *see also* Gross profit
Gross profit, 196–197

Hartley, W. C. F., 105

Improvements, 202
Income, 30, 33, 38–39, 40, 43–45, 54, 188–190
Income statement, 44, 236–238, 239–242
Incorporation, 183–185
Industry ratios, 257–259, 266
Installment sales receivable, 120–121
Insurance expense, 205
Interest expense, 203
Internal Revenue Service
　Form 1040, Schedule C, 169, 170, 172
　publications, 20
Inventory, 32–33, 127–134, 195
　finished goods, 128
　perpetual system, 129–131
　raw materials, 128
　retail, 133–134
　work in process, 128
Inventory identification, 195
Inventory ratios, 270–271
　net sales to inventory, 270–271
Inventory trial balance adjustments, 225, 230
Inventory valuation, 131–133, 195–196
　conventional retail inventory valuation, 133–134
　FIFO (first-in, first-out), 131–133
　LIFO (last-in, first-out), 131–133
　standard costs, 196
　weighted average, 131

Investment tax credit, 137–140
 depreciable tangible personal property, 138–139
 employee stock ownership plan, 138
 real property, 139
 useful life limitations, 139–140

Journal, 34, 49–50
 abbreviations, 79

Kiting, 107

Lapping, 107
Ledger, 51, 77
 format, 78–81
Leverage; *see* Financial leverage
Liabilities, 29, 33, 38–39, 40, 43–45, 52, 53, 147–148
 current, 29, 147–148
 fixed, 29
 long-term, 29, 148
 noncurrent, 148
Liability entries, 164–166
Limited partnership, 175–176

Management cash control, 107–109
Money float, 109–111
 negative, 111
 positive, 111

Net profit, 44, 239
Nickerson, Clarence, 31

Office fund voucher, 14–16
Operating expenses, 30–32, 34, 38–39, 40, 43–45, 52, 54, 197–206
Operations ratios, 268–270
 fixed assets to tangible net worth, 269–270
 net profit on net sales, 268–269
Optimizing, 109
Original transaction documents, 6–9
Owner's equity, 29, 33, 53

P & L, 44
Packing slips, 16
Partnership, 172–176
 accounting, 173–175
Payment stimulation techniques, 118–120
Payroll records, 20–23
Period journal entry, 45–46
"Perks," 17
Permanent accounts, 47
Perpetual inventory system, 129–130
Perquisites, 17
Personal bad debt, 119
Petty cash, 14–16
Positive float, 111
Post reference, 79
Preferred stock, 182–183
Profit and loss statement, 44, 239
Purchase order, 16
Purchases journal, 75–76
Purchasing documents, 16–17

Real property tax, 205
Receivables, 111–122
Rental expense, 201
Repairs expense, 202
Replacement expense, 202
Reserve for bad debts, 119–120
Restrictive endorsement, 11
Retail selling price, 133
Retained earnings, 29–30, 33, 44, 241, 246
Revenue, 30, 188–190

Sales, 188–190
Sales discounts, 189–190
Sales documents, 6
Sales journal, 71–74
Sales returns, 190
Salvage value, 141–142
Selling expenses, 199–206
Social Security tax, 22
Sole proprietorship, 29, 169–172
 accounting, 172

Index

Statement of retained earnings, 248–251
Subchapter S corporation, 176–177
Supplies, 128

Tax expense, 205–206
Temporary accounts, 45–47
Time price differential, 160–161
Transportation expense, 17–19, 202–204
Travel and entertainment records, 17–19

Travel expense, 202–203
Trial balance, 77, 211–216
   account adjustments, 220–230
   completion, 230–235
   entries, 213–216
   format, 211–212
Trial balance sheet, 216–220
Trial income statement, 216–218

Uncollectible accounts, 112
Useful life, 141

Wages and salaries, 199–201

AIM FOR THE BEST
WITH BUSINESS BOOKS
FROM BERKLEY

__ 0-425-10173-8	**COMMUNICATE LIKE A PRO** Nido R. Qubein	$3.95
__ 0-425-09110-4	**CORPORATE COMBAT** William E. Peacock	$3.95
__ 0-425-08537-6	**GET THE BEST FROM YOURSELF** Nido R. Qubein	$3.50
__ 0-425-10150-9	**PEAK PERFORMANCE PRINCIPLES FOR HIGH ACHIEVERS** John R. Noe	$4.75
__ 0-425-09394-8	**GAME PLANS: SPORTS STRATEGIES FOR BUSINESS** Robert W. Keidel	$3.95
__ 0-425-08776-X	**THE GREATEST MANAGEMENT PRINCIPLES IN THE WORLD** Michael LeBoeuf (Trade Paperback)	$6.95
__ 0-425-07653-9	**NIDO QUBEIN'S PROFESSIONAL SELLING TECHNIQUES** Nido R. Qubein (Trade Paperback)	$5.95
__ 0-425-09847-8	**THE ONE MINUTE MANAGER** Kenneth Blanchard, Ph.D. & Spencer Johnson, M.D. (Trade Paperback)	$7.95
__ 0-425-07757-8	**PUTTING THE ONE MINUTE MANAGER TO WORK** Kenneth Blanchard, Ph.D. & Robert Lorber, Ph.D. (Trade Paperback)	$6.95
__ 0-425-08102-8	**ZIG ZIGLAR'S SECRETS OF CLOSING THE SALE** Zig Ziglar (Trade Paperback)	$7.95
__ 0-425-09644-0	**13 FATAL ERRORS MANAGERS MAKE*** ***AND HOW YOU CAN AVOID THEM** W. Steven Brown	$3.95
__ 0-425-09559-2	**PAULA NELSON'S GUIDE TO GETTING RICH** Paula Nelson	$3.95
__ 0-425-09803-6	**SPEAK THE LANGUAGE OF SUCCESS** Gloria Hoffman and Pauline Graivier	$4.75

Available at your local bookstore or return this form to:

BERKLEY
THE BERKLEY PUBLISHING GROUP, Dept. B
390 Murray Hill Parkway, East Rutherford, NJ 07073

Please send me the titles checked above. I enclose _____. Include $1.00 for postage and handling if one book is ordered; add 25¢ per book for two or more not to exceed $1.75. CA, IL, NJ, NY, PA, and TN residents please add sales tax. Prices subject to change without notice and may be higher in Canada. Do not send cash.

NAME _____

ADDRESS _____

CITY _____ STATE/ZIP _____

(Allow six weeks for delivery.)

THE BEST BUSINESS GUIDES AVAILABLE TODAY FROM JOVE PAPERBACKS

_____	08805-6	**SIMPLIFIED ACCOUNTING FOR NON-ACCOUNTANTS** Rick Stephan Hayes and C. Richard Baker	$3.95
_____	08737-8	**HOW TO BE RICH** J. Paul Getty	$3.50
_____	09048-4	**HOW TO MAKE MEETINGS WORK** Doyle & Straus	$3.95
_____	07617-1	**OWNING YOUR HOME COMPUTER** Robert L. Perry	$4.95
_____	09079-4	**THE FAMILY INVESTMENT GUIDE**	$3.50

Available at your local bookstore or return this form to:

JOVE
THE BERKLEY PUBLISHING GROUP, Dept. B
390 Murray Hill Parkway, East Rutherford, NJ 07073

Please send me the titles checked above. I enclose _____. Include $1.00 for postage and handling if one book is ordered; add 25¢ per book for two or more not to exceed $1.75. CA, IL, NJ, NY, PA, and TN residents please add sales tax. Prices subject to change without notice and may be higher in Canada. Do not send cash.

NAME_____

ADDRESS_____

CITY_____ STATE/ZIP_____

(Allow six weeks for delivery.)

NAM. BRAVO COMPANY.

THE EXPLOSIVE NEW FILM— AND NOW, THE SEARING NEW NOVEL!

PLATOON
a novel by Dale A. Dye
based on a screenplay by Oliver Stone

_____ 0-441-67069-5 $3.50

Available at your local bookstore or return this form to:

CHARTER
THE BERKLEY PUBLISHING GROUP, Dept. B
390 Murray Hill Parkway, East Rutherford, NJ 07073

Please send me the titles checked above. I enclose _____. Include $1.00 for postage and handling if one book is ordered; add 25¢ per book for two or more not to exceed $1.75. CA, IL, NJ, NY, PA, and TN residents please add sales tax. Prices subject to change without notice and may be higher in Canada. Do not send cash.

NAME_____
ADDRESS_____
CITY_____STATE/ZIP_____
(Allow six weeks for delivery.)   C6A

Top Performance

ZIG ZIGLAR

THE BESTSELLING AUTHOR OF ZIG ZIGLAR'S SECRETS OF CLOSING THE SALE REVEALS MORE SECRETS IN GAINING UNBEATABLE RESULTS!

HOW TO DEVELOP EXCELLENCE IN YOURSELF AND OTHERS

> "To call Zig Ziglar a 'super salesman' would be an understatement."
> — RICHARD M. DeVOS, PRESIDENT, AMWAY CORPORATION

America's #1 motivator shows you the formulas, principles and techniques that will take you to the top!

- ★ 17 maxims to unlock top performance
- ★ 10 commandments for running a meeting
- ★ 5 management myths that should be exploded
- ★ 6 key work attitudes
- ★ 22 principles to meet a person's needs
- ★ The 7-step goal setting formula
- ★ 3 ways to build healthy self-esteem
- ★ And much more!

__**TOP PERFORMANCE: HOW TO DEVELOP EXCELLENCE IN YOURSELF AND OTHERS** (trade edition) 0-425-09973-3/$7.95

Available at your local bookstore or return this form to:

BERKLEY
THE BERKLEY PUBLISHING GROUP, Dept. B
390 Murray Hill Parkway, East Rutherford, NJ 07073

Please send me the titles checked above. I enclose _____ Include $1.00 for postage and handling if one book is ordered; add 25¢ per book for two or more not to exceed $1.75. CA, IL, NJ, NY, PA, and TN residents please add sales tax. Prices subject to change without notice and may be higher in Canada. Do not send cash.

NAME_____

ADDRESS_____

CITY_____STATE/ZIP_____

(Allow six weeks for delivery.)   B504